A SKETCH GRAMMAR OF PONDI

A SKETCH GRAMMAR OF PONDI

RUSSELL BARLOW

PRESS

ASIA-PACIFIC LINGUISTICS

Published by ANU Press
The Australian National University
Acton ACT 2601, Australia
Email: anupress@anu.edu.au

Available to download for free at press.anu.edu.au

ISBN (print): 9781760463830
ISBN (online): 9781760463847

WorldCat (print): 1175268620
WorldCat (online): 1175268668

DOI: 10.22459/SGP.2020

This title is published under a Creative Commons Attribution-NonCommercial-NoDerivatives 4.0 International (CC BY-NC-ND 4.0).

The full licence terms are available at
creativecommons.org/licenses/by-nc-nd/4.0/legalcode

Cover design and layout by ANU Press. Cover photograph by Russell Barlow.

This edition © 2020 ANU Press

CONTENTS

Acknowledgements ix
List of abbreviations xi
List of maps, figures, and tables xiii

1. Introduction. 1
   1.1   Organisation. 1
   1.2   Previous research on the language. 2
   1.3   Methodology 2
   1.4   Orthography and presentation 3
   1.5   Pondi: The language and its speakers 3
        1.5.1   The name of the language. 4
        1.5.2   The environment 4
        1.5.3   Langam village 5
        1.5.4   The people 6
        1.5.5   Relationships with neighbouring villages
                     and borrowing. 8
        1.5.6   Variation 11
   1.6   Language vitality. 11
        1.6.1   UNESCO's nine factors 12
        1.6.2   EGIDS. 12
        1.6.3   LEI 13
   1.7   Classification 14
   1.8   Typological overview. 18
2. Phonetics and phonology 21
   2.1   Consonants 21
        2.1.1   Voiceless stops. 22
        2.1.2   Prenasalised voiced stops. 23
        2.1.3   Prenasalised voiced affricate 24
        2.1.4   Nasals. 25
        2.1.5   Liquid 26

	2.1.6	Fricative 27
	2.1.7	Glides 28
2.2	Vowels 29	
	2.2.1	The high front unrounded vowel /i/ 29
	2.2.2	The mid front unrounded vowel /e/ 30
	2.2.3	The low central unrounded vowel /a/............. 30
	2.2.4	The mid back rounded vowel /o/................. 31
	2.2.5	The high back rounded vowel /u/ 31
	2.2.6	The high central unrounded vowel /ɨ/ 31
	2.2.7	Diphthongs................................... 32
2.3	Syllable structure 33	
2.4	Stress 35	
2.5	Morphophonemic processes 36	
	2.5.1	Vowel coalescence 36
	2.5.2	Glide formation 36
	2.5.3	Vowel degemination (or shortening).............. 37
	2.5.4	High central vowel deletion 37
	2.5.5	High vowel gliding............................ 37
	2.5.6	Glide insertion............................... 38
	2.5.7	Monophthongisation 39
	2.5.8	Degemination and quasi-degemination 40
	2.5.9	Sibilant voicing 41
2.6	Metathesis... 41	
2.7	Lexically determined alternations 42	
3. Nominal morphology (number)............................ 43		
3.1	Plurals ending in -*al* 44	
3.2	Plurals ending in -*il* 46	
3.3	Plurals ending in -*e*................................. 47	
3.4	Plurals ending in -*se*................................ 49	
3.5	Plurals ending in -*ate* 51	
3.6	Plurals ending in -*ange*............................. 51	
3.7	Plurals ending in -*une*.............................. 52	
3.8	Non-plural -*mo*, plural -*me* 52	
3.9	Plural ending in -*mbe* 53	
3.10	Non-plurals ending in -*m* (singulative suffix) 54	
3.11	Suppletive forms 55	
3.12	Additional remarks on nominal number................. 55	
4. Verbal morphology 59		
4.1	Basic verbal morphology 59	

	4.2	The imperfective aspect 63
	4.3	The perfective aspect 64
	4.4	The irrealis mood 65
	4.5	The imperative mood 66
	4.6	The perfect prefix *a-* 67
	4.7	The detransitiviser prefix *l-* 68
	4.8	Nonfinite verb forms 71
	4.9	The simultaneous suffix *-e* 71
	4.10	The conditional suffix *-se* 72
	4.11	The locative verb *p-* 'be (at)' 73
	4.12	The motion verbs *i-* 'come' and *mal-* 'go' 74
5.	Other word classes 75
	5.1	Adjectives 75
		5.1.1 Adjectival number morphology 77
		5.1.2 The derivational suffix *-wï* '-like' 78
	5.2	Pronouns 79
		5.2.1 Personal pronouns 79
		5.2.2 Reflexive/reciprocal pronouns 80
		5.2.3 Possessive pronouns 81
		5.2.4 Intensive pronouns 83
		5.2.5 Indefinite/interrogative pronouns 84
	5.3	Determiners 85
		5.3.1 Deictic demonstratives 85
		5.3.2 Subject markers and object markers 87
		5.3.3 Quantifiers 88
	5.4	Postpositions 90
	5.5	Adverbs 94
		5.5.1 Temporal adverbs 95
		5.5.2 Locative adverbs 97
		5.5.3 Other adverbs 98
	5.6	Negators 100
	5.7	Interrogative words 100
	5.8	Conjunctions 101
	5.9	Numerals 103
6.	Phrase-level syntax 109
	6.1	Noun phrases 109
		6.1.1 Nominal number 110
		6.1.2 Possession 112

- 6.2 Verb phrases 113
  - 6.2.1 Auxiliary verbs 113
  - 6.2.2 Compound verbs 118
  - 6.2.3 Equational constructions 121
- 6.3 Adpositional phrases 122
7. Clause-level syntax 125
  - 7.1 Basic constituent order 125
  - 7.2 Core argument alignment 127
  - 7.3 Obliques 128
  - 7.4 Ditransitive alignment? 131
  - 7.5 Monoclausal (or simple) sentences 134
8. The syntax of sentences 135
  - 8.1 Complex sentences 135
    - 8.1.1 Coordination 135
    - 8.1.2 The functional equivalent of relative clauses 136
    - 8.1.3 Permissive constructions 137
    - 8.1.4 Subordination 138
    - 8.1.5 Simultaneous action 139
    - 8.1.6 Parataxis 140
  - 8.2 Questions 141
  - 8.3 Commands and requests 145
  - 8.4 Negation 149
  - 8.5 Reported speech 151
  - 8.6 Conditional sentences 154
9. Lexicon 157
  - 9.1 Pondi-to-English word list 157
  - 9.2 English-to-Pondi finder list 170

Swadesh 100-word list 181

Swadesh 200-word list 185

Standard SIL–PNG word list (190 items) 191

References 197

ACKNOWLEDGEMENTS

Above all, I have to thank the Pondi speakers who patiently and enthusiastically shared their language with me—in particular, Clement Katram, Bonny Koiama, and Robert Kupoa. I must also thank Mr Thomas Ambata and Mrs Betty Ambata of the Manu Primary School for accommodating us while we worked on documenting the language.

Some of the research that led to this sketch grammar was conducted while I was a PhD student at the University of Hawai'i at Mānoa. Thanks to my amazing dissertation committee for teaching me how to write a reference grammar, and above all to Lyle Campbell. My field research in Papua New Guinea in 2016 was supported in part by a Firebird Foundation fellowship, for which I am also grateful.

The remainder of the research leading to this grammar I undertook as a postdoctoral researcher at the Department of Linguistic and Cultural Evolution at the Max Planck Institute for the Science of Human History in Jena, Germany. I would especially like to thank Russell Gray for his continued support and encouragement.

Thanks also to Bill Foley for coaxing me to the Sepik in the first place, and to Timothy Usher for our lively discussions about the linguistic prehistory of the region and for his helpful comments on an earlier draft.

The present work has been greatly improved by the comments of Bruno Olsson as well as an anonymous reviewer.

LIST OF ABBREVIATIONS

The following abbreviations have been used in the glosses of Pondi. Wherever possible, the conventions of the Leipzig Glossing Rules (Comrie et al. 2008) have been followed.

1	1st person	OBJ	object (or 'non-subject')
2	2nd person	OBL	oblique
3	3rd person	PFV	perfective
COND	conditional	PL	plural (or 'more than two')
DETR	detransitiviser	POSS	possessive
DU	dual	PRF	perfect
FUT	(immediate) future	PROH	prohibitive
IMP	imperative	Q	question
INDF	indefinite	REFL	reflexive
INT	intensive	SG	singular
IPFV	imperfective	SIM	simultaneous
IRR	irrealis	SUBJ	subject
NEG	negative/negator	VOL	volitive
NPL	non-plural ('less than three')		

The following is a list of other abbreviations used in this book.

EGIDS	Expanded Graded Intergenerational Disruption Scale
EXCL	exclusive
F	feminine
INCL	inclusive
IPA	International Phonetic Alphabet
ISO	International Organization for Standardization
LEI	Language Endangerment Index
M	masculine
NP	noun phrase
PARADISEC	Pacific and Regional Archive for Digital Sources in Endangered Cultures
PNG	Papua New Guinea
PP	postpositional phrase

sp.	species (not necessarily used in a scientific sense)
SVC	serial verb construction
TAM	tense-aspect-mood
TP	Tok Pisin
VP	verb phrase

LIST OF MAPS, FIGURES, AND TABLES

Maps

Map 1.1. Papua New Guinea 5
Map 1.2. Langam village and its neighbours. 6

Figures

Figure 1.1. The Keram family. 17

Tables

Table 1.1. Pondi's endangerment according to UNESCO's nine factors 12
Table 1.2. Pondi's endangerment according to the LEI 13
Table 1.3. Keram pronouns 15
Table 1.4. Proto-Keram pronouns compared with non-cognate forms 16
Table 1.5. Keram deictics 16
Table 1.6. Keram suppletive alternation for the word 'thing'. 16
Table 1.7. Keram TAM suffixes 17
Table 2.1. Pondi consonants (in practical orthography) 22
Table 2.2. Pondi vowels (in practical orthography) 29
Table 3.1. Final segments in Pondi nominal plurals 56

Table 3.2. Final segments in Pondi nominal plurals
(grouped allomorphically) 56

Table 4.1. Basic TAM suffixes in Pondi. 60

Table 4.2. Paradigms for verbs with nasal-final stems 61

Table 4.3. Paradigms for verbs with stems ending in (covert) -m..... 61

Table 4.4. Verbal prefixes 62

Table 4.5. Paradigms for *i-* 'come' and *mal-* 'go' 74

Table 5.1. Adjectives. 76

Table 5.2. Irregular adjectives 78

Table 5.3. The derivational suffix *-wi* '-like' 78

Table 5.4. Personal pronouns 80

Table 5.5. Reflexive/reciprocal pronouns 80

Table 5.6. Possessive pronouns for non-plural possessum 81

Table 5.7. Possessive pronouns for plural possessum.............. 82

Table 5.8. Intensive pronouns 83

Table 5.9. Intensive words 84

Table 5.10. Deictic demonstratives.......................... 85

Table 5.11. Quantifiers.................................... 88

Table 5.12. Postpositions 90

Table 5.13. Temporal adverbs............................... 95

Table 5.14. Locative adverbs. 97

Table 5.15. Other adverbs 98

Table 5.16. Negators 100

Table 5.17. Interrogative words 100

Table 5.18. Conjunctions................................. 101

Table 5.19. Pondi numerals up to twenty-four 104

Table 5.20. Pondi higher numerals.......................... 105

Table 6.1. Auxiliary verbs................................. 114

Table 8.1. Paradigms for verbs of speaking 151

1
INTRODUCTION

This is a grammatical sketch of Pondi [ISO 639-3 lnm, Glottocode lang1328], a severely endangered language spoken by fewer than 300 people, almost all of whom live in a single village in the Sepik region of Papua New Guinea (PNG). Pondi is a non-Austronesian (i.e. Papuan) language, belonging to the Ulmapo branch of the Keram family.

1.1 Organisation

In this introductory chapter, I briefly describe the previous research on the language (§1.2) and my own research methodology (§1.3), before explaining the orthography and presentation of examples in this grammar (§1.4). Then I provide some extralinguistic context for the Pondi language and people (§1.5), describe its level of endangerment (§1.6), and discuss its genetic classification (§1.7). Chapter 1 concludes with a typological overview of Pondi's grammar (§1.8). Chapter 2 covers matters of phonetics and phonology. Then I discuss the morphology of two very important word classes: nouns (Chapter 3) and verbs (Chapter 4). After this, I cover other, smaller word classes, including pronouns, determiners, and postpositions (Chapter 5). In Chapter 6, I consider syntactic phenomena that exist at the level of the phrase, including nominal number and possession (for noun phrases) and compound verbs and equational constructions (for verb phrases). Then, in Chapter 7, I turn to clausal syntax, looking at basic constituent order, alignment, core arguments and obliques, and monoclausal sentences. The focus of Chapter 8 is the syntax of the Pondi sentence, beginning with a discussion of complex sentences before turning to a number of syntactic topics—namely, questions, commands, negation, reported speech, and conditional sentences. Finally, Chapter 9 provides a lexicon of over 600 Pondi words, presented both as a Pondi-to-English word list and as an English-to-Pondi finder list. I have also included Swadesh and SIL word lists to serve as handy reference for crosslinguistic comparison.

1.2 Previous research on the language

Prior to 2016, there was only minimal linguistic research concerning the Pondi language. Donald Laycock (1973:36) first identified the language (as 'Langam') in the linguistic literature, following a survey trip in 1971, during which he produced 21 pages of handwritten field notes, including a word list of about 200 words and some basic sentences that he had elicited. These have never been published, but digital copies of his field notebooks (including these notes on Pondi) are available through the PARADISEC online archive (Laycock 1971).

Pondi's two closest relatives are Ulwa and Mwakai. Barlow (2018) is a reference grammar of Ulwa. Barlow (2020) offers grammatical notes on Mwakai.

1.3 Methodology

The descriptions and analyses here are based on two field trips. On the first field trip (July 2016), I visited Langam village, where Pondi is spoken. I spent about 12 hours eliciting words and sentences over the course of two days. My three consultants then were Bonny Koiama (born 1966), Clement Katram (born 1973), and Robert Kupoa (born around 1965). On the second field trip (August 2018), I met with just Bonny Koiama and Clement Katram, who travelled to Manu village (about a day's walk away from Langam) to work with me. There I spent about 18 hours eliciting data over the course of three days. In total, I have recorded about 27 hours of Pondi digital audio data, which is archived with PARADISEC (Barlow 2016). Elicitation was conducted by using Tok Pisin as a contact language (all examples included in this grammar are taken from elicited sentences). It goes without saying that, given the limited time spent with consultants and the absence of a corpus of naturalistic texts, the descriptions found in this book are simply the best I can offer, given the quantity and quality of data.

1.4 Orthography and presentation

The working orthography has been chosen here so as to avoid less common (or more difficult to type) characters (such as <ⁿdʒ>) as well as to facilitate phonological comparison with Pondi's sister languages Ulwa (Barlow 2018) and Mwakai (Barlow 2020). Although phonetic realisations differ, the same basic set of graphemes is used for all three languages, with the only exception that Mwakai uses <r> where Pondi and Ulwa use <l> to represent the single liquid phoneme.

The graphemes used in this orthography mostly match those found in the IPA. The exceptions are as follows: <mb> = /ᵐb/, <nd> = /ⁿd/, <ng> = /ᵑg/, <nj> = /ⁿdʒ/, and <ï> = /i/.

Pondi examples are presented in four lines: the first is a phonemic transcription, the second is a morpheme-by-morpheme morphological analysis of the utterance, the third is a morphological gloss, and the fourth is a translation of the utterance into English. In the first line, the working orthography is used to transcribe words as they are pronounced following any phonological rules. In the second line, morphemes are separated such that a tabbed space comes between phonological words, an equal sign (=) comes between clitics and their host words, and a hyphen (-) comes between bound morphemes within a single word. In the third line, I have followed, wherever possible, the conventions of the Leipzig Glossing Rules (Comrie et al. 2008). In the fourth line—the English translation—I have attempted to be as literal as possible. Where further clarification or a more literal translation is deemed helpful, this is provided parenthetically, following the translation.

Pondi words that appear within the English text are written in *italics*. A hyphen at the end of a verb indicates that the form presented is an uninflected root; a hyphen at the end of a nominal (i.e. a noun or adjective) indicates that the form presented is not marked in any way for number.

1.5 Pondi: The language and its speakers

In the following subsections I provide some basic contextual information on the name of the language (§1.5.1), the environment in which it is spoken (§1.5.2)—in particular the village Langam (§1.5.3)—the Pondi people (§1.5.4), their relationships with speakers of other languages and possible lexical borrowing (§1.5.5), and linguistic variation (§1.5.6).

1.5.1 The name of the language

It is my impression that, until recently, it was not common for language communities in the region to have well-established names for their languages. To refer to Pondi, Laycock (1973:36) used the exonym *Langam*, which is the Tok Pisin name for the village where Pondi is spoken.[1] When I asked speakers in 2016 what their language was called, some could think of no name, some offered *Pondi*, and others offered *Mwa*. The word *mwa*, which means 'no' or 'nothing', seems to have been patterned on the names of nearby languages such as Ap Ma (in which language *ap ma* means 'no, nothing'). Indeed, there seems to be a recent trend of linguistic communities adopting endonyms based on their respective words for 'no' or 'nothing': other cases include Kanda (Lower Sepik family) and Ulwa (Keram family). However, I have avoided using Mwa as a glottonym, since *mwa* also means 'no, nothing' in Pondi's sister language Mwakai (in which language *mwakai* is an emphatic form of *mwa*). The name Pondi, on the other hand, which is said to have been the name of a traditional founder figure, refers to the collective linguistic community. I have chosen to use it as the name of the language in accordance with the wishes of the majority of speakers with whom I have discussed the matter. It also has the advantage of differentiating the name of the village (Langam) from the name of the language (Pondi), without resorting to locally unfamiliar derivations (e.g. *Langamese*).

1.5.2 The environment

The environment in which the Pondi people live is tropical swampy rainforest. The nearest year-round navigable river is the Yuat, which is about 4 km (2.5 miles) west of Langam (as the crow flies), and can be reached via a creek when the water levels are high enough—that is, in the rainy season. The Yuat River is a tributary of the Sepik, the mighty serpentine river that serves as the major highway running through the swamps and jungles of the province.

Map 1.1 depicts PNG. The East Sepik Province (where Pondi is spoken) is located towards the north-west of the country.

---

[1] This glottonym (Langam) has been adopted by *Ethnologue* and, as of the 23rd edition, is still used to refer to the language (Eberhard et al. 2020). *Glottolog* (version 4.2.1) uses the name Pondi (Hammarström et al. 2020).

1. INTRODUCTION

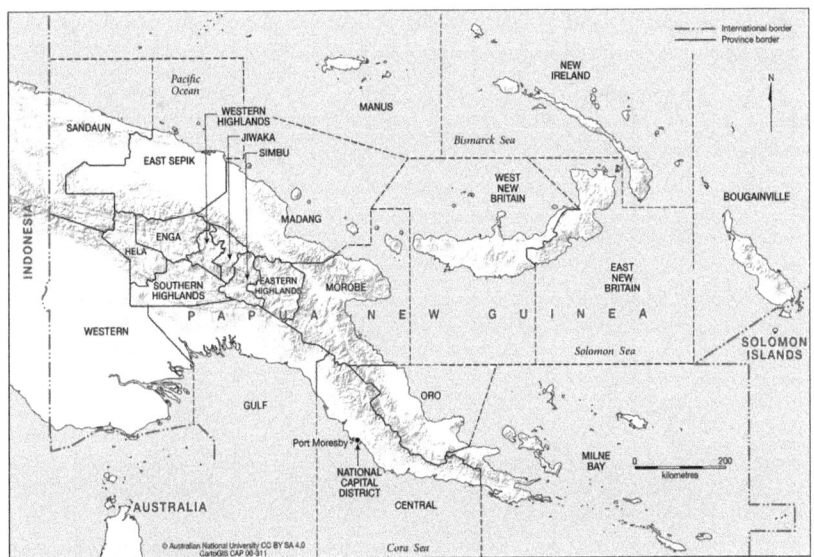

Map 1.1. Papua New Guinea.
Source: Map reproduced with the permission of CartoGIS Services, ANU College of Asia and the Pacific, The Australian National University. Available online at asiapacific.anu.edu.au/mapsonline/base-maps/png-provinces.

1.5.3 Langam village

Langam village, where almost all Pondi speakers live, is located in the Keram Rural Local-Level Government area of Angoram District, East Sepik Province, PNG. The geographic coordinates of Langam are 4°18'15"S, 143°53'5"E (-4.304, 143.885). The endonym for the village is Amonan. Langam lies about 7 km (4 miles) south-west of Kaimbal and Mongol (the two Mwakai-speaking villages), about 13 km (8 miles) north-west of Maruat, Dimiri, and Yaul (the closest Ulwa-speaking villages), and about 25 km (16 miles) north-west of Manu (the fourth and farthest Ulwa-speaking village). The other nearest villages include some Kanda-speaking villages to the north and west, Mundukumo-speaking villages to the west and south, and Ap Ma-speaking villages to the south and east.

The village has no health clinic and no school. A primary school was founded in 2010, but is currently defunct, awaiting official certification, materials, and teachers. There are two churches in the village: one Catholic and the other Assemblies of God.

The village consists of 87 houses, sitting on either side of a single path that runs about 0.8 km (0.5 miles) from end to end.

Map 1.2 depicts the location of Langam village and its neighbouring villages, with different colours indicating the different languages traditionally spoken in these villages.

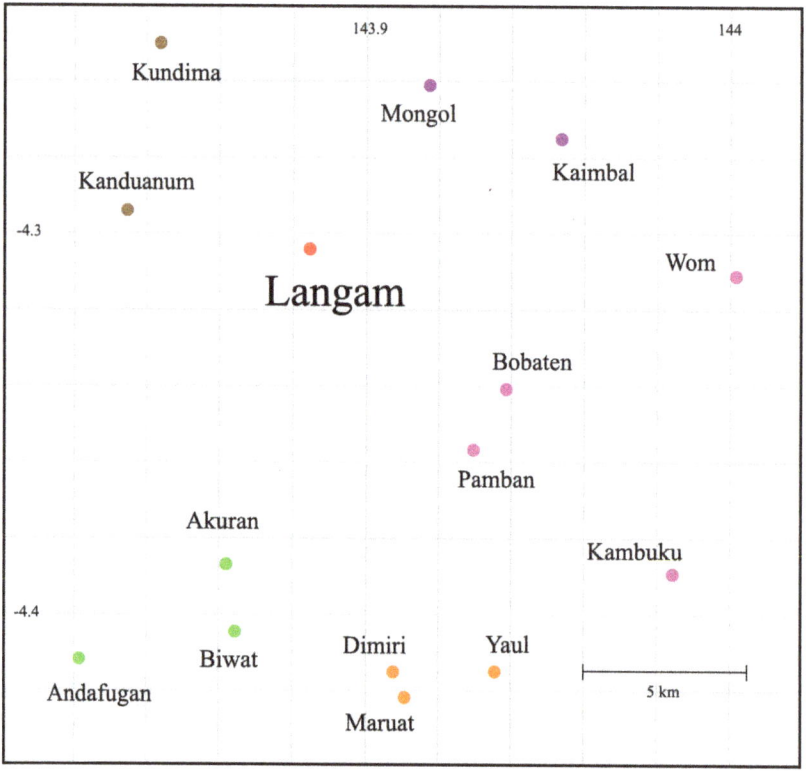

Map 1.2. Langam village and its neighbours.

Six languages are spoken in this small area: Pondi [lnm] (Langam), Kanda [aog] (Kundima, Kanduanum), Mwakai [mgt] (Mongol, Kaimbal), Ap Ma [kbx] (Wom, Bobaten, Pamban, Kambuku), Mundukumo [bwm] (Akuran, Biwat, Andafugan), Ulwa [yla] (Dimiri, Yaul, Maruat).
Source: Author's depiction.

1.5.4 The people

There are about 600 ethnic Pondis, almost all of whom live in Langam village. There they subsist on a combination of hunting, gathering, fishing, and horticulture. The most important staple carbohydrate and single greatest source of food energy is sago, a starch that must be painstakingly extracted from various species of palms of the *Metroxylon* genus, processed and strained to form a flour (*ilas* in Pondi), and then prepared either by frying to create a chewy pancake (*kïmï*) or—more commonly—by mixing with boiling water to create a jelly (*ke*). This is eaten with almost every meal (indeed, *ke* 'jellied sago' is also the general Pondi word for 'food'). The work of processing sago is traditionally the domain of women. Some people maintain small banana and coconut plantations. Bananas (generally of the starchy plantain variety, which need to be cooked) are another source of carbohydrates. Coconuts are a major source of dietary fats. Protein, when available, mostly comes from the creek that runs near the village. People fish with traps, nets, and sometimes just their bare hands. Protein also comes in the form of grubs, which are harvested from the stems of certain palm species. The men of the village also occasionally hunt with spears: pigs, bandicoots, and crocodiles are the most common game. Finally, various leafy green vegetables are gathered from the surrounding jungle.

The favourite recreational drug of the Pondi people is betel nut (the fruit of the *Areca catechu* palm), which is chewed with lime (calcium hydroxide) along with the leaf or flower of the *Piper betle* vine ('betel pepper') to produce the effects of a mild stimulant.

Although the Pondi people meet most of their needs with what they can find and make in the jungle, a small amount of cash does enter the community. Some people produce surplus sago, which they transport via canoe to sell in the town of Angoram. People use cash to buy things like clothes, soap, pots, and non-perishable food items, such as rice, canned fish, and salt.

The Pondi people all identify as being Christian. Most people belong either to the Catholic Church or to the Assemblies of God congregation, each of which has a designated church structure found within Langam village. A few people are members of the Christian Revival Church, although this has no physical place of worship in Langam.

A census conducted in July 2016 at my behest revealed that there were 616 residents of Langam village. Of these, all but one were ethnic Pondis, born and raised in Langam village (the one exception was a woman from the Mwakai-speaking Mongol village who had married a Pondi man and moved to his village). I was told that there were only two ethnic Pondis who were living outside Langam village (a man living in the Kanda-speaking Magendo village and a woman living in the Mundukumo-speaking Biwat village). Of these 616 people, 265 were estimated to be around 30 years old or older, 66 between around 20 and 30 years old, and 285 younger than 20 years old (people in Langam tend not to know exact ages, including their own). At that time (2016), I estimated that people older than 30 tended to be fluent speakers (of varying degrees of proficiency), whereas people in their twenties only seemed capable of producing basic phrases (although their comprehension might have been quite good). It struck me that people younger than 20 could neither produce nor understand Pondi.

1.5.5 Relationships with neighbouring villages and borrowing

The village closest to the Pondi-speaking community (as the crow flies) is Kanduanum, on the Yuat River, about 5.5 km (3.4 miles) to the west of Langam. The people of Kanduanum traditionally speak the Kanda language (also known as Angoram [aog, ango1255]), which belongs to the Lower Sepik family. Farther north, along the Yuat River, there are other Kanda villages (such as Kundima), and, farther north still, past the confluence with the Sepik River, is the Kanda village of Kambrindo, an important way station for river travel. The second-closest village to the Pondi village of Langam is Mongol, about 6.0 km (3.7 miles) north-east, as the crow flies. The Mongol population traditionally spoke Pondi's sister language Mwakai (also known as Mongol [mgt, mong1344]). Today, the village is mostly vacant, as the majority of its inhabitants abandoned the village in the 1970s, fleeing inhospitable conditions (including a lack of potable water) for settlements in the outskirts of Angoram town. Slightly further to the east is the other Mwakai-speaking village, Kaimbal, whose population is more robust. The third-closest village to the Pondis is Bobaten, about 7.0 km (4.4 miles) south-east, as the crow flies. The people of Bobaten traditionally speak Ap Ma (also known as Kambot or Botin [kbx, apma1241]), which also belongs to the Keram family. There are several other Ap Ma villages farther to the south and to the east, the closest of which are Pamban, Kambuku, and Wom. Bobaten and Wom serve as two important way stations when navigating the bayous and creeks connecting Langam village to the Sepik River. To the west and south are villages that speak Mundukumo (also known as Biwat [bwm, biwa1243]), which belongs to the Yuat family. Also, not too far from Pondi are villages that speak Pondi's sister language Ulwa (also known as Yaul [yla, yaul1241]).

1. INTRODUCTION

It is thus not uncommon for Pondi speakers to have contact with members of other villages (and, as a result, with speakers of other languages). Whether travelling by foot or by boat, Pondi speakers can reach a number of different linguistic communities within a day (and, vice versa, visitors from a number of different linguistic communities can visit Pondi speakers relatively easily). In practice, it is much more common for men to travel than for women to do so. Accordingly, there are (or at least used to be) more multilingual men than multilingual women. It is my impression, however, that nowadays very few Pondis speak the languages of neighbouring communities at all fluently. Before the spread of Tok Pisin in the previous century, it must have been common for people of the region to speak multiple regional languages. As the new lingua franca par excellence, however, Tok Pisin seems to have obviated the need for multilingualism.

That said, the two neighbouring languages that Pondis most commonly report to have some familiarity with are Kanda and Ap Ma. This is unsurprising, considering the much greater size and influence of these two languages: Kanda is spoken in 22 villages, reportedly by 8,220 people (Eberhard et al. 2020, citing '2003 SIL'); and Ap Ma is spoken in 15 villages, reportedly by 10,000 people (Eberhard et al. 2020, citing '2010 PBT'). While no Pondi speakers seem to know more than just a few words in Mwakai or Ulwa (Pondi's two closest sister languages), people are aware of the similarities among these three languages and enjoy pointing out cognates.

Given the presumably long period of cultural dominance of the Kanda and Ap Ma people, we would expect at least some amount of lexical borrowing in Pondi (if not also structural changes caused by prolonged contact and areal diffusion of features). Perhaps in part due to the paucity of lexical data available for these languages, however, it is not particularly easy to find many obvious borrowings. Still, there are a few forms that stick out. From Kanda, Pondi seems to have borrowed words for 'fishing net' (*yuwali* < Kanda *yuwali*) and 'string bag' (*mandïn* < Kanda *mandïm*).[2] The directionality of borrowing is, in both cases, most likely to be from Kanda to Pondi (and not vice versa), both because this accords with the

---

2   The Kanda forms presented here are taken from my fieldwork with the Maramba dialect. Until its 21st edition, *Ethnologue* erroneously classified this Kanda dialect as its own language ('Maramba' [myd], supposedly belonging to the Yuat family). The people of Maramba village, however, speak Kanda (of the Lower Sepik family), and the ISO code [myd] has been retired.

sociolinguistic context of the Kanda speakers being culturally dominant and—more importantly—because the Pondi forms are not cognate with their Ulwa or Mwakai[3] equivalents. The suppletive non-plural form of the word 'dog' (*ndindi*, §3.11) likely comes from Kanda *ndanda* 'dog'.[4]

The only possible loan from Ap Ma with which I am familiar is Pondi *momwï* 'grandmother', which may be from Ap Ma *mom* 'old woman' (presumably with the Pondi suffix *-wï* '-like', §5.1.2).[5]

There may also be some loans from Mwakai or Ulwa, but—given the genetic relation among the three languages and the often-uncertain sound changes that have produced reflexes of proto-words—it is not at all a simple task discerning language-family-internal borrowings from lexemes inherited from the proto-language.

Finally, the Pondi lexicon contains some words that have certainly been borrowed, but it is impossible to discern whence exactly, since they are words that have diffused (sometimes widely) through the region. A word for 'axe' (or other cutting tool, but generally referring to a metal implement, not a stone tool) seems to have diffused through the immediate area, for example. In Pondi, the word for '(metal) axe' is *sanglama*. In nearby (related) Mwakai, we find the term *sangïlama*, and in the Maruat-Dimiri-Yaul dialect of Ulwa: *sakanma*. The Manu dialect of Ulwa does not use anything similar for 'axe' per se, but does have *sakïma* as 'adze (for carving canoes)'. The Magendo dialect of Kanda has *sakarïma* 'axe', and Mundukumo has *sakanma* 'axe'.

A term for 'tobacco' seems to have diffused over an even greater geographical expanse. In Pondi, 'tobacco' is *sakwe*, a form that is very similar to words for this plant in many languages of the Sepik and even into the Highlands of New Guinea. Pondi's sister languages exhibit the words *sokoy* (Ulwa), *soke* (Mwakai), *soke* (Ap Ma), and *tʃukwe* (Ambakich) for 'tobacco', but it is unlikely that there was a proto-Keram word for 'tobacco', unless the proto-language was still spoken at the time of the plant's introduction to the region. Pondi's neighbouring (unrelated) languages exhibit the following words for 'tobacco': *sokwe* (Kanda) and *sakwe* (Mundukumo).

---

3   In the case of 'string bag', however, whereas Ulwa has the non-cognate form *ani* (Manu dialect) or *ali* (Maruat-Dimiri-Yaul dialect), Mwakai does have a similar-looking form, *mandapa* 'string bag', but this, too, seems to have been borrowed from Kanda.
4   This Kanda form is taken from the Magendo dialect.
5   The Ap Ma form is from the Yamen dialect.

Indeed, very many languages of New Guinea have similar words for 'tobacco': these forms perhaps all derive from Malay *sugeh* or *sogeh* or *sugi* 'quid (of tobacco …)' (Wilkinson 1959:1128).

1.5.6 Variation

Pondi is spoken (and, as far as anyone knows, has always been spoken) in just one small village. Unsurprisingly, there do not seem to be any discernible regional dialects. The Pondi people consider themselves to constitute a single eponymous clan, but this clan can be divided into four traditionally recognised subclans. These subclans are not known to correspond to any distinct linguistic varieties. Rather, the most significant variation found among Pondi speakers is age-determined: older speakers are more fluent. The younger speakers who can and do use some Pondi tend to introduce more words and calques from Tok Pisin.

1.6 Language vitality

Pondi is severely endangered. My impression is that—compared to its two closest sister languages, Mwakai and Ulwa—it is relatively vital, since a greater percentage of the community are speakers and the language appears to be used more commonly. Still, although intergenerational transmission may have continued until a later date here than for Ulwa or Mwakai, it is certainly no longer occurring, nor has it been for the past two decades, as there are no Pondi speakers younger than 20 years old. Therefore, unless there are changes in teaching or acquisition, Pondi is moribund and will most likely not be spoken by anyone in the next century.

The single greatest factor in the decline of Pondi is the linguistic domination of Tok Pisin, the English-based creole that serves as PNG's lingua franca and is one of the nation's three official languages. I have been told that there are (or were in 2016) a few monolingual Pondi speakers, but I have not met them and doubt that there are truly any Pondis who do not know any Tok Pisin. As far as I can tell, everyone in the area is fluent in Tok Pisin, and for an increasing number of people, this is becoming their dominant (or only) language. A rapid shift to Tok Pisin is pervasive among the linguistic communities around the lower Sepik River, including Pondi.

In the following subsections, I assess the language's vitality according to three common metrics: UNESCO's nine factors (§1.6.1), the EGIDS (§1.6.2), and the LEI (§1.6.3).

1.6.1 UNESCO's nine factors

Based on UNESCO's (2003) framework, Pondi would be considered endangered. Table 1.1 presents Pondi's endangerment status according to each of UNESCO's nine factors.

Table 1.1. Pondi's endangerment according to UNESCO's nine factors.

Factor	Description	Pondi's status
1	Intergenerational language transmission	'definitively endangered' (3)
2	Absolute number of speakers	'at risk'
3	Proportion of speakers within the total population	'severely endangered' (2)
4	Trends in existing language domains	'limited or formal domains' (2)
5	Response to new domains and media	'inactive' (0)
6	Materials for language education and literacy	'no orthography available to the community' (0)
7	Governmental and institutional language attitudes and polices, including official status and use	'equal support' (5)
8	Community members' attitudes toward their own language	'most members support language maintenance' (4)
9	Amount and quality of documentation	'fragmentary' (2)

Source: Author's summary, based on UNESCO 2003.

The first six factors are meant to be taken together to indicate the language's vitality. Factor 2 does not have a grade associated with it. Of the remaining five, Pondi averages a grade of 3.2 out of 5.0 (with a lower number indicating greater endangerment).

1.6.2 EGIDS

According to the EGIDS (Expanded Graded Intergenerational Disruption Scale) (Lewis & Simons 2010), Pondi may be assumed to be either 'Level 7: shifting' or 'Level 8a: moribund'. If semi-speakers are admitted into the set of people who 'can' use the language, then 'Level 7' applies ('The child-bearing generation can use the language among themselves, but it is not being transmitted to children'). If, however, a higher proficiency in the language is required to qualify one as a speaker, then 'Level 8a' seems more appropriate ('The only remaining active users of the language are members of the grandparent generation and older').

1.6.3 LEI

Finally, according to the LEI (Language Endangerment Index) (Lee & Van Way 2016; 2018), Pondi would be classified as 'severely endangered', receiving an endangerment score of 64 per cent ('severely endangered' = 61–80 per cent, with a higher percentile indicating greater endangerment). The LEI assessment of Pondi is summarised in Table 1.2.

Table 1.2. Pondi's endangerment according to the LEI.

	LEI factor	Pondi's status	Description in LEI	Notes on Pondi
1	Intergenerational transmission	3: endangered	'Some adults in the community are speakers, but the language is not spoken by children.'	Only older adults tend to be fluent, and there are no children speakers.
2	Absolute number of speakers	3: endangered	'100–999 speakers'	There are fewer than 300 fluent speakers.
3	Speaker number trends	3: endangered	'Only about half of community members speak the language. Speaker numbers are decreasing steadily, but not at an accelerated pace.'	While almost half of the community are speakers, absolutely no children are acquiring the language, so numbers *will* decrease rapidly.
4	Domains of use	4: severely endangered	'Used mainly just in the home and/or with family, and may not be the primary language even in these domains for many community members.'	Pondi is not used for any wider communication, nor is it the primary language in any domain for any community member.
	calculation of factors: $[(f_1 \times 2) + f_2 + f_3 + f_4] \div 25$	$[(3 \times 2) + 3 + 3 + 4] \div 25 = 64\%$	'80–61% = Severely Endangered'	Pondi is severely endangered.

Source: Author's summary based on Lee & Van Way 2016; 2018.

1.7 Classification

Pondi is a member of the small Ulmapo subgroup, consisting of itself, Mwakai, and Ulwa. There is no precise metric established for determining *just how related* members of a given family are (although it is common to draw impressionistic comparisons such as: 'as related as the members of Romance' or 'as related as the members of Indo-European', etc.). In case comparisons of so-called basic lexical items can offer any guide, then I can say that Pondi, Mwakai, and Ulwa each share about 40 per cent cognate vocabulary (of a Swadesh 100-word list) with each of the other two languages. I tentatively propose that Pondi and Mwakai form a subgroup within Ulmapo, but this classification is, admittedly, based more on a slightly greater number of overall cognates between Mwakai and Pondi and on innovations in Ulwa, rather than on shared innovations in Mwakai-Pondi. That is, it is possible that either Ulwa-Mwakai or Ulwa-Pondi indeed form a legitimate subgroup, only that Ulwa subsequently innovated or borrowed more rapidly.

Generations of contact and horizontal transmission have obscured the historical picture of the languages in the region. Although there are a sufficient number of basic vocabulary items shared by the three languages to establish genetic relation, as well as a few regular sound correspondences, it is nevertheless difficult to find a great number of regular sound correspondences, likely due at least in part to family-internal borrowing.

The Ulmapo subgroup belongs to the Keram family (Usher n.d.), which consists of Ulmapo as well as two other languages, Ap Ma (also known as Kambot or Botin [kbx, apma1241]) and Ambakich (also known as Aion [aew, amba1269]). These latter two languages may form an East Keram subgroup, although the evidence for this is less clear than for the Ulmapo branch. The relationships between Ulmapo and either Ap Ma or Ambakich are deeper and therefore weaker. Again, if basic vocabulary can be any guide, then we can say that, of a Swadesh 100-word list, Ulmapo shares around 30 per cent cognate vocabulary with Ambakich and less than 20 per cent cognate vocabulary with Ap Ma, the most lexically divergent member of the family. Moreover, these cognates are often much more different in phonetic form (as compared to the cognates found within Ulmapo), due to the greater number of sound changes affecting the lexica.

The cognacy of pronouns, deictic markers, suppletive alternations, and bound TAM morphology, however, are strong pieces of evidence for the Keram family. A more detailed discussion of the history and classification of the family is forthcoming, but here it may suffice to present some morphological evidence. Table 1.3 provides the personal pronouns for the Keram family, as well as tentative reconstructions of the proto-forms (all in IPA). For Ulwa and Pondi I present non-subject forms, which I believe better to reflect the most archaic forms in each of these languages. The two contemporary Mwakai dialects (Kaimbal and Mongol) both exhibit great variation in the realisation of personal pronouns. The forms I provide for Mwakai are what I believe to be the oldest forms for that language; they are all attested in the contemporary language, aside from 1PL *an (the contemporary Kaimbal dialect has *kani* and *kan*, and the contemporary Mongol dialect has *ari*, *ara*, and *ar*).

Table 1.3. Keram pronouns.

	Ulwa	Mwakai	Pondi	Ambakich	Ap Ma	*Keram
1SG	nɨ	ni	ɲi	ɲi	ɲi	*ni
2SG	u	u	u	mbɨ	u	*u
3SG	ma	ma	ma	mɨ	ma	*ma
1PL	an	*an	an	anɨ	ni	*anɨ
2PL	un	un	wan	onɨ	nu	*unɨ
3PL	ⁿdɨ	ⁿdə	ⁿdɨ	alɨ	li	*ⁿdɨ

Source: Author's field notes.

The odd-looking 2SG Ambakich form may be compared to a common alternate Ap Ma 2SG form *uᵐba*. The 3PL Ambakich and Ap Ma forms with /l/ are probably derived from a proto-Keram plural distal deictic marker (cf. Ulwa *ala*, Mwakai *ara*, and Pondi *ala* 'those'). Also, Ap Ma has lost most initial syllables in multisyllabic words (apparent throughout the lexicon), thus explaining 1PL *ni* (< *anɨ*) and 2PL *nu* (< *unɨ*, or perhaps *unu*).

These forms may be compared with those of some of the nearest languages belonging to different language families (Table 1.4, original orthographies maintained): Mundukumo (also known as Biwat) and Kyenele (also known as Miyak [kql, kyen1243]) (both from the Yuat family) (Foley 2018:227), Kanda (also known as Angoram) and Tabriak (also known as Karawari [tzx, tabr1243]) (both from the Lower Sepik family) (Foley 2005:113), and Tayap (also known as Taiap or Gapun [gpn, taia1239], an isolate) (Kulick & Terrill 2019:84–85). The Keram forms exhibit no significant similarities to the Yuat, Lower Sepik, or Tayap forms.

Table 1.4. Proto-Keram pronouns compared with non-cognate forms.

	*Keram	Mundukumo	Kyenele	Kanda	Tabriak	Tayap
1SG	*ni	ŋə	ŋə	ami	ama	ŋa
2SG	*u	də	də	mi	mi	yu
3SG	*ma	u	u	mɨn	mɨn	ŋgu (F), ŋi (M)
1PL	*anɨ	i (EXCL), abə (INCL)	ni (EXCL), aba (INCL)	paŋgir	apia	yim
2PL	*unɨ	ya	be	ipwe	ipa	yum
3PL	*ⁿdɨ	wa	vara	pum	mpu	ŋgɨ

Source: Author's summary, based on Foley 2005, Foley 2018, and Kulick & Terrill 2019.

Table 1.5 (in IPA) provides the singular deictic forms for the members of the Keram family, again with tentative reconstructions.

Table 1.5. Keram deictics.

	Ulwa	Mwakai	Pondi	Ambakich	Ap Ma	*Keram
proximate	ⁿga	ⁿga	ⁿdʒa	ga	ⁿga	*ⁿga
distal	aⁿda	ⁿda	aⁿda	aⁿda	ⁿda	*aⁿda

Source: Author's field notes.

Table 1.6 (in IPA) shows a suppletive alternation between the singular (or non-plural, cf. Chapter 3) and plural forms of the word 'thing'. The Ap Ma data come from Wade (1984).[6] Ulwa and Ambakich do not exhibit any number distinction for the word 'thing'.

Table 1.6. Keram suppletive alternation for the word 'thing'.

	Ulwa	Mwakai	Pondi	Ambakich	Ap Ma	*Keram
'thing [SG]'	ⁿdʒi	ⁿdʒi	ⁿdʒin	oⁿdɨ	ⁿdʒi	*ⁿdʒi
'thing [PL]'	–	si	se	–	si	*si

Source: Author's field notes and Wade 1984.

---

6   In her original orthography, the singular form of 'thing' is <ji>.

1. INTRODUCTION

Finally, Table 1.7 shows the basic TAM verbal morphology for each of the members of the Keram family. What I identify as 'perfective' aspect in the first four languages presented corresponds to what Wade (1984) calls 'completed' aspect for Ap Ma. Similarly, what I identify as 'imperfective' aspect, Wade calls 'continuative' aspect for Ap Ma. The third TAM category, however, which marks irrealis mood in the first four languages, Wade describes as marking 'incomplete' aspect. It is likely that the grammatical function of this third proto-suffix has changed over time.

Table 1.7. Keram TAM suffixes.

	Ulwa	Mwakai	Pondi	Ambakich	Ap Ma	*Keram
perfective	-p	-p	-apɨ	-ap	-ap	*-ap[i]
imperfective	-Ø, -e	-Ø, -i	-i	-i, -a	-(V)l	*-V
irrealis	-na	-ra	-la	-l	-la	*-la

Figure 1.1 is a tree depicting what I believe to be the most likely subgroupings of the Keram family.

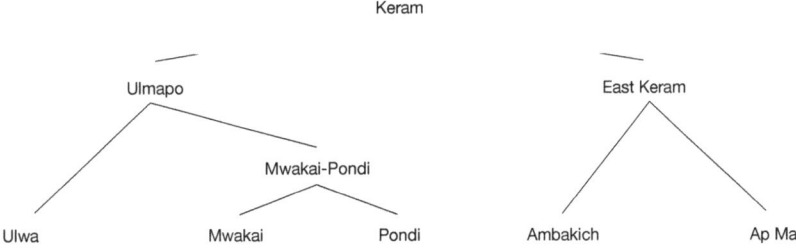

Figure 1.1. The Keram family.

Finally, there is some evidence to suggest that the Keram family of five languages is related to the Ramu family of some 21 to 25 languages spoken to the east of the Keram family, although the details of this genetic affiliation remain to be worked out. I have yet to see any convincing evidence for a genetic relationship between the Ramu family and the Lower Sepik family of six languages.

1.8 Typological overview

Pondi has a small consonant inventory (13 consonants, §2.1) and an average-sized vowel inventory (6 vowels, §2.2).[7] Pondi thus has a 'moderately low' consonant-to-vowel ratio of 2.17 (Maddieson 2013c). Pondi distinguishes plosives in three places of articulation: labial, alveolar, and velar. In each place of articulation, there is a contrast in voicing. All voiced stops are prenasalised (a common feature for the region). The only palatal obstruent is the affricate /ⁿdʒ/. It has no voiceless counterpart (i.e. no */tʃ/ or */ʃ/); the sole fricative in the language, /s/ (which can be realised as [ʃ]), may however be viewed as filling this gap in the consonant inventory. The nasal series matches the four places of the obstruent series, with the exception that there is no phonemic velar nasal (thus: /m, n, ɲ/).[8] There are no uvular consonants, nor are there glottalised consonants, nor consonants with any other types of secondary manners of articulation. There is one lateral consonant: a voiced alveolar /l/, which, only rarely, may be realised as a rhotic, [ɾ]. The vowel inventory consists of the five standard vowels plus the high central vowel /ɨ/. The two back vowels are rounded; and the two front vowels are unrounded. There are no phonemic nasal vowels. Syllable structure is generally simple. A few consonant clusters are permitted (more so in onsets than in codas), but there are never more than two consecutive consonants in a syllable (§2.3). There is no phonemic tone and no phonemic stress (§2.4).

Pondi is a mostly analytic (i.e. isolating) language. The word class that nevertheless shows the most inflectional morphology is the verb, which receives TAM suffixes and may also receive prefixes (Chapter 4). Nouns may inflect for number, generally by means of suffixation. Often, however, the alternations between the two numbers are so irregular that it is difficult to discern a single, distinct root to which a plural suffix is attached (Chapter 3). In general, though, it is safe to say that Pondi is a mostly suffixing (as opposed to prefixing) language. There may be one, marginal, example of infixation, although this is unclear (§5.1.1). There

---

7   In Maddieson's (2013a) sample of 562 languages, the average size for a consonant inventory is 22.7. Maddieson (2013b) describes the crosslinguistic average size for a vowel inventory as being 'just fractionally below 6'.

8   Velar nasals occur phonetically: as part of the prenasalised voiced velar stop and when an underlying alveolar nasal precedes the voiceless velar stop. The palatal nasal [ɲ] has a very limited distribution, and its phonemic status is questionable at best (it is not included among the count of 13 consonants): generally, it can be analysed as a series of two phonemes: /ny/.

are no known processes of suprasegmental modification or reduplication. Suppletion is found both among nouns (§3.11) and among verbs (§4.12). Pondi is more dependent-marking than head-marking: the dependents (objects) in adpositional phrases are marked to reflect their status as grammatical objects (§6.3); and the dependents (possessors) in possessive NPs are marked as such by a suffix (on pronouns) or a possessive determiner (on full NPs) (§6.1.2). Based on an admittedly small sample of verbs, Pondi has an 'indeterminate' valence orientation (Nichols et al. 2004), since the correspondences between 'plain' and 'induced' verbs are generally of the suppletive variety (e.g. the verbs meaning 'die' and 'kill'; 'burn, catch fire' and 'burn, set fire'; and 'fall' and 'drop' all form pairs of distinct, underived verbs).

Nouns are not marked in any way for person, gender, or case. They do inflect for number, however, exhibiting a highly unusual alternation between a category that encodes 'one or two' referents and a category that encodes 'more than two' referents (§6.1.1).[9] Pronouns, however, exhibit a crosslinguistically much more common three-way number contrast: singular vs dual vs plural (§5.2.1). Also, subject NPs and non-subject NPs alike can receive determiners that indicate number (singular, dual, or plural), as well as grammatical relation (§5.3.2). Non-core NPs can be indicated as such by an oblique-marker enclitic (§7.3). Possession is generally marked by a separate possessive modifier, which directly precedes the possessum (§5.2.3). There are no obligatorily possessed nouns, nor is there any grammatical distinction made between alienable and inalienable possession.

The basic paradigm of personal pronouns consists of nine items (in a matrix of three persons and three numbers) (§5.2.1). Overt (albeit slight) formal distinctions between subject and non-subject forms are present in the 2SG, 3SG, and 3PL pronominal forms. There is no distinction between inclusive and exclusive among the first person non-singular forms. Gender is not marked in any way in pronouns, nor are there any politeness distinctions made among pronouns. The same forms that are used as indefinite pronouns are also used as interrogative pronouns (at least those that refer to human referents) (§5.2.5); and the same forms that are used as plural reflexive pronouns are also used as reciprocal pronouns (§5.2.2).

---

9   For simplicity's sake, these may be referred to as 'non-plural' and 'plural', respectively.

Verbs are obligatorily marked for various aspect and mood distinctions by suffixes (§4.1). There is a basic three-way contrast among imperfective, perfective, and irrealis forms. There is no grammatical evidentiality, nor is tense (as opposed to aspect) a major formal feature. Verbs in dependent clauses can be marked to signal simultaneous action with an event in the associated main clause (§4.9), or to signal conditionality (i.e. that the clause to which they belong is the protasis of a conditional sentence) (§4.10). There is a small set of auxiliary verbs. These immediately follow the main verb, which, when followed by such an auxiliary verb, is always marked as irrealis (§6.2.1).

The order of basic constituents is subject-object-verb (SOV) (§7.1). This order is rigid. Oblique phrases either precede or follow the subject, but generally do not follow the object and never follow the verb (i.e. either XSOV or SXOV). Negators follow subjects and precede objects (i.e. S-NEG-O-V). Adpositions always follow their NPs (that is, there are only postpositions, no prepositions). In possessive constructions, the possessor (genitive) precedes the possessum (possessed). Adjectives follows the nouns that they modify. Demonstratives and numerals also follow nouns. Pondi thus conforms very neatly to the typological expectations of OV languages.

Pondi has nominative-accusative morphosyntactic alignment (§7.2). There are no indications of ergativity, whether morphological or syntactic, in any aspect of the grammar. Unlike many Papuan languages, Pondi does not make robust use of serial verb constructions. There are, however, some compound verb constructions, in which a nominal adjunct combines with a semantically weak verb to create a verbal meaning (§6.2.2). Nouns and adjectives can function as predicate complements—always without an overt copula (§6.2.3). Polar questions are formed by applying a rising intonation to a declarative statement, and content questions are formed with the interrogative word in the position expected of its grammatical function in the sentence (i.e. there is no *wh*-movement) (§8.2). Coordination of clauses is mostly formed paratactically (§8.1.1); subordination is also often accomplished this way, but may also be formed with medial verb constructions (§8.1.4).

2
PHONETICS AND PHONOLOGY

In this chapter I discuss the phonemic inventory of Pondi, describing the general phonetic realisation of its phonemes. In the discussion of consonants (§2.1) and of vowels (§2.2), I provide minimal pairs as much as possible. I also briefly describe syllable structure (§2.3) and stress (§2.4), and conclude with analyses of some of the morphophonemic processes that occur in the language (§2.5), a discussion of metathesis (§2.6), and a look at lexically determined alternations (§2.7).

There are 19 phonemes in Pondi, consisting of 13 consonants and 6 vowels.

2.1 Consonants

The consonant inventory of Pondi consists of six stops (three voiced and three voiceless), one (voiced) affricate, two or three nasals, a single (sibilant) fricative, a single (lateral) liquid, and two glides (or semivowels). Table 2.1 shows these 13 consonants, presented in the practical orthography; where this differs from the conventions of the IPA, the IPA equivalent is also given (in parentheses). The palatal nasal, which has a very limited distribution (and has, at best, only marginal status as a phoneme) is included in brackets.

Table 2.1. Pondi consonants (in practical orthography).

	Labial	Alveolar	Palatal	Velar
Voiceless stops	p	t		k
Prenasalised voiced stops	mb (ᵐb)	nd (ⁿd)		ng (ⁿg)
Prenasalised voiced affricate			nj (ⁿdʒ)	
Nasals	m	n	[ny (ɲ)]	
Liquid		l		
Fricative		s		
Glides	w		y (j)	

2.1.1 Voiceless stops

There is a three-way place distinction among voiceless stops: labial /p/, alveolar /t/, and velar /k/. All three are slightly aspirated (there is no phonemic contrast in the language between aspirated and unaspirated stops). The /p/ is bilabial, produced between the lips; the alveolar /t/ is a plain 't' (that is, neither dental nor postalveolar); and the /k/ is generally a prototypical voiceless velar stop, although it may occasionally be labialised.

The following minimal pairs (and near-minimal pairs) illustrate contrasts among voiceless stops in word-initial position (2.01). There are not many examples of /t/-initial words in my lexicon, hence the paucity of comparisons between /t/ and the other two voiceless stops.

(2.01) **p**ïn   'pot'   **t**ïndïmo 'testicle'   **k**ïn   'inside'
        pïtï   'cane grass' **t**ïtï   'often, always'   **k**ït   'bottom'
        patale   'lime'   **t**atï   'papa'   **k**atïl 'old, hard'
        pal   'far'   **k**al   'mosquito net'
        pemo   'arrow'   **k**e   'jellied sago'
        pisï   'ladle'   **k**isïm 'jungle'
        polas   'scab'   **k**oke   'clavicle'
        pul   'flatus'   **k**ul   'wind, breath'

The following words (2.02) illustrate contrasts among the three voiceless stops in intervocalic position.

(2.02) kï**p**akï   'earlier'   kï**t**al   'sago sp.'   kï**k**al   'ear'
        ka**p**atupa 'hawk'   ka**t**al   'laughter'   ka**k**al   'centipede'
        a**p**usï   'sago pith' matu**k**ul 'cut it'   sa**k**un   'stomach'

2. PHONETICS AND PHONOLOGY

It is possible for the voiceless stops /p/ and /t/ to occur word-finally as well, as seen in (2.03). The velar stop /k/, however, is not known to close a syllable, aside from in one lexical item, the postposition *lak* 'for the sake of', which derives from Tok Pisin *laik* 'want (to)'.

(2.03) kïtupu**p** 'wasp sp.' ku**t** 'neck'
  kula**p** 'fishing spear' ipa**t** 'back of the hand' la**k** 'for the sake of'

The voiceless labial and velar stops are sometimes labialised. Thus, speakers occasionally produce forms such as [yapʷə] for /i-apï/ 'come [PFV]' and [kokʷe] for /koke/ 'clavicle'. These should be distinguished from underlying consonant clusters of /pw/ and /kw/, respectively (§2.3).

2.1.2 Prenasalised voiced stops

Matching the three voiceless stops in place of articulation are three voiced stops. These are all prenasalised—that is, each is preceded by a homorganic nasal. They are: labial /ᵐb/, alveolar /ⁿd/, and velar /ᵑg/. In the practical orthography, these are written <mb>, <nd>, and <ng>, respectively.

The following words (2.04) illustrate contrasts among prenasalised stops in word-initial position. There are not many examples of word-initial /ng/ in my lexicon.

(2.04) **mb**atï 'but' **nd**at 'above them [PL]' **ng**am 'ring'
  mbole 'maybe' **nd**ole 'hear them [PL] [IPFV]' **ng**ol 'village'
  mbïn 'also' **nd**ïn 'they [PL]'
  mbingamï 'steps' **nd**indi 'dog'

The following words (2.05) illustrate contrasts among the prenasalised voiced stops in intervocalic position. In this position as well, these consonants are realised as single segments, not as sequences of nasal-plus-stop.

(2.05) ka**mb**ama 'knee' ka**nd**am 'sugarcane' ka**ng**ane 'back'
  kata**mb**us 'dull' ka**nd**ul 'cress' na**ng**un 'mosquito'
  kula**mb**ïn 'flat' ma**nd**ïn 'string bag' amba**ng**ïn 'ground'
  pu**mb**um 'bird sp.' mu**nd**u 'tongs' nu**ng**ul 'grass'

Voiced stops do not occur word-finally in Pondi.

The three voiced stops may be contrasted with the three corresponding voiceless stops, as shown in the following sets of words (2.06).

(2.06) **mb**atï   'but'   **p**atale   'lime'
       mbole   'maybe'   **p**olas   'scab'
       a**mb**ï   'spirit house'   a**p**ïn   'fire'
       ndïn   'they [PL]'   **t**ïndïmo   'testicle'
       ka**nd**am   'sugarcane'   a**t**amate   'bad'
       ngam   'ring'   **k**amo   'betel nut'
       ngol   'village'   **k**olwe   'bedbug'
       mo**ng**am   'young'   mo**k**an   'all'

There are no plain voiced stops in Pondi—that is, every voiced stop must be preceded by a homorganic nasal.

When in intervocalic position, the voiced velar stop may optionally be realised as a plain velar nasal [ŋ].

2.1.3 Prenasalised voiced affricate

There is one affricate in Pondi. It is a prenasalised voiced palato-alveolar affricate /ⁿdʒ/. In the practical orthography, it is written <nj>. Like the prenasalised voice stops, this affricate may occur word-initially or intervocalically but not word-finally. It occurs word-initially in the following words (2.07).

(2.07) **nj**a   'this'
       njakï   'here'
       njimoka   'tree'

The following words (2.08) show the prenasalised voiced affricate as it occurs word-medially.

(2.08) pa**nj**ï   'piece'
       kwa**nj**imo   'egg'
       imba**nj**e   'liver'
       mi**nj**amo   'banana'
       imu**nj**ï   'betel pepper'

The following words (2.09) show this phoneme contrasting with the other voiced obstruents in the language—that is, the three prenasalised voiced stops.

(2.09) **nj**a   'this'   **mb**an   'basket'   **nd**am   '3PL.INT'   **ng**am   'ring'
       njin   'thing'   **mb**isa-   'say'   **nd**indi   'dog'
       kwa**nj**angat 'left'   a**mb**angïn 'ground'   kwa**nd**ap   'one'   ma**ng**al   'thatch'
       a**nj**in   'our [PL]' na**mb**i   'water'   a**nd**im-   'look'   sa**ng**ine   'trap'

2.1.4 Nasals

There are three nasals in Pondi: bilabial /m/, alveolar /n/, and palatal /ɲ/ (written here as <ny>). They may all occur word-initially, intervocalically, and word-finally.[1] The following words (2.10) contain these nasals in initial position (the only known forms that begin with the palatal nasal are related to or derived from the first person singular personal pronoun).

(2.10)	**m**ï	'he, she, it'	**n**ï	'banana tree'	**ny**ï	'I'
	mangal	'thatch'	**n**angal	'navel'	**ny**anï	'give me!'
	mi	'faeces'	**n**im	'canoe'[2]	**ny**is	'my'
	mundu	'tongs'	**n**ungakï	'banana flower'	**ny**un	'with me'

The following words (2.11) contain nasals in medial position.

(2.11)	ka**m**al	'head'	ka**n**am	'now'	ki**ny**al	'coconut [PL]'
	ya**m**ïn	'all'	**n**a**n**ï	'mama'	**n**a**ny**ï	'wash [IPFV]'[3]
	su**m**am	'fat'	ku**n**ï	'buttocks'	u**ny**ï	'put [IPFV]'

The following words (2.12) contain nasals in final position. There are very few words in my lexicon that end with the palatal nasal (and these are likely derived forms).

(2.12)	ni**m**	'canoe'	i**n**in	'two'	mama**ny**	'correct'
	kala**m**	'sky'	nï**m**an	'man'	wa**ny**	'you [DU]'
	mo**m**	'fruit'	mo**n**	'louse'		
	pumbu**m**	'crowned pigeon'	kïlïmbu**n**	'shin'		

The three nasal phonemes correspond in place of articulation to three of the four prenasalised voiced obstruents in the language: the stops /mb/ and /nd/ and the affricate /nj/. The third prenasalised voiced stop, the velar /ng/, has no nasal equivalent (i.e. there is no /ŋ/); however, when intervocalic, the phoneme /ng/ has the optional allophone [ŋ] (§2.1.2).

The series of nasals and prenasalised voiced stops may be contrasted with each other in the following words (2.13).

---

1 The palatal nasal, however, has a very limited distribution. Its status as a phoneme may be questioned.
2 The underlying form of this word may be /nïm/, but surface realisations both of [nïm] and of [nim] seem to be common.
3 This verbal form, along with the one immediately following, is likely derived from a root ending in -*n* plus a suffix -*yï* (§4.1).

(2.13) m**i**ngwï   'grub sp.'   **mb**ingamï   'steps'
       a**m**am   '(one)self'   a**mb**am   'arrowhead'
       nim   'canoe'   **nd**indi   'dog'
       ka**n**am   'now'   ka**nd**am   'sugarcane'
       nyï   'I'   **nj**ï   'this'[4]
       ki**ny**al   'coconut [PL]'   mi**nj**amo   'banana'

2.1.5 Liquid

There is one liquid consonant in Pondi, the voiced alveolar lateral approximant /l/. While this phoneme is almost always pronounced as a lateral [l], it has as an allophone the voiced alveolar rhotic flap [ɾ] when immediately following /t/. Also, some speakers occasionally pronounce word-final /l/ as [ɾ], though generally never in careful speech. The liquid /l/ occurs word-initially, intervocalically, and word-finally. The following words (2.14) illustrate word-initial position.

(2.14) **l**ambom   'scar'
       lem   'nest'
       lim   'palm sp.'
       lokom   'throat'
       lukep   'lips'
       lïl   'river'

The following words (2.15) illustrate /l/ as it occurs intervocalically.

(2.15) ma**l**am   'fly'
       ama**l**o   'mother'
       ke**l**a   'rattan'
       i**l**as   'sago flour'
       ku**l**un   'wallaby'
       mï**l**ïm   'tongue'

The following words (2.16) exemplify /l/ in final position.

(2.16) ma**l**   'sago sp.'
       ale**l**   'spear'
       ngo**l**   'village'
       ku**l**   'wind, breath'
       isï**l**   'ash'

---

4 The form [njï] is a reduced form of /nja/, but it is the common (unstressed) pronunciation of this demonstrative word.

The alveolar lateral approximant /l/ may be contrasted with the nasal /n/, the other alveolar sonorant in the language, as seen in the following pairs of words (2.17).

(2.17)
lim	'palm sp.'	**n**im	'canoe'
lum-	'carve'	**n**um	'*garamut* drum'
ka**l**am	'sky'	ka**n**am	'now'
mbo**l**e	'maybe'	mo**n**e	'louse [PL]'
kï**l**	'cassowary'	kï**n**	'inside'
mu**l**	'boil [PL]'	mu**n**	'hunger'

Despite minimal pairs such as those in (2.17), the relationship between /l/ and /n/ is nevertheless not entirely clear-cut. The two phonemes appear to be not entirely stable, in that speakers sometimes replace one with the other. Some lexical items even have two equally acceptable variants, one with /n/, the other with /l/, as in the words for 'good' and 'big' (§2.7). The somewhat fluid relationship between /l/ and /n/ appears to be an areal feature.

Along with the labial-velar glide /w/, the liquid /l/ is one of only two consonants permitted as the second segment in a consonant cluster. It may follow bilabial or velar stops (/p, mb, k, ng/) (§2.3).

2.1.6 Fricative

There is a single fricative phoneme in Pondi, the sibilant voiceless alveolar fricative /s/. This consonant may optionally be palatalised before the high front vowel /i/ to become [ʃ]. The fricative /s/ occurs word-initially, intervocalically, and word-finally. The following words (2.18) illustrate word-initial position.

(2.18)
sal	'mouth'
se	'cry [IPFV]'
sim	'sago shoot'
sumam	'fat'
sïlïm	'ladder'

The following words (2.19) illustrate /s/ as it occurs intervocalically.

(2.19)
ka**s**ane	'older sister'
ala**s**is	'bee'
ko**s**unï	'caterpillar'
ku**s**am	'yam'
kï**s**ïl	'vine'

The following words (2.20) exemplify /s/ in final position.

(2.20) as   'tail'
      pi**s**   'leg'
      apmo**s** 'heart'
      yaku**s** 'machete'

The alveolar fricative /s/ may be contrasted with the stop /t/, the other voiceless alveolar consonant in the language, as seen in the following pairs of words (2.21).

(2.21) **s**aw   'bamboo'   **t**aw   'fence'
      se   'mouth [PL]'   **t**e   'be about to'
      kwa**s**ï 'bow'   mba**t**ï   'but'
      a**s**   'tail'   a**t**   'top'
      u**s**-   'build'   u**t**-   'grind'

2.1.7 Glides

There are two glides (or semivowels) in Pondi, a labial-velar /w/ and a palatal /j/ (written here as \<y\>). The following words (2.22) contain word-initial glides.[5]

(2.22) **y**an   'eye'   **w**an   'you [PL]'
      yul   'hair'   **w**owe   'middle'
      yin   'snake sp.'

The following words (2.23) contain intervocalic glides.

(2.23) me**y**anga   'yesterday'   la**w**an   'flying fox'
      ande**y**al   'many'   mïnange**w**ï 'green'
      kali**y**e   'frog'   **w**o**w**e   'middle'
      angwali**y**ï 'woman'   atï**w**ï   'father'
      sambe**y**o   'eel'   ku**w**al   'fish trap [PL]'
      kondi**y**am   'palm sp.'   i**w**alam   'garden'

The following words (2.24) contain word-final glides.

(2.24) a**y**   'father's sister'   a**w**   'how?'
      kula**y** 'lie [PL]'   kapa**w** 'cassowary casque'

---

5   Although it is possible that these words contain underlying VV sequences, it is unlikely, given that the language avoids such vowel sequences (cf. §2.5.2). I therefore assume that no Pondi root contains VV sequences.

The labial-velar glide is (along with /l/) one of only two segments permitted as the second element in a consonant cluster. It may follow any labial or velar consonant, aside from itself (/m, p, mb, k, ng/) (§2.3).

2.2 Vowels

The vowel inventory of Pondi consists of six monophthongs: two front vowels, two central vowels, and two back vowels. Table 2.2 shows these six vowels, presented in the practical orthography. The only major difference between this practical orthography and the IPA is found in the high central vowel (<ï> for /ɨ/). Also, the grapheme <a>—as is common in linguistic literature—represents a low central vowel, and not a low front vowel, as the IPA vowel chart might suggest.

Table 2.2. Pondi vowels (in practical orthography).

	Front	Central	Back
High	i	ï (ɨ)	u
Mid	e		o
Low		a	

2.2.1 The high front unrounded vowel /i/

The high front unrounded vowel /i/ is rarely pronounced as the cardinal vowel [i], but is rather more often realised as the lax vowel [ɪ], or even as the high central vowel [ɨ], especially when unstressed. The high front vowel has a wide distribution. The following words (2.25) show it contrasting with the high back vowel /u/.

(2.25) isï 'sago sp.' usï 'build [IPFV]'
ingamo 'man' ungapï 'put [PFV]'
kin '*kundu* drum' kun 'fan'
ndindi 'dog' mundu 'tongs'

The following words (2.26) show the high front vowel /i/ contrasting with the mid front vowel /e/.

(2.26) ki 'name' ke 'jellied sago'
lim 'palm sp.' lem 'nest'
kalami 'black' kame 'betel nut [PL]'

2.2.2 The mid front unrounded vowel /e/

The mid front unrounded vowel /e/ is rarely pronounced as the cardinal vowel [e], but is rather more often realised as the lax vowel [ɛ], or even as the mid central vowel [ə], especially when unstressed. An immediately following palatal glide /y/ very often raises this vowel, such that it may even approach [i], as in [miyo] for /meyo/ 'dog [PL]'. The only word in my data that begins with /e/ is the monosyllabic (and monophonemic) word *e* 'blood' (generally pronounced [ɛ]). §2.2.1 shows contrasts between /e/ and the other front vowel, /i/. The following words (2.27) show the mid front vowel /e/ contrasting with the mid back vowel /o/.

(2.27) **e** 'blood' **o** 'you [SG]'
  m**a**l**e** 'fog' m**a**l**o** 'waistcloth'
  yakam**e** 'finger [PL]' yakam**o** 'finger'
  k**e**kal 'waist' k**o**kal 'clavicle [PL]'

2.2.3 The low central unrounded vowel /a/

The low central unrounded vowel /a/ is generally pronounced as [a]. It may, however, be pronounced a bit higher, as [ɐ], or even as the mid central vowel [ə], especially when unstressed. Thus, in casual speech, the phonemes /e/ and /a/ may neutralise to [ə] (cf. §2.2.2). The low vowel /a/ has a wide distribution. It may be contrasted with the two other non-high vowels in Pondi, /e/ and /o/. The following words (2.28) show the low central vowel /a/ contrasting with the mid front vowel /e/.

(2.28) k**a**lam 'sky' k**e**la 'rattan'
  kul**a**l 'vomit' **a**l**e**l 'spear'
  kilw**a**ta 'worm' k**a**w**a**t**e** 'chicken [PL]'
  ol**a** 'don't!' ol**e** 'hear [IPFV]'

The following words (2.29) show the low central vowel /a/ contrasting with the mid back vowel /o/.

(2.29) **a**le 'sun' **o**le 'hear [IPFV]'
  k**a**ndul 'cress' k**o**ndiyam 'palm sp.'
  m**a**n 'with it (instrumental)' m**o**n 'louse'
  mïl**a** 'go [IRR]' mïl**o** 'tongue [PL]'

2.2.4 The mid back rounded vowel /o/

The mid back rounded vowel /o/ is rarely pronounced as the cardinal vowel [o]. In fact, it is often relatively high in the vowel space, even approaching [u], especially when word-final. When following a labial consonant—that is, /p, mb, m, w/—it may be pronounced lower, as [ɔ]. §2.2.3 shows contrasts between /o/ and the other mid vowel, /e/. The following words (2.30) show the mid back vowel /o/ contrasting with the high back vowel /u/, which is also the only other rounded vowel in Pondi.

(2.30) **o**   'you [SG]'   **u**   'fish sp.'
        k**o**sunï   'caterpillar'   k**u**suwate   'full'
        k**o**k**o**mï 'heavy'   k**u**k**u**l   'semen'
        mï**o**   'tongue [PL]'   kul**u**   'lie'

2.2.5 The high back rounded vowel /u/

The high back rounded vowel /u/ is rarely pronounced as the cardinal vowel [u], but is rather more often realised as the lax vowel [ʊ], or even as the high central vowel [ɨ], especially when unstressed. Thus, in casual speech, the phonemes /i/ and /u/ (and /ɨ/) may neutralise to [ɨ] (cf. §2.2.1). The high back vowel has a wide distribution. §2.2.4 shows contrasts between /u/ and the other back vowel, /o/. §2.2.1 shows contrasts between /u/ and another high vowel, /i/. §2.2.6 shows contrasts between /u/ and the other remaining high vowel, /ɨ/.

2.2.6 The high central unrounded vowel /ɨ/

The high central unrounded vowel /ɨ/ is written in the practical orthography as <ï>. It has a relatively limited distribution, as it is the only vowel that never occurs word-initially. In word-final position, it is realised by the allophone [ə] (that is, it is pronounced lower when in an open syllable). This means that the other central vowel, /a/, which may be pronounced a bit higher, often neutralises with the high central vowel when in open syllables (cf. §2.2.3). Also, both of the other high vowels, /i/ and /u/, may be pronounced more centrally when unstressed, thereby also neutralising with /ɨ/ (cf. §2.2.1, §2.2.5). Finally, the high central vowel often serves an epenthetic function, breaking up forbidden (or disfavoured) consonant clusters. Despite these common causes of ambiguity, however, there are undoubtedly phonemic occurrences of the high central unrounded vowel /ï/, since it forms minimal pairs with the other vowels in the language, as demonstrated by the following examples.

(2.31) /ï/ vs /i/
    kï   'at, in, on'   ki   'name'
    mï   'he, she, it'   mi   'faeces'
    kïn   'inside'   kin   '*kundu* drum'

(2.32) /ï/ vs /e/
    kï   'at, in, on'   ke   'jellied sago'
    tatï   'papa'   kawate   'chicken [PL]'
    kïkal   'ear'   kekal   'waist'

(2.33) /ï/ vs /a/
    mwï   'forehead, face'   mwa   'no'
    katïl   'old, hard'   katal   'laughter'
    kïl   'cassowary'   kal   'mosquito net'

(2.34) /ï/ vs /o/
    minjamï   'palm sp.'   minjamo   'banana'
    malï   'go [IPFV]'   malo   'waistcloth'
    kïte   'sago sp. [PL]'   kote   'small'

(2.35) /ï/ vs /u/
    kït   'bottom'   kut   'neck'
    kïl   'cassowary'   kul   'wind, breath'
    kïn   'inside'   kun   'fan'

2.2.7 Diphthongs

In addition to the six monophthongs described in §2.2.1–6, there are two diphthongs in Pondi, /aw/ and /ay/. Each is formed by the combination of the low central vowel /a/ and one of the two glides in the language, /w/ and /y/. The following words and phrases (2.36) contain diphthongs.

(2.36) **ay**   'father's sister'   **aw**   'how?'
    ayndana   'dragonfly'   **aw**mo   'tooth'
    p**ay**ne   'packet'   k**aw**n   'vegetable sp. (TP *aibika*)'
    k**ay**wï   'sharp'   y**aw**le   'three'
    mun m**ay**   'he is hungry'   kap**aw**   'cassowary casque'

2.3 Syllable structure

Pondi permits a variety of syllable shapes: there are syllables that contain onsets, codas, both, and neither. Complex onsets and complex codas, however, are both rare.

The following words (2.37) exemplify syllables that have neither onsets nor codas: each word consist entirely of a nucleus (i.e. a single vowel (V)).

(2.37) Syllables without onsets or codas (V)
e	'blood'	u	'fish sp.'
o	'you [SG]'		

Set (2.38) consists of longer words with initial simple V syllables. Since prenasalised voiced stops do not occur in coda position, it can be assumed in each example that each stop is serving as the onset to the second syllable.

(2.38) Syllables without onsets or codas (in longer words) (V)
a.mbam	'arrowhead'	i.nga.mo	'man'
a.nda	'that'	u.nda	'put [IRR]'
i.mba.nje	'liver'	u.nga.pï	'put [PFV]'

The following set (2.39) shows clear examples of CV syllables, since each word is monosyllabic, beginning with a consonant.

(2.39) Syllables with simple onsets (CV)
ke	'jellied sago'	nja	'this'
lo	'song'	nyï	'I'
mi	'faeces'	se	'cry [IPFV]'
mï	'he, she, it'	sï	'these'[6]
mo	'boil'	pa	'grandfather'
nï	'banana tree'	po	'chest'

Syllables may also contain codas. The following set (2.40) contains examples of syllables with no onset, but with codas (which may be glides). Disyllabic words may have initial VC syllables, as illustrated by words such as *alwe* 'good [PL]'. Note also that a glide may form the coda of VC syllable, as in *aw* 'how?' or *ay* 'father's sister'.

---

6   The form [sï] is a reduced form of /sa/, but it is the common (unstressed) pronunciation of this demonstrative word.

(2.40) Syllables with simple coda and no onset (VC)

al	'maggot'	aw	'how?'
am	'where?'	ay	'father's sister'
an	'we [PL]'	in	'two'
ap	'mother's sister'	un	'with'
as	'tail'	al.we	'good [PL]'

The following set (2.41) consists of monosyllabic CVC words. Note that glides may form the onset of a syllable, as in *wan* 'you [PL]' and *yan* 'eye'.

(2.41) Syllables with both onset and coda (CVC)

kal	'mosquito net'	ndïn	'they [PL]'
kaw	'year'	ngam	'ring'
kin	'*kundu* drum'	ngol	'village'
kun	'fan'	njin	'thing'
kut	'neck'	pal	'far'
kïp	'nose'	sal	'mouth'
lem	'nest'	saw	'bamboo'
lïl	'river'	sim	'sago shoot'
mal	'sago sp.'	wan	'you [PL]'
mom	'fruit'	yan	'eye'
mban	'basket'	yul	'hair'

Only a few types of complex onset are permitted. There are no examples in my data of more than two consonants in a cluster. In all the permitted CCs, the second consonant is either /l/ or /w/. The first consonant may be either a bilabial stop (/p, mb/) or a velar stop (/k, ng/), or—only when the second element is /w/—a bilabial nasal (/m/). Thus, the only observed consonant clusters in the language are /pl, mbl, kl, ngl, pw, mbw, kw, ngw, mw/, as seen in the following words (2.42).

(2.42) Syllables with complex onsets (CCV or CCVC)

ple	'speech'	kwan	'a'
a.mbla	'themselves [PL]'	kwa.sï	'bow'
ko.mblam	'child'	ngwam	'sago sp.'
klal	'ripe'	mi.ngwï	'grub sp.'
sa.ngla.ma	'axe'	mwa	'no'
pwas	'soft'	mwal	'forehead [PL]'
ka.ta.mbwa.se	'snail [PL]'		

Even among this rather small set of permitted CCs, there is a general preference for avoiding consonant clusters. Thus, it is common for an epenthetic [ɨ] or [ə] to interrupt underlying CCs (especially, it seems, when the second consonant is /l/ as opposed to /w/). Therefore, we find pronunciations such as those in (2.43).

(2.43) [pilɛ]   for   /plɛ/   'speech'
      [katapɨlam] for   /kataplam/ 'dry'
      [kəlal]   for   /klal/   'ripe'
      [mukəli]   for   /mukli/   'vegetable sp. (TP *tulip*)'
      [sangəlamə] for   /sanglama/ 'axe'

Complex codas are even rarer. There are two examples of codas composed of /mp/ (2.44), both of which seem derived from underlying stems ending in */mb-/ (and both seem capable of being pronounced alternatively with just a final [-m]).

(2.44) inimp   'vulva'
      nump   '*garamut* drum'

Additionally, there are some CC codas that begin with the labial-velar glide /w/. These are almost certainly derived from diphthongs (the second vowel being */u/). In fact, some speakers seem to have a resistance to diphthongisation in the pronunciation of certain words, resulting in (what are otherwise unusual for the language) VV structures (e.g. [wa.ul] for *wawl* 'scale'). Both words in (2.45) contain /n/ as the second consonant, and may thus derive from forms ending in */-un/.

(2.45) pawn   'vegetable sp. (TP *balbal*)'
      kawn   'vegetable sp. (TP *aibika*)'

2.4 Stress

Stress in Pondi is not phonemic. In single-word utterances, disyllabic words may receive stress either on the ultima or on the penult, although there is perhaps a slight preference for penultimate (trochaic) stress. In longer words and phrases, pragmatic factors play a significant role in stress assignment, although there is nevertheless a tendency for stress to fall on alternating syllables. There is no phonemic tone, nor are there other suprasegmental phonemic distinctions found in the language.

2.5 Morphophonemic processes

A number of morphophonemic processes can be observed in Pondi. Although it seems that many of these can occur across word boundaries (at least optionally so), the processes discussed here all seem to be fairly regular (and generally obligatory) within phonological words. Thus, I mostly limit the following discussion to phonological rules occurring across morpheme boundaries within words.

2.5.1 Vowel coalescence

The underlying sequence of vowels /aï/ is realised as [e]. This is probably a process of vowel coalescence, whereby the low vowel /a/ and the high vowel /ï/ coalesce to form the mid vowel [e]. This may be formalised as in (2.46).

(2.46) a + ï → e

This change can be witnessed in the imperfective form (suffix -*ï*) of verbs that have stems ending in -*a*, such as in the words in (2.47).

(2.47) ole   'hear [IPFV]'   < /ola-ï/   cf. olala 'hear [IRR]' (suffix: -*la*)
       numle   'throw [IPFV]'   < /numla-ï/   cf. numlala 'throw [IRR]'
       use   'tie [IPFV]'   < /usa-ï/   cf. usala 'tie [IRR]'
       se   'cry [IPFV]'   < /sa-ï/   cf. sala 'cry [IRR]'
       apïn we 'burn [IPFV]'   < apïn wa-ï/ cf. apïn wala 'burn [IRR]'

2.5.2 Glide formation

An underlying sequence of low vowel plus high vowel produces a diphthong. Thus /ai/ is realised as [ay] and /au/ is realised as [aw]. The sequence /aï/ does *not*, however, produce a diphthong; rather the two vowels coalesce according to the phonological process outlined in §2.5.1. This process may be formalised as in (2.48).

(2.48) V [+high] → [-syl] / V [+low]_

This process may be even more general than just described, affecting sequences of low vowel plus mid vowel as well. This holds for forms like *mun may* 'he is hungry' (from *mun ma=e* [ultimately from /mun ma=a-ï/])— that is, it implies diphthongisation of /ae/ → [ay].

2.5.3 Vowel degemination (or shortening)

Pondi has no phonemic vowel length. An underlying sequence of two like vowels results in the deletion of one vowel (2.49).

(2.49) $V_i \rightarrow \emptyset\ /\ \_\ V_i$

This can be seen in forms such as the following (2.50).

(2.50) mïnapï   'rot [PFV]'   < /mïna-apï/
      lapï   'put [PFV]'   < /la-apï/
      sinangapï 'stand [PFV]'   < /sinanga-apï/
      un   'with you [SG]'   < /u=un/

2.5.4 High central vowel deletion

There is also a more general vowel deletion process affecting the high central vowel /ï/, which deletes before *any* following vowel (2.51).

(2.51) $ï \rightarrow \emptyset\ /\ \_\ V$

This can be seen in forms such as the following (2.52).

(2.52) ndam   'eat them [PL]'   < ndï=am
      nyala   'see me'   < nyï=ala
      nduse   'tie them [PL]'   < ndï=usa
      nyun   'with me'   < nyï=un
      ndo   'after them [PL]' < ndï=o
      nyo   'after me'   < nyï=o

These forms may be compared to forms such as *ndï=tïny* 'count them [PL]', *ndï=mal* 'go to them [PL]', and *nyï=to* 'from me', in which the high central vowel is preserved when immediately followed by a consonant.

2.5.5 High vowel gliding

The high back vowel /u/ becomes a glide when before a vowel occurring in the same syllable (2.53).

(2.53) $u \rightarrow w\ /\ \_\ V]\sigma$

This can be seen in the 2SG.OBJ marker (*u=*) when it cliticises to a following vowel-initial verb, as in the following (2.54).

(2.54) wale   'see you [SG] [IPFV]'   < /u=ala-ï/ cf. utukulï 'cut you [SG]
                                                              [IPFV]'
       mun winda 'you [SG] hunger   < /u=i-nda/ cf. mun mininda 'they [DU]
                  [IRR]'   hunger [IRR]'

In practice, this change only occurs when the underlying /u/ is word-initial. Otherwise, the two vowels would fall across a syllable boundary and (instead of /u/ fortifying to [w]), an epenthetic [w] would be inserted (§2.5.6).

Furthermore, this rule must be ordered after the vowel shortening rule (§2.5.3), since that rule bleeds the change *u → w / _ u (i.e. we see forms like [un] from /u=un/, as opposed to *[wun]).

The high front vowel /i/ can behave similarly, but there is more variation in its realisation when it comes before a vowel occurring in the same syllable—namely, it may either become a glide (in this case, [y]) or it may remain, with an epenthetic glide being inserted to separate it from the following vowel (2.55).

(2.55) i → y / _ V]σ
       OR
       ∅ → y / i _ V]σ

Both possibilities can be seen in alternative realisations of the perfective form of the verb *i-* 'come' (2.56).

(2.56) yapï   'come [PFV]'   < /i-apï/
       iyapï   'come [PFV]'   < /i-apï/

When /i/ is not word-initial, then the only option for handling this vowel when it immediately precedes an unlike vowel is glide insertion (§2.5.6).

2.5.6 Glide insertion

Thus, all underlying vowel sequences beginning with /a/ undergo some form of change: if the second vowel is non-low then they form a diphthong (/ai/ → [ay] and /au/ → [aw], as well as probably /ae/ → [ay] and /ao/ → [aw]) or they coalesce (/aï/ → [e]); when the second vowel is also low, then the sequence degeminates (/aa/ → [a]). Underlying vowel sequences beginning with the other central vowel, /ï/, also change: the initial high central vowel always deletes (/ïV/ → [V]). When the first vowel is /u/, then this vowel becomes a glide ([w]), provided that the second vowel occurs in the same syllable; and when the first vowel is /i/, then either it may become a glide ([y]), or the glide [y] may be inserted.

All remaining underlying sequences of unlike vowels are broken up with an epenthetic glide. That is, in non-identical vowel sequences occurring within a syllable that begin with non-central vowels, either a [w] or a [y] is inserted, depending on the backness of the first vowel (front vowels /i, e/ causing [y] to be inserted and back vowels /u, o/ causing [w] to be inserted) (2.57).

(2.57) Ø → [-syl, -cons, αback] / V [αback] _ V
      (assuming this rule is ordered after all the previously mentioned rules)

Glide insertion can be seen in the following words and phrases (2.58).

(2.58) lo oleyapï   'sing [PFV]'   < /lo ole-apï/
      meyo   'dog [PL]'   < /*me-o/
      asiyï   'hit [IPFV]'   < /asi-ï/
      oliyapï   'cut [PFV]'   < /oli-apï/
      luwï   'carve [IPFV]'   < /lu-ï/
      luwapï   'carve [PFV]'   < /lu-apï/

2.5.7 Monophthongisation

Sequences of /a + w/ and /a + y/ may optionally become [o] and [e], respectively, when not immediately followed by a vowel. This process is quite common in the contemporary Tok Pisin of the area and could conceivably be a borrowed phonological process (although it is crosslinguistically not uncommon). One indication of a non-native origin of this morphophonemic process is the fact that the Tok Pisin word *laik* [laɪk] 'want' has been borrowed as [lak] and not *[lek], presumably some time ago, thereby suggesting an earlier aversion not only to the diphthong [aɪ], but also to its monophthongisation to [e]. This optional monophthongisation rule can occur even when the underlying forms are /a + u/ or /a + i/ (that is, it may follow the glide formation rule, §2.5.2), as in the following phrases (2.59).

(2.59) mosapï   'build it [PFV]'   < mawsapï < /ma=us-apï/   ([mawsapï] is also attested)
      mun me   'he is hungry'   < mun may < /mun ma=a-ï/   ([mun may] is also attested)

This may be formalised as in (2.60).

(2.60) aw → (o) / _ {$C_#$} (optional)
ay → (e) / _ {$C_#$} (optional)

Variations of this sort can also be seen within lexical items (as in /mokaw/ 'little' which may also be pronounced as [moko]), although there may be an aversion to monophthongisation within a morpheme, perhaps especially when it could obliterate a meaningful phonological distinction. Thus, we find minimal pairs such as the following (2.61).

(2.61) aw   'how?'   vs   o   'you [SG]'
       ay   'father's sister'   vs   e   'blood'

2.5.8 Degemination and quasi-degemination

Consecutive like consonants are reduced to single segments (2.62).

(2.62) C_i → ∅ / _ C_i

Thus, we find the following forms (2.63).

(2.63) [katala-]   'laugh'   < /katal la-/ (literally 'laughter-put')
       [kulala-]   'vomit'   < /kulal la-/ (literally 'vomitus-put')
       mina-   'give them [DU]' < /min=na-/

In these first two examples, the consecutive consonants occur across a word boundary; although they commonly degeminate here, this is not obligatory.

There is also a process of quasi-degemination, a shortening of a homorganic nasal-plus-prenasalised voice stop (or affricate) sequence, such that it is realised simply as a prenasalised voiced stop (or affricate) (2.64).

(2.64) [+nasal, αplace] → ∅ / _ [+nasal, αplace]

This process may be seen in some possessive forms such as the following (2.65).

(2.65) wanjin   '2PL-POSS.NPL'   < wan-njin
       ambinjin   'NPL.REFL-POSS.NPL' < ambin-njin

It may also be witnessed in the irrealis forms of the verbs 'take' and 'give', as in (2.66).

(2.66) nda   'take [IRR]'   < n-nda
      anda   'give [IRR]'   < an-nda
      wanda   'give you [SG] [IRR]'   < u=an-nda

2.5.9 Sibilant voicing

Following nasals, the voiceless (alveolar) sibilant /s/ becomes voiced to the (palato-alveolar) affricate /ⁿdʒ/ (2.67).

(2.67) s → ⁿdʒ / [+nasal] _

This can be seen in some plural noun forms, such as the following (2.68).

(2.68) simomnje   'kidney [PL]'   < /simom-se/
       malamnje   'fly [PL]'   < /malam-se/

It can also be seen in the following verb form (2.69).

(2.69) andimnje   'see [COND]'   < /andim-se/

2.6 Metathesis

Although I know of no productive phonological rule of metathesis in Pondi, it does seem to be a common feature of the language. Sometimes metathesis reveals itself in the form of speech errors. At least in some instances, however, the act of metathesis seems to have instigated a successful diachronic change. For example, the verb *kwa- ~ kaw-* 'hoe, break up (ground)' appears to exhibit metathesis in its stem, because the perfective form is *kwa-apï*, whereas the irrealis form is *kaw-la*.

The verb *mwas-* 'show' seems to exhibit metathesis within its stem when preceded by proclitics ending in a vowel, as seen in the following alternation (2.70).

(2.70) momatï   'show to him [IPFV]': /ma=mwat-ï/ > *mawmatï* > [momatï]
       vs
       minmwatï 'show to them [DU] [IPFV]'

In the first form (with a 3SG object), the /m/ and /w/ of the stem metathesise, enabling the creation of the diphthong *aw* with the preceding low vowel; this in turn monophthongises to [o].

2.7 Lexically determined alternations

Finally, there are some lexical items that vary between two pronunciations, sometimes even within the speech of an individual speaker. Examples include the following (2.71).

(2.71) almwan ~ anmwan 'good'
alïmbam ~ anïmbam 'big'
meyamba ~ meyanga 'yesterday'

The first two examples illustrate an alternation between /l/ and /n/, which is a difference found between the two major dialects of Ulwa (Barlow 2018:23).

3
NOMINAL MORPHOLOGY (NUMBER)

Nouns in Pondi constitute a large, open lexical class. They serve as the heads of noun phrases, which in turn may serve as grammatical subjects, direct objects of verbs, or objects of postpositions. These NPs may also contain determiners, adjectives, or numerals. Unlike verbs, nouns are not inflected in any way for tense, aspect, or mood. Nor do Pondi nouns exhibit grammatical gender or case. They are, however, marked for number. This chapter describes nominal number inflection in Pondi, covering the topic in some detail, since the morphology of nominal number is of particular interest to the study of languages of the Sepik area.

Whereas pronouns and determiners exhibit a three-way number distinction (singular vs dual vs plural), nouns exhibit a two-way number distinction. Interestingly, this is *not* a contrast between singular and non-singular (i.e. a category covering both dual and plural), but rather a contrast between plural and non-plural (i.e. a category covering both singular and dual). Similar typologically unusual nominal systems are present elsewhere in the region, for example in the Ramu language Chini (also known as Akrukay [afi, akru1241]) (Brooks 2016). This number feature may represent an areal feature, or it may reflect an old (inherited) nominal number system, perhaps in origin differentiating two categories: 'many' and 'not many'. Generally, for convenience, the glosses 'PL' (for 'plural') and 'NPL' (for 'non-plural') are used to refer to nominal morphology, but it should be kept in mind that 'PL' denotes a category that implies more than two referents and 'NPL' denotes a category that implies one or two referents.

There is no single, simple, agglutinative 'plural' or 'non-plural' morpheme; rather, Pondi nouns exhibit alternations between non-plural and plural forms that can be reduced to a number of classes (plus exceptions and suppletive forms). Some of the nouns in some of these classes appear to reflect semantic patterns, but I believe that these semantic patterns result from compounding rather than from a (lost) nominal gender (or noun class) system. Whether due to complex gender systems or not, the presence of irregular nominal number marking is an areal feature of the languages around the Sepik and Ramu rivers. Synchronically, at least, Pondi nouns do not constitute a noun class system, since they do not reflect any patterns of grammatical agreement (Corbett 1991). That is, although nouns can be grouped into categories based on formal (and in some instances semantic) similarities, these groupings do not represent any structurally coherent grammatical categories. Although adjectives also exhibit non-plural-vs-plural alternations, these are (as for nouns) lexically determined. Although adjectives agree with nouns in terms of number, they do *not* agree in terms of any sort of 'gender' or 'class' (i.e. the plural form of any given adjective is the same regardless of the form of the noun with which it agrees). Thus, in using the term 'class' to refer to sets of Pondi nouns I do not mean to suggest 'class' in the sense of grammatical gender—these 'classes' are, rather, convenient ways to group nouns together based on phonologically similar patterns of declension between non-plural and plural forms.

In the following sections I present my best attempt at sorting Pondi nouns into a relatively small set of classes, determined by shared patterns of phonological forms. These are mostly organised according to the phonological shape of the plural forms, since—roughly speaking—it is easier to predict a non-plural form given the associated plural form than vice versa. Often, it is the plural form that suggests what the earlier phonological shape of the stem of the noun must have been.

3.1 Plurals ending in *-al*

A relatively large number of nouns have plural forms ending in *-al*. A subset of these exhibit non-plural (or base) forms ending in *-s* (thus NPL: *-s*, PL: *-sal*), as in the following words (3.01).

(3.01)

	non-plural	plural
'heart'	apmos	apmos**al**
'leg'	pis	pis**al**
'vine sp.'	imïngas	imïngas**al**
'breast'	kwas	kwas**al**

Many of these non-plural forms (such as *imïngas* 'betel pepper vine') may be (diachronically) analysable as containing the element *as* 'tail'. A number of these forms refer to long, thin entities, so it almost seems as though the form *-al* reflects a semantically determined class of long, thin nouns. The following words (3.02) further illustrate this pattern.

(3.02)

	non-plural	plural
'tail'	as	as**al**
'bone'	kalwas	kalwas**al**
'tusk'	kïkïlas	kïkïlas**al**

However, there are many other Pondi nouns with plurals ending in *-al* that do *not* have non-plural forms ending in *-as* and do *not* encode particularly long or thin referents. Thus, it is more likely that these words ending in *-as* are simply compounds, containing the element *as* 'tail'.

The following words (3.03) exhibit the plural suffix *-al* following stems ending in /ï/ (phonetically [ə]). This vowel deletes before the following /a/ in the plural suffix.

(3.03)

	non-plural	plural
'crocodile'	yuwï	yuw**al**
'leaf'	papï	pap**al**
'coconut'	kinyï	kiny**al**
'house'	kapï	kap**al**
'banana tree'	nï	n**al**

The word *saw* 'bamboo' forms its plural by affixing *-al* (i.e. *saw**al*** 'bamboo [PL]'); for the word *alaw* 'paddle', however, the /aw/ ending is replaced by [-al] in the plural (i.e. *al**al*** 'paddle [PL]').

There are also several irregular non-plural/plural nominal alternations that may profitably be categorised here, since their plural forms all end with *-al*. They include the following (3.04).

(3.04)

	non-plural	plural
'back of hand'	ipat	ipas**al**
'eye'	ya**n**	yuw**al**

3.2 Plurals ending in *-ïl*

Perhaps related to the set of nouns with plurals ending in *-al* (its members at least bear a phonological resemblance) is a set of nouns whose plural forms end in *-ïl*. Although the high central vowel often serves an epenthetic function (breaking up illicit CCs), I do not believe that this explains the presence of this segment in the following plural forms, since it, in some instances, alternates with other vowels. That is, there are some vowel-final stems that lose their final vowels when the plural ending /ïl/ affixes to the stem; were this form to be underlyingly */l/, however, then we would expect the vowel of the stem to remain, so as to prevent the illicit consonant cluster.

In a subset of these nouns with plurals ending in *-ïl* we find non-plural forms (and, I assume, noun stems) that end in *-im* or *-ïm*, such as the following (3.05).

(3.05)		non-plural	plural
	'sago shoot'	sim	simïl
	'stinger'	lïm	lïmïl

In another subset, the non-plural form reflects a final vowel not seen in the plural form, as in the following (3.06).

(3.06)		non-plural	plural
	'liver'	imbanje	imbanjïl
	'tongs'	mundu	mundïl
	'girl'	iye (/ie/)	il (< /i-ïl/)

In a third subset, I assume the noun stems to end in /-nd/. Voiced stops are not allowed by Pondi's phonotactics, and so these appear as *-n* in the non-plural forms (i.e. the prenasalised stops are weakened to nasals). The plural forms reveal the full ending *-ndïl*, as in (3.07).

(3.07)		non-plural	plural	(stem)
	'shoulder'	kamun	kamundïl	(/kamund-/)
	'ghost'	namban	nambandïl	(/namband-/)

One of several words for 'mother' seems to belong to this class, although it is more irregular, its stem seeming to alternate between *amalo-* in the non-plural and *amand-* in the plural, as seen in (3.08).

(3.08)		non-plural	plural
	'mother'	amalo	amand**ïl**

The word for 'fat' also seems related to this class (3.09): it has the ending *-njïl* (with an epenthetic *i*).

(3.09)		non-plural	plural
	'fat'	sumam	sumam**injïl**

3.3 Plurals ending in -e

One of the largest and most transparent classes of nouns comprises those with plurals ending in *-e*. In these nouns, there is little or no alternation among the non-plural forms—that is, the non-plural forms are identical to the nominal root, to which the plural suffix *-e* attaches. A number of these nouns have roots ending in *-n*, such as the following (3.10).

(3.10)		non-plural	plural
	'louse'	mon	mon**e**
	'snake'	kokun	kokun**e**
	'basket'	mban	mban**e**
	'string bag'	mandïn	mandïn**e**

At least two forms have stems ending in *-t* (3.11).

(3.11)		non-plural	plural
	'neck'	kut	kut**e**
	'top of foot'	pisapat	pisapat**e**

Some nouns form their plural with *-i* as opposed to *-e*. This latter suffix may be a phonologically conditioned allomorph of the former, since, in all instances of its occurrence, the nominal root ends in a labial (*m* or *p*), and there are no attested instances of a root ending in a labial that has the plural suffix *-e*. The following words (3.12) illustrate this allomorph.

(3.12)		non-plural	plural
	'fruit'	mom	mom**i**
	'canoe'	nïm	nïm**i**
	'nose'	kïp	kïp**i**
	'sternum'	ingip	ingip**i**

The labial-velar glide *w* also seems to condition this final high front vowel. The examples that reflect this, however, also exhibit irregularity between the non-plural and plural forms: either a /w/ of the plural form corresponds to [m] in the non-plural, as in 'boy', or a final /n/ of the non-plural is lost in the plural, as in 'vegetable sp. (TP *aibika*)' (3.13).

(3.13)
	non-plural	plural
'boy'	kula**m**	kulaw**i**
'vegetable sp.'	kaw**n**	kaw**i**

These irregularities may be explainable, in part, by a non-productive singulative suffix **-m* (§3.10) and perhaps also a bygone singulative suffix **-n*.

A rather interesting subset of nouns with plurals ending in *-e* consists of non-plural forms that end in *-al*. This sequence [al] does not occur at all in the plural. This is interesting because the form /al/ is itself a fairly common nominal plural marker (§3.1). It is also typologically highly unusual for a non-plural form to be longer than its plural equivalent. Nouns of this pattern include the following (3.14).

(3.14)
	non-plural	plural
'ear'	kïk**al**	kïk**e**
'navel'	nang**al**	nang**e**
'mouth'	s**al**	s**e**
'pig'	nam**al**	nam**e**
'thatch'	mang**al**	mang**e**
'palm flower'	lak**al**	lak**e**

Nouns such as these seem in some way to be treating *-al* as an inverse suffix, such as is found in the American language Kiowa (Wonderly et al. 1954, Corbett 2000:159). That is, the suffix is not functioning as a marker of plurality per se, but rather inverts whatever basic number meaning belongs to the stem. Although, semantically, this accords nicely with nouns like 'thatch' (which comes in many woven strands) or 'palm flower', since many occur together on the same palm, it seems unusual with nouns like 'navel' and 'mouth', for which we would imagine a non-plural default number reference. Another explanation could be that the plural forms originally contained /al/ but simply lost it (e.g. **nagal-e* 'navel [PL]'). One indication that this might be the case is the fact that the preceding [m] in *name* 'pig [PL]' fails to condition the plural allomorph [-i].

3.4 Plurals ending in -se

A number of nouns have plural forms that end in -*se* (3.15). In many of these the stem ends in /a/, which, in the non-plural forms may be reduced to [ï]. At least one form, however, (*yapiyapo* 'butterfly') ends in /o/. In one of the words for 'woman', *angwaliyï*, the stem ends in /i/; here, the non-plural form has an extra -*(y)ï*.

(3.15)		non-plural	plural
	'knee'	kambama	kambama**se**
	'old woman'	katmana	katmana**se**
	'millipede'	kamuliyaka	kamuliyaka**se**
	'dragonfly'	ayndana	ayndana**se**
	'butterfly'	yapiyapo	yapiyapo**se**
	'woman'	angwaliy**ï**	angwali**se**

Stems ending in -*m* exhibit the plural allomorph -*nje*, as in (3.16) (cf. §2.5.9).

(3.16)		non-plural	plural
	'kidney'	simom	simom**nje**
	'fly'	malam	malam**nje**

In some nouns, the non-plural form ends in -*i*, whereas the plural ends in -*se* (or -*si*). All of these have stems ending in -*l*, as in (3.17).

(3.17)		non-plural	plural
	'armband'	mol**i**	mol**se**
	'creek'	nïml**i**	nïmïl**se**
	'net'	yuwal**i**	yuwal**si**

Note that the plural form of 'creek' has an epenthetic [ï] that breaks up the unwanted consonant cluster of /mls/. Also, the plural form of 'net' shows the allomorph [-si] (as opposed to [-se]). While this form seems mostly conditioned by preceding labials (cf. the examples in §3.3), it appears with some other forms as well.

In other cases, however, it seems that /i/ is actually part of the root, as it occurs both in the non-plural and in the plural forms, as in the word for 'small knife' (3.18).

(3.18)		non-plural	plural
	'small knife'	kïtam**i**	kïtam**isi**

In yet other cases, we find [i] in the plural form, but *not* in the associated non-plural form. This could have arisen as a strengthening of an epenthetic *ï*. The nouns of this pattern all have labial-final stems. Interestingly, these labial consonants trigger the allomorphic form with high vowel *i* even though the /s/ of the suffix precedes this vowel. These forms include those in (3.19).

(3.19)	non-plural	plural
'fishing spear'	kulap	kulap**isi**
'throat'	lokom	lokom**isi**
'vulva'	inimp	inimb**isi**

Note that the underlying form /inimb/ 'vulva' is rendered [inimp] to fit Pondi's phonotactic constraint against word-final voiced stops.

Further variations within this noun class include non-plural/plural alternations of *-l / -se, -l / -ase, -lum / -se, -lam / -(w)ase, -one / -ase,* and *-li / -isi*, as seen in the following words (3.20).

(3.20)	non-plural	plural
'rat sp.'	kolwa**l**	kolwa**se**
'scale'	waw**l**	wawa**se**
'wildfowl'	kunaw**lum**	kunaw**se**
'frog sp.'	yawku**lam**	yawkuwa**se**
'frog sp.'	minjam**one**	minjam**ase**
'anus'	mïm**li**	mïm**isi**

As with *-al* (§3.1) and *-mo / -me* (§3.8), it is likely that the morpheme *-se* has emerged from compounding, in this case between the nominal root and the plural form of *njin / se* 'thing' (§3.11). If so, we might expect (on semantic grounds) that this group of nouns includes only inanimate referents (or, at least, only non-human) referents. However, words like *katmana* 'old woman' and *angwaliyï* 'woman', which belong to this class, contradict this assumption.

3.5 Plurals ending in *-ate*

Another set of nouns shows plurals ending in *-ate*. These include the words in (3.21).

(3.21)   non-plural   plural
    'sago sp.'   mal   mal**ate**
    'centipede'   kakal   kakal**ate**

A final vowel of the non-plural form may be lost in the plural, as in (3.22).

(3.22)   non-plural   plural
    'lower leg'   pisangan**e**   pisangan**ate**
    'axe'   sanglam**a**   sanglam**ate**
    'feather'   awmbam**e**   awmbam**ate**

Variations of this class include non-plural/plural alternations of *-al / -ate*, *-ale / -late*, and *-akïn / -ate*, as shown in (3.23).

(3.23)   non-plural   plural
    'head'   kam**al**   kam**ate**
    'chicken'   kaw**al**   kaw**ate**
    'shell'   kamb**ale**   kamb**late**
    'grub sp.'   kïm**akïn**   kïm**ate**

3.6 Plurals ending in *-ange*

The set of nouns with plurals ending in *-ange* includes the following words (3.24). The non-plural forms all end with *ï*, which is lost in the plural.

(3.24)   non-plural   plural
    'bandicoot'   al**ï**   al**ange**
    'bow'   kwas**ï**   kwas**ange**
    'woman'   am**wï**   am**ange**

The non-plural form for 'woman' seems, further, to have developed a labial-velar glide between the labial /m/ and final high central vowel.

There is also at least one plural form that appears to have derived from a weakening of this form, from **-ange* to *-ane* (3.25).

(3.25)   non-plural   plural
    'fish'   kimb**e**   kimb**ane**

One frequently used word for 'mother' seems to have undergone further reduction in its plural form (that is, *-ange > -ane > -an) (3.26).

(3.26) | non-plural | plural
'mother' | anungwï | anungw**an**

Of course, alternative etymologies for the plural forms for 'mother' and 'fish' are also possible.

3.7 Plurals ending in *-une*

Some nouns have plurals ending in *-une*. In the following examples (3.27), I assume the root of *'garamut* drum' to be *numb-* (with devoicing of the stop articulation in the final /mb/ in the non-plural) and the root of 'palm sp.' to be *kondiyamb-* (with a complete loss of the stop articulation of the final /mb/ in the non-plural). Indeed, some speakers follow the same rule as seen in *kondiyam* 'palm sp.' in pronouncing *num(p)* '*garamut* drum' (that is, they pronounce it without any stop articulation at all).

(3.27) | non-plural | plural | (stem)
'*garamut* drum' | num(p) | numb**une** | (/numb-/)
'palm sp.' | kondiyam | kondiyamb**une** | (/kondiyamb-/)

3.8 Non-plural *-mo*, plural *-me*

There is a set of nouns that show an alternation between non-plural forms ending with *-mo* and plural forms ending with *-me*. Since the /m/ is found in both forms, these nouns could have been classified as exhibiting an alternation between *-o* and *-e* (and thus constituting a subset of nouns with plurals ending in *-e*, §3.3). I am, however, treating them separately, since I believe the forms *mo* / *me* to have a diachronic explanation. I believe that they have developed from a form meaning 'fruit'. Indeed, most of the nouns in this class refer to small, (mostly) round objects. (Actually, the shared semantic trait that is perhaps more robust among this set is that each referent belongs to a logical, generally naturally defined group: thus, although 'ribs' and 'bananas' are not particularly round, they both are found in natural groupings; this might also explain the inclusion of one word for 'man', i.e. 'man as member of a family'.[1]) Thus, I take it that a form like *mo (plural *me) 'fruit' first developed into a sort of conjunct in compound nouns. The form then came to be generalised to include referents that are not necessarily small or round, but belong to natural groups or bunches. It should be noted, though, that these -mo nouns (along with all the other sets of nouns in the language) cannot be considered to constitute a grammatical gender, since there is no agreement with other parts of speech (cf. on the other hand, the grammatical category of number, which does show concord with adjectives). There are many nouns that belong to this category. Some of them include the following (3.28).

(3.28)

	non-plural	plural
'tooth'	aw**mo**	aw**me**
'finger'	yaka**mo**	yaka**me**
'rib'	pal**mo**	pal**me**
'testicle'	tïndï**mo**	tïndï**me**
'betel nut'	ka**mo**	ka**me**
'banana'	minja**mo**	minja**me**
'arrow'	pe**mo**	pe**me**
'man'	inga**mo**	inga**me**

The word for 'egg' shows a slightly irregular plural in *-ne* (3.29).

(3.29)

	non-plural	plural
'egg'	kwanji**mo**	kwanji**ne**

Synchronically, the word for 'fruit' (or 'seed') in Pondi is *mom*, plural *momi* (cf. Ulwa *mu* 'fruit, seed' and Mwakai *mu* 'vegetable(s)'.

3.9 Plural ending in *-mbe*

There is one noun that shows an ending in *-mbe* (3.30): a word for 'man' (that is, an adult male human, often referring to a spouse), which has a non-plural form ending in *-man* (or *-an* if we assume a plural derivation of *nïmbe < *nïm-mbe*).

(3.30)

	non-plural	plural
'man'	nï**man**	nï**mbe**

---

1 Indeed, *ingamo* 'man' almost certainly derives from proto-Keram *inga* 'affine, in-law'.

3.10 Non-plurals ending in -*m* (singulative suffix)

In addition to the various plural suffixes discussed in §3.1–9, there is evidence that Pondi once had a singulative suffix, inherited from proto-Keram, which is no longer productive in the language. In Pondi's closest relative, Mwakai, this singulative suffix -*m* is still visible, for example in the word 'shield', which has the plural form *para* and the non-plural form *param*. That is, the plural form is identical to the nominal root, whereas the non-plural form is created by addition of a suffix (-*m*). The Pondi nouns in question, however, are no longer so transparently analysable. It seems that the singulative function of -*m* has been lost, requiring of a base, as it were, to include a plural suffix when encoding plurality. This can be seen in the following nouns (3.31), in which the non-plural suffix -*m* alternates with the plural suffix -*al* (§3.1) (and the assumed underlying double vowel is shortened, §2.5.3).

(3.31)
	non-plural	plural
'pandanus'	mïna**m**	mïna**l** (/mïna-al/)
'garden'	iwala**m**	iwala**l** (/iwala-al/)
'shield'	pala**m**	pala**l** (/pala-al/)

Note that the root /pala-/ 'shield' is cognate with Mwakai *para*- 'shield'.

Another group of Pondi nouns shows an even stranger alternation, one between -*m* in the non-plural and -*w* (or -*o*) in the plural. In seven of the nine classes mentioned so far (§3.3–9), the plural form ends with an *e* (allomorph *i*). In the other two classes (§3.1–2), the final phoneme of the plural form is *l*. Thus, these nouns are particularly unusual in that they have plural forms ending with *w* as the final segment (I assume here that the plural forms ending in [o] have /w/ as the underlying suffix, which, coalesces with the final /ï/ of the stem to yield [o]). They, too, seem to have their origins in a reanalysis of old singulative forms. They include the following (3.32).

(3.32)
	non-plural	plural
'yam'	kusa**m**	kusa**w**
'sugarcane'	kanda**m**	kanda**w**
'tongue'	mïlï**m**	mïl**o** (< /mïlïw/?)
'ironwood tree'	yalï**m**	yal**o** (< /yalïw/?)
'jungle'	kisï**m**	kis**o** (< /kisïw/?)

For some of these nouns, the cognates in Mwakai are very instructive, since they maintain the singulative suffix -*m* more transparently, as in *kusim* 'yam [SG]' vs *kusi* 'yam [PL]' and *kisim* 'jungle [SG]' vs *kisi* 'jungle [PL]'. In Pondi, however, it seems that the plural forms of these nouns have come to be viewed as morphologically lacking, as it were, thus in need of some form of emphatic strengthening, in this case by means of the ending -*w*, otherwise unknown as a plural marker.

3.11 Suppletive forms

There are at least four nouns that show suppletive non-plural forms—that is, the roots for these non-plural forms are completely unrelated to and phonologically different from the roots found in their associated plural forms. I present these nouns in (3.33), along with what I believe the older (supplanted) non-plural forms might have been.

(3.33)		non-plural	plural	older non-plural form?
	'thing'	njin	se	*nji (proto-Keram)
	'dog'	ndindi	meyo	*mem? (stem: *me-)
	'tree'	njimoka	yame	*yamo? (stem: *yam-)
	'bird'	njinulam	sewawi	?

The first of these words, 'thing', represents an alternation already present in proto-Keram: **nji* 'thing [NPL]'/ **si* 'thing [PL]' (§1.7). The last of these words, 'bird', seems to reflect this same alternation and may thus be a compound (i.e. *njin-ulam* and *se-wawi*).

3.12 Additional remarks on nominal number

Although there is great diversity among plural forms, there are definitely some notable and significant patterns, foremost the frequency with which plural nouns end with a final -*e* or -*l*. Of 168 known plural noun forms in my lexicon, more than half end with -*e* and about a third end with -*l*. The 168 plural forms exhibit the following final segments (Table 3.1).

When we consider that [-i] is an allomorph of /-e/ and that [-o] is an allomorph of /-w/, then the breakdown looks as follows (Table 3.2).

Table 3.1. Final segments in Pondi nominal plurals.

Segment	Count	% of total
-e	91	54%
-l	55	33%
-i	13	8%
-w	4	2%
-o	4	2%
-n	1	1%
Total	168	100%

Table 3.2. Final segments in Pondi nominal plurals (grouped allomorphically).

Segment	Count	% of total
-e/-i	104	62%
-l	55	33%
-w/-o	8	5%
-n	1	1%
Total	168	100%

It is also notable that several Pondi nouns have plural forms that are phonologically shorter than their non-plural equivalents. These include several nouns that have non-plural forms ending in *-al* and plural forms ending in *-e* (i.e. the non-plural form has one segment more than the plural form). Thus, for example *lakal* 'palm flower [NPL]' is longer than *lake* 'palm flower [PL]'. Also—at least in terms of surface realisation—a few nouns with plurals ending in *-o* are longer in their non-plural inflections. Underlyingly, however, it may be that non-plural and plural forms have the same number of segments, only that the non-plural form receives an epenthetic vowel to break up an unwanted consonant cluster. For example, *mïlïm* 'tongue [NPL]' has more segments than *mïlo* 'tongue [PL]', but, if we assume there to be underlying forms of /mïl-m/ and /mïl-o/, then the difference of length exists only on the surface level. In addition, at least two nouns that exhibit suppletion have longer (suppletive) non-plural forms than their plural equivalents: *njinulam* 'bird [NPL]' (seven phonemes) vs *sewawi* 'bird [PL]' (six phonemes), and *njimoka* 'tree [NPL]' (six phonemes and three syllables) vs *yame* 'tree [PL]' (four phonemes and two syllables).

It should also be noted that the forms presented here almost certainly do not exhaust the diversity of Pondi nominal number morphology, considering the fact that I have gathered only a limited lexicon. Also, among adjectives, which are morphosyntactically very similar to nouns in Pondi, there are plural endings that have not been covered in the present chapter, namely *-we*, *-use*, and *-sime*, in addition to an apparent infix *-e-*, which is found in the word meaning 'bad' (§5.1.1).

Finally, although I have presented only one plural form for each noun, there is not always consistent usage among (or even within) speakers. This could reflect simple idiolectal differences, analogical levelling of irregular forms, or grammatical attrition caused by language shift. For example, some speakers give as the plural of *kut* 'neck' the form *kute* 'neck [PL]', whereas others give the form *kutïl* 'neck [PL]'. Also, it seems that some of the plural forms are being reanalysed as 'non-plural' (or 'unmarked'). For example, it is rare ever to encounter *kwas* 'breast [NPL]'. Rather, *kwas-al* 'breast-PL' is often used with singular/dual reference, and the form *kwas-al-e* 'breast-PL-PL' has been coined to replace the original plural form.

4
VERBAL MORPHOLOGY

This chapter focuses on the morphology of the Pondi verb. The structure of verb phrases is covered in (§6.2).

4.1 Basic verbal morphology

A verb in Pondi consists, minimally, of a verb stem. Verbs generally also contain a single suffix, typically either one of three finite suffixes that indicate tense-aspect-mood (TAM)[1] distinctions or a dependent-marking suffix that affixes to a medial verb. (Only some imperatives and some medial verbs may occur without any overt suffix.) Although there seems to exist just a single morphological slot available for suffixes, there is a small, closed class of auxiliary verbs, which follow the main verb with which they are associated (§6.2.1). The degree to which these are independent words, however, as opposed to, say, suffixes may be a diachronic question. Preceding the verb stem there is also a slot available for prefixes, the functions of which are not entirely clear. Object-marker proclitics may come before the affixed verb, cliticising typically to the beginning of the verb stem (when no prefix is present) or to the prefix (when present) (§5.3.2).

---

1 The label 'TAM' is overly general for the Pondi verbal categories, since the three basic suffixes encode only aspect and mood—not tense. It is used here given its usefulness in crosslinguistic comparison.

Pondi exhibits a basic three-way TAM distinction, which corresponds to a set of three basic verbal suffixes. The three basic categories are imperfective (§4.2), perfective (§4.3), and irrealis (§4.4). The associated morphemes for these grammatical categories are presented in Table 4.1.

Table 4.1. Basic TAM suffixes in Pondi.

Aspect/mood	Verbal suffix
imperfective [IPFV]	-ï ~ yï
perfective [PFV]	-apï ~ -ngapï
irrealis [IRR]	-la ~ -nda ~ -(y)a

Since, phonetically, word-final -ï is always pronounced [ə] (§2.2.6), it should be noted that the surface forms for the imperfective and perfective suffixes are [ə] and [apə] ~ [ngapə], respectively.

The irrealis suffix has the allomorph -nda, which occurs when following a nasal. Similar irrealis suffix allomorphy is found in Ulwa, where the alternation is between -na and -nda, the latter occurring whenever the preceding consonant is a sonorant. The conditions for -nda in Pondi are, however, slightly different, as they are conditioned by the immediately preceding segment (whether a consonant or a vowel) and they are conditioned not by all sonorants (liquids and glides do not trigger the allomorph -nda), but rather by nasals alone. Additionally, the form -ya sometimes occurs as an allomorph of the irrealis suffix -la. It is seen in verbs with stems ending in -l plus a high vowel, such as kïli- 'die' and oli- 'cut, chop', and seems to represent a sort of haplology taking the form of palatalisation (i.e. l → y / l V [+high] _). In other words, underlying forms such as /kïlila/ and /olila/, are realised as [kïliya] and [oliya], respectively. In an alternative analysis, the /l/ is simply deleted, and the [y] emerges as an epenthetic glide (§2.5.6).[2]

The perfective suffix -apï has a phonologically conditioned allomorph -ngapï, which appears with verbs whose stems end in a nasal. (There is no apparent general phonological rule underpinning this allomorphy, as this alternation does not appear elsewhere in the grammar of the language.) For example, the verb am- 'eat' has the form amï in the imperfective, but the form amngapï in the perfective. Similarly, the verb nan- 'wash' has the form nangapï in the perfective. Note that the alveolar nasal assimilates and

---

2   The stem-final front vowel /i/ or /ï/ does seem to play a role in conditioning this allomorph, though, since we do not find such haplology in verbs like la-la 'put [IRR]' or the several compounds containing it (§6.2.2).

deletes before a following prenasalised velar stop. A similar phonological process occurs in the irrealis forms: all stem-final nasals successfully trigger the irrealis allomorph *-nda*, but alveolar nasals delete before the following prenasalised alveolar stop. Furthermore, verbs with stems ending in the alveolar nasal *-n* exhibit the imperfective suffix [yï] as an allomorph of /ï/—that is, the final nasal palatalises before the imperfective suffix. This allomorphy is unique to this suffix; it does not occur with the homophonous imperative ending [-ï] (§4.5). These changes are all illustrated in the paradigms for verbs with nasal-final stems (Table 4.2). Here, the examples of verbs with stem-final alveolar nasals ('give' and 'take') are both irregular, exhibiting suppletive or missing forms (shown with brackets and a null sign, respectively). Note also that the bilabial nasal does not delete before heterorganic prenasalised stops (thus the perfective and irrealis forms for 'eat').

Table 4.2. Paradigms for verbs with nasal-final stems.

Gloss	Verb stem	Imperfective	Perfective	Irrealis
'eat'	am-	amï	amngapï	amnda
'wash'	nan-	nanyï	nangapï	nanda
'cough'	kusan-	kusanyï	kusangapï	kusanda
'count'	tïn-	tïnyï	tïngapï	tïnda
'give'	an-	[ale] (< ala-)	Ø	anda
'take'	n-	[liyï] (< li-)	Ø	nda

Verbs that exhibit nonfinite forms ending in *-m* (§4.8, §8.1.4) also exhibit this allomorphy. It is thus not clear whether [m] is a nonfinite suffix or part of the verb stem. The verbs whose stems putatively end in *-m* are presented in Table 4.3 (note that brackets indicate suppletive forms, and the null sign indicates a missing form).

Table 4.3. Paradigms for verbs with stems ending in (covert) -m.

Gloss	Verb stem	Imperfective	Perfective	Irrealis	Nonfinite
'sew'	ka(m)-	ke[3]	kangapï	kanda	?
'see'	andi(m)-	[ale]	Ø	andinda	andim
'hit/kill'	asi(m)-	asiyï	asingapï	asinda	asim
'carve/blow'	lu(m)-	luwï	luwapï	lumunda[4]	lum

---

3   /a + ï/ → [e] (§2.5.1).
4   This irrealis form is anomalous in that it retains the /m/, adding an epenthetic [u] to separate the /mnd/ cluster.

The available data are unfortunately limited. First, I do not have any examples in my corpus of *ka(m)-* 'sew' being used in a nonfinite way, nor with the ending *-m*, so its inclusion is speculative. Second, the verb *asi(m)-* 'hit, kill' exhibits variation in the perfective form: my corpus contains some examples of this verb with the *-apï* suffix and some examples with the *-ngapï* suffix, without any apparent semantic difference.[5] Nevertheless, based on the current state of the evidence, I offer what I see as the best account of the data: there is a small set of verbs ending in a covert *-(m)*. This underlying final nasal is seen in the surface forms of nonfinite verb forms, but otherwise is not overtly present, even though it triggers suffix allomorphy in the perfective and irrealis finite forms. The verb *am-* 'eat' does not belong to this class, since the status of its final *m* is not in question (it is always present). The variability seen in the perfective form of *asi(m)-* 'hit, kill' may reflect the loss (perhaps due to grammatical attrition) of this underlying final *-(m)*.

Finally, some allomorphy is also apparent in the imperfective suffix. A phonological rule of vowel coalescence produces the ending *-e* in the form *ke* 'sew [IPFV]', from the root *ka-* 'sew': /a/ + /i/ = [e]. Also, glide insertion results in forms such as *usiyï* 'split [IPFV]', from the root *usi-* 'split'.

In addition to these three basic finite TAM suffixes, there are medial verb suffixes, which affix to verbs heading the predicate of dependent clauses. These include the simultaneous suffix *-e* (§4.9) and the conditional suffix *-se* (§4.10).

The prefix slot may include one of the following prefixes (Table 4.4).

Table 4.4. Verbal prefixes.

Prefix	Function?
a-	perfect [PRF]
l-	detransitiviser [DETR]

The functions of these two prefixes remain largely obscure to me. The prefix *a-* is discussed in §4.6 and the prefix *l-* is discussed in §4.7.

---

[5] The form *asiyï* (which looks morphologically imperfective and is indeed the form used to encode imperfective aspect) is frequently used with apparent perfective meaning. This behaviour is similar to that of some deponent verbs, which lack designated perfective forms, instead relying on imperfective morphology to encode both imperfective and perfective meaning (cf. *mal-ï* 'go [IPFV/PFV]', §4.12).

4.2 The imperfective aspect

The imperfective aspect presents states and events as unbounded in time. The imperfective suffix -*ï* signals that the event or state to which the verb refers is or was continuous, habitual, iterative, or otherwise without defined end. Imperfective-marked verbs are not encoded in any way for tense: they may refer either to past or present time (they may not, however, refer to future time, since future time is always indicated with the irrealis suffix).

The following examples illustrate some uses of the imperfective aspect.

An uncompleted event.

(4.01) meyamba tatï kapï **usï**
        meyamba   tatï   kapï   us-**ï**
        yesterday   papa   house   build-IPFV
        'Yesterday papa was building a house (but he didn't finish it).'

A habitual event.

(4.02) mï kandam nambi **amï**
        mï   kandam   nambi   am-**ï**
        3SG.SUBJ   sugarcane   water   eat-IPFV
        'He eats (tends to eat) sugar.' (literally 'water-eats', i.e. 'drinks')

An iterative action.

(4.03) alkï kulam mï **lasiyï**
        alkï   kulam   mï   l-asi-**ï**
        person   boy   3SG.SUBJ   DETR-hit-IPFV
        'The person is hitting the boy.'

A continuous or progressive action.

(4.04) anale kanam minjame **ndamï**
        anale   kanam   minjame   ndï=am-**ï**
        woman.PL   now   banana.PL   3PL.OBJ=eat-IPFV
        'The women are eating bananas now.'

4.3 The perfective aspect

The perfective aspect, on the other hand, is applied to events that are viewed as having reached their logical conclusion. The perfective suffix *-apï ~ -ngapï* signals that the event to which the verb refers has concluded. Like the imperfective aspect (§4.2), the perfective aspect does not encode tense per se, although it is almost always associated with past time. When perfective-marked verbs occur with adverbs like *kanam* 'now', the event is most likely being viewed by the speaker as having just occurred. The perfective aspect can—also like the imperfective aspect—never refer to future time.

The following sentences illustrate some uses of the perfective aspect.

A completed event.

(4.05) meyamba tatï kapï **mawsapï**
    meyamba   tatï   kapï   ma=us-**apï**
    yesterday   papa   house   3SG.OBJ=build-PFV
    'Yesterday papa built the house.'

A past action with present consequence.

(4.06) o awse **amngapï**
    o   aw-se   am-**ngapï**
    2SG.SUBJ   Q-thing.PL   eat-PFV
    'What have you eaten?'

An action that has immediately transpired.

(4.07) kanam alkï kulam mï **lasiyapï**
    kanam   alkï   kulam   mï   l-asi-**apï**
    now   person   boy   3SG.SUBJ   DETR-hit-PFV
    'Just now, the person hit the boy.'

4.4 The irrealis mood

In contrast to the two other major TAM suffixes, the irrealis suffix *-la ~ -nda* does not encode aspect, but rather mood. While the irrealis suffix is the only verbal suffix available to the speaker when referring to future time, this same suffix can also be used when referring to present or past time. It is used whenever encoding something nonfactual (events in future time are necessarily nonfactual). The following sentences illustrate some uses of the irrealis mood.

Future time/prediction.

(4.08) kïmbïlo alkï kulam mï **lasinda**
 kïmbïlo alkï kulam mï l-asi-**nda**
 tomorrow person boy 3SG.SUBJ DETR-hit-IRR
 'The person will hit the boy tomorrow.'

Future time/intention.

(4.09) kïmbïlo nyï name **asinda**
 kïmbïlo nyï name asi-**nda**
 tomorrow 1SG pig.PL hit-IRR
 'I'll kill lots of pigs tomorrow.'

Volition ('want', 'would like', etc.).

(4.10) wan kandam nambi **amnda**
 wan kandam nambi am-**nda**
 2PL sugarcane water eat-IRR
 'Would you like to eat some sugarcane?' (literally 'drink')

Necessity ('should', 'must', etc.).

(4.11) kanam nyï kapï **usïla**
 kanam nyï kapï us-**la**
 now 1SG house build-IRR
 'I should build a house now.'

Ability ('can', 'could', etc.).

(4.12) kanam nyinjin kulam ambo **kawla**
 kanam nyi-njin kulam ambo kaw-**la**
 now 1SG-POSS.NPL boy NEG sleep-IRR
 'My son can't sleep now.'

4.5 The imperative mood

The imperative form of a verb is (generally) simply the verb stem—that is, there is often no overt TAM suffix on the verb, as seen in the following example.

(4.13) kapï **maws**
kapï   ma=**us**
house   3SG.OBJ=build
'Build the house!'

Although imperative forms generally take no suffix, the prefix *a-* (§4.6) may appear on the verb, as in the following.

(4.14) ke **alik**
ke   **a**-lik
sago   PRF-prepare
'Prepare the sago!'

Verb stems that end in a covert *-m* exhibit this final segment in their imperative forms, as seen in examples (4.15) and (4.16).

(4.15) **anandim**
an=**andim**
1PL=see
'Look at us!'

(4.16) namal **asim**
namal   **asim**
pig   hit
'Hit the pig!'

An epenthetic suffix *ï* may occur at the end of the imperative forms following certain consonants (such as /l/), presumably to aid in pronunciation or add stress to the final segment, as in the following.

(4.17) **amalï**
a-mal-ï
PRF-go-IMP
'Go!'

The irregular imperative form of *p-* 'be (at)' is discussed in §4.11. The verb *am-* 'eat' also seems to have an irregular imperative form. It appears to have the detransitiviser prefix *l-* (§4.7) fossilised to the verb root (cf. the basic TAM paradigm for Ulwa 'eat': *am* [IPFV], *amap* [PFV], *landa* [IRR]). To confuse matters, it seems that the verb *am-* 'eat' always takes the perfect prefix *a-* in its imperative forms, giving the appearance (perhaps only superficially) that the prefixes *a-* and *l-* are co-occurring. The following sentences exemplify the imperative forms of 'eat'.

(4.18) minjamo **alam**
 minjamo **a-lam**
 banana PRF-eat.IMP
 'Eat a banana!'

(4.19) **malam**
 ma=**a-lam**
 3SG.OBJ=PRF-eat.IMP
 'Eat!' (literally 'Eat it!')

More examples of imperatives are provided in §8.3.

4.6 The perfect prefix *a-*

The prefix *a-* is one of only two prefixes in the language (the other, *l-*, is discussed in §4.7). It only occurs with perfective or imperative forms in my corpus, and it never seems to be obligatory. Perhaps cognate with the Ulwa adverb *ta* 'already', this prefix may indicate that an event occurs or occurred before some reference point (i.e. perfect aspect). Its exact aspectual nuances are, however, not fully known, and it could perhaps instead be considered a completive marker. The fact that it is morphologically part of the verb (and not simply an adverb meaning 'already' that precedes the verb) is apparent in example (4.19), since it (along with the verb stem) hosts the object-marker proclitic. The following pairs of sentences contrast perfective-marked verbs that contain this prefix (4.21, 4.22) with those that do not (4.20, 4.23).

(4.20) tatï nïm luwapï
 tatï nïm lu-apï
 papa canoe carve-PFV
 'Papa carved the canoe.'

(4.21) tatï nïm **aluwapï**
   tatï   nïm   **a**-lu-apï
   papa   canoe   PRF-carve-PFV
   'Papa already carved the canoe.'

(4.22) Peter ngol **ayï**
   Peter   ngol   **a**-i-ï
   [name]   village   PRF-come-IPFV
   'Has Peter already come home?'

(4.23) meyamba mï ngol iyï
   meyamba   mï   ngol   i-ï
   yesterday   3SG.SUBJ   village   come-IPFV
   'He came home yesterday.' (This is the response to the question in example 4.22.)

The perfect prefix *a-* may serve the clarifying function of marking perfective aspects in verbs that make no morphological distinction between perfective and imperfective forms (such as for the verb *i-* 'come', as in examples 4.22 and 4.23; see §4.12). For example, the verb *si-* 'sit' is deponent in that it only has the two basic TAM forms: *si-ï* 'sit-IPFV' and *si-la* 'sit-IRR', lacking a designated perfective form. The perfect prefix may thus help signal perfective aspect, as in the following example.

(4.24) kulam min **asiyï**
   kulam   min   **a**-si-ï
   boy   3DU   PRF-sit-IPFV
   'The (two) boys have already sat down.'

In imperatives, I assume that the prefix *a-* adds some urgency to the command (i.e. 'do it already!') (§8.3).

4.7 The detransitiviser prefix *I-*

Pondi has no known morphological means of increasing valency. There are no applicatives in the language, nor does it seem that causatives can be formed with less than two clauses (this is, however, speculative, based solely on how permissive constructions are formed in the language, §8.1.3). There may, however, be a morphological means of decreasing valency (or, perhaps better put, of signalling a relatively low level of semantic transitivity). I do not know whether passive constructions (of any sort) exist in the language,[6] but there do seem to be some constructions that resemble antipassives. The prefix *l*-, which is glossed here as 'DETR' ('detransitiviser') is indeed hard to decipher. Based on its likely cognacy with Ulwa *na*- 'DETR',[7] I present here a discussion of some of its possible morphosyntactic functions.

In Ulwa, the presence of an immediately preverbal oblique necessitates the demotion of the logical object to oblique status (Barlow 2019b). In Ulwa this demotion to oblique status is signalled through an oblique-marking enclitic (=*n*) on the demoted object, without any additional verbal morphology. The transitivity-reducing prefix *na*-, on the other hand, is typically employed in Ulwa *without* any demoted object. In Pondi, too, the presence of an immediately preverbal oblique can trigger a sort of valency reduction. Here, however, no oblique marking is necessary on the logical object;[8] rather, the prefix *l*- appears on the verb.

The following pair of sentences seems to illustrate this sort of 'detransitivisation'. Here, the verb *nambi pu*- 'bathe' has a grammatical object when it functions as a transitive verb (e.g. 'bathe the child'); the theme argument (that which is bathed) occurs between the two elements (4.25); when, however, the theme is not in this position, the verb takes the prefix *l*- (here exhibiting a phonologically conditioned allomorph *lï*-, with the high central vowel breaking up the word-initial consonant cluster /lp-/) (4.26).

(4.25) meyamba nanï **nambi kulam** mapwapï
       meyamba   nanï   **nambi**   **kulam**   ma=pu-apï
       yesterday   mama   water   boy   3SG.OBJ=bathe-PFV
       'Mama bathed the boy yesterday.'

(4.26) meyamba nanï kulam nambi **lïpwapï**
       meyamba   nanï   **kulam**   **nambi**   l-pu-apï
       yesterday   mama   boy   water   DETR-bathe-PFV
       'Mama bathed the boy yesterday.'

---

6   See Barlow (2019a) for discussion of the typologically unusual 'syntactic passive' construction in Pondi's sister language Ulwa.
7   The prefix *na*- in Ulwa functions much like an antipassive marker, signalling that the event encoded by the verb has reduced transitivity—that is, that it deviates from the common semantic properties of prototypical transitive clauses (Barlow 2019b).
8   It must be pointed out that overt oblique marking is only permitted on pronouns and determiners (§7.3), and I do not have examples of 'detransitivised' sentences with demoted object NPs containing such word classes.

The following pair of sentences illustrates a similar detransitivisation. In (4.27), the oblique argument *pemo* 'arrow' appears in the canonical position following the subject but preceding the object. In (4.28), on the other hand, the oblique is fronted to immediately preverbal position. Here the detransitiviser prefix *l-* appears on the verb. While the logical object (*njinulam* 'bird') appears to have been demoted to an oblique, it seems that the oblique argument *pemo* 'arrow' has been promoted not to an object but rather to a second subject (as signalled by the subject marker *mï*). This, too, which is difficult to explain fully, seems to parallel a similar phenomenon in Ulwa (Barlow 2019a), perhaps one akin to double nominative constructions in languages like Japanese.

(4.27) tatï **pemo njinulam** masiyï

tatï	**pemo**	**njinulam**	ma=asi-ï
papa	arrow	bird	3SG.OBJ=hit-IPFV

'Papa shot the bird with an arrow.'

(4.28) tatï **njinulam pemo mï lasiyï**

tatï	**njinulam**	**pemo**	**mï**	l-asi-ï
papa	bird	arrow	3SG.SUBJ	DETR-hit-IPFV

'Papa shot the bird with an arrow.'

(For other examples of this phenomenon, see 4.03, 4.07, 4.08, and 8.24.)

Other uses of the prefix *l-*, however, are harder to account for in terms of any reduction in valency or transitivity. Furthermore, there are also instances in which one might expect the presence of *l-* (based on its presence elsewhere with orderings of logical objects preceding obliques), but no such prefix is found, as in the following example (which may be compared with 4.28).

(4.29) tatï **sewawi pemo** ndasiyï

tatï	**sewawi**	**pemo**	ndï=asi-ï
papa	bird.PL	arrow	3PL.OBJ=hit-IPFV

'Papa shot the birds with an arrow.'

Perhaps the detransitiviser prefix only appears when the logical object is non-plural (whereas here it is plural: 'birds'). It is also interesting to note that, in (4.29), it seems that the object-marker proclitic refers to the logical object *sewawi* 'birds' (despite being separated from the verb) and *not* to the immediately preceding oblique *pemo* 'arrow' (the plural form of this noun is *peme* 'arrows'). The grammar of this sentence is thus not entirely accounted for.

4.8 Nonfinite verb forms

Nonfinite verb forms in Pondi are here understood to be those that are unmarked for TAM. I exclude imperative forms (§4.5), which, although sometimes lacking overt suffixation, are understood to have a particular modal force. Also, auxiliary verbs, two of which may occur without TAM marking, are discussed separately (§6.2.1).

In certain medial verb constructions, there is a finite verb (marked for TAM), which sits at the end of a sentence, while—somewhere in the middle—sits a nonfinite (medial) verb (unmarked for TAM). In such constructions, the action encoded by the medial, nonfinite verb is understood to precede that of the finite verb at the end of the main clause. Verbs with otherwise covert final *-m* in their stems (§4.1) exhibit this final consonant in their nonfinite forms. Nonfinite verb forms are covered in greater detail in the discussion of subordination in §8.1.4 (see examples 8.10, 8.11, 8.12, and 8.13).

4.9 The simultaneous suffix -e

Although medial verbs, which imply a sequential temporal relationship with a final verb, are unmarked for TAM distinctions (§4.8), verbs in dependent clauses that imply a simultaneous temporal relationship with the verb in a main clause receive the simultaneous suffix *-e*. This suffix affixes to the verb in the dependent clause, without any other suffix permitted. The following sentences illustrate the use of the simultaneous suffix *-e*.

(4.30) o **kawe** name ngol ol amalï
o kaw-**e** name ngol ol a-mal-ï
2SG.SUBJ sleep-SIM pig.PL village from PRF-go-IPFV
'While you were sleeping, the pigs left the village.'

(4.31) nyï minjamo **ame** kokun kapï iyï
nyï minjamo am-**e** kokun kapï i-ï
1SG banana eat-SIM snake house come-IPFV
'When I was eating a banana, a snake came into the house.'

(4.32) komblam moko **male** alkï ndindi asiyï
       komblam   moko   mal-**e**   alkï   ndindi   asi-ï
       child   little   go-SIM   person   dog   hit-IPFV
       'The person hit the dog when the child went.'

Simultaneous clauses are discussed further in §8.1.5.

4.10 The conditional suffix -se

There is at least one other dependent-marking verbal suffix: the conditional suffix *-se*, which affixes to the verb in the protasis of a conditional sentence. This suffix, which takes the same slot as the simultaneous suffix (§4.9), indicates that the verb to which it affixes forms (part of) the predicate of a protasis in a conditional sentence (§8.6). As this suffix (generally) affixes directly to the verb stem, the verb is not in any way marked for tense, aspect, or mood (e.g. forms such as 'if it rained' and 'if it is raining' would be expressed with the same verb forms).

The conditional suffix *-se* may, perhaps, be analysable as containing a conditional element *-s(a)* plus the simultaneous suffix *-e*. Under this assumption, the conditional element would likely be cognate with the conditional suffix *-ta* in Ulwa (there are other *s*:*t* correspondences found between cognate forms in Pondi and Ulwa). The following sentences illustrate the use of the conditional suffix *-se*.

(4.33) kin **lapïse** nyï kapï mapïla
       kin   lap-**se**   nyï   kapï   ma=p-la
       rain   fall-COND   1SG   house   3SG.OBJ=be-IRR
       'If it's raining, I'll stay home.'

(4.34) o ambo ke **amngase** mun winda
       o   ambo   ke   amnga-**se**   mun   u=i-nda
       2SG.SUBJ   NEG   sago   eat-COND   hunger   2SG.OBJ=hit?-IRR
       'If you don't eat, you'll be hungry.' (literally 'eat sago')

In this second example, it seems that the stem *am-* 'eat' has been reanalysed (by analogy from the perfective form *amngasi*) as being *amnga-* 'eat'.

More examples of conditional sentences are provided in §8.6.

4.11 The locative verb *p-* 'be (at)'

The common locative verb *p-* 'be (at)' shows some minor stem variation. Although the imperfective form simply adds the regular ending *-ï* to the stem *p-* (4.35), the perfective form exhibits the stem *pi-*, producing the form /pi-apï/ ([piyapï]), as opposed to the expected form /p-apï/ ([papï]) (4.36). The irrealis form is regular in that it adds the ending *-la*, although it is common for speakers to pronounce the form as [pïla] as opposed to [pla] (4.37)—that is, these speakers insert an epenthetic *ï* despite the fact that /pl/ is generally a permitted consonant cluster (§2.3).

(4.35) tatï ambo kapï **pï**

tatï	ambo	kapï	**p-ï**
papa	NEG	house	be-IPFV

'Papa is not at home.'

(4.36) mï Angoram **piyapï**

mï	Angoram	**pi-apï**
3SG.SUBJ	[place]	be-PFV

'He was in Angoram.'

(4.37) mï Madang **pïla**

mï	Madang	**p-la**
3SG.SUBJ	[place]	be-IRR

'He will be in Madang.'

The imperative of the verb *p-* 'be at' has the irregular form *alap*, as seen in (4.38) and (4.39).

(4.38) o ambinjin kapï **alap**

o	ambin-njin	kapï	**alap**
2SG.SUBJ	NPL.REFL-POSS.NPL	house	be.IMP

'Stay in your own house!'

(4.39) **malap**

ma=**alap**
3SG.OBJ=be.IMP
'Wait!' (literally 'Be here!')

4.12 The motion verbs *i-* 'come' and *mal-* 'go'

Two very common verbs of motion (*i-* 'come and *mal-* 'go') display interesting suppletive behaviour in Pondi and thus deserve special attention. Morphologically, they have the following forms (Table 4.5).

Table 4.5. Paradigms for *i-* 'come' and *mal-* 'go'.

Gloss	Verb stem	Imperfective	Perfective	Irrealis
'come'	i-	iyï (/i-ï/)	ayï (/a-i-ï/)[9]	ila (/i-la/)
'go'	mal-	malï (/mal-ï/)	(i)yapï (/i-apï/)[10]	mïla (/mal-la/)

The imperfective and irrealis forms of *i-* 'come' are entirely regular. This verb, however, lacks a designated perfective form. It is not alone in having such a deficit, as there are several other verbs that are deponent and use imperfective morphology to encode both imperfective and perfective aspect. Interestingly, in the case of 'come', however, this perfective form has migrated to become the (suppletive) perfective form of the verb *mal-* 'go'. This verb *mal-* 'go' forms its imperfective quite regularly (*mali*), but has the suppletive perfective form /i-apï/. The irrealis form shows vowel mutation in the stem, a change which I believe serves a practical function. Without any such stem change, the irrealis form would be pronounced (after degemination of the consecutive *l* consonants) as *mala; and, since final /a/ is usually reduced to [ï], this would often lead to the form *malï, thereby creating a confusing homophony with the imperfective form of the same verb. The irregular change in the stem vowel of the irrealis form, however, prevents this confusion and results in an interesting metathetic relationship between *malï* 'go [IPFV]' and *mïla* 'go [IRR]'.

The adoption of **(i)yapï* 'come [PFV]' as the suppletive form to fill the perfective gap in the *mal-* 'go' paradigm seems, however, not to have been fully accepted, as speakers sometimes use the imperfective form *mali* with perfective meaning (sometimes even adding the perfect prefix *a-* to clarify its perfective aspect). Similarly, as alluded to in §4.6, the perfect prefix can also be used with the morphologically imperfective form of *i-* 'come' to clarify that it has perfective meaning (the morphologically perfective form of *i-* 'come' would be, of course, unusable, since it has developed the meaning of 'go' instead).

---

9   This is the imperfective form plus the perfect prefix *a-*.
10 This is a suppletive perfective form (< *i-* 'come'); *(a)malï* may also be used to mean 'go [PFV]'.

5
OTHER WORD CLASSES

In the following sections I discuss other word classes, namely adjectives (§5.1), pronouns (§5.2), determiners (§5.3), postpositions (§5.4), adverbs (§5.5), negators (§5.6), question words (§5.7), conjunctions (§5.8), and numerals (§5.9).

5.1 Adjectives

Compared to nouns and verbs, adjectives are much harder to define on morphosyntactic grounds. The semantic prototype of the adjective is a word denoting a property. Based on structural and distributional criteria, property-denoting words tend to pattern more closely with nouns than with verbs in Pondi. The only suggestions that they may form a distinct class (if perhaps only a subclass of nouns) are the fact that they exhibit agreement for number with head nouns and the fact that they always follow the noun that they modify when functioning attributively. Although it is possible that 'adjectives' might not form a distinct word class in Pondi, I include this section for the sake of crosslinguistic comparison and to illustrate how concord functions in the language. (When no distinction between nouns and adjectives is pertinent, I may refer to them together as 'nominals'.)

Structurally, adjectives are decidedly unlike verbs, since they never receive TAM suffixes or any other verbal morphology. When considering distributional properties, we may note that adjectives may either appear within a noun phrase (i.e. as attributive adjectives) or clause-finally as predicates (in which case they behave much the same as predicate nouns).

Like nouns, adjectives inflect (often with irregular morphology) for two number categories. The two forms are set (i.e. lexically determined) for any given adjective. That is, the morphological inflection for number that adjectives exhibit does not indicate gender agreement in any way with the nouns with which they agree, but rather they are stable (i.e. although the irregular nominal number morphological distinctions may have developed diachronically from a gender system, the different 'classes' of nouns represented by the grammar do not currently represent different genders, §3.12). Some of the patterns seen in the alternations between non-plural and plural adjectival forms are the same as those found for some nouns.

Table 5.1 presents examples of property-denoting words (or adjectives) in Pondi.

Table 5.1. Adjectives.

Gloss	Non-plural	Plural	Gloss	Non-plural	Plural
'good'	almwan	alwe	'old (person)'	katïl	katiyal
'bad'	atal	ateyal	'young'	mongam	mongal
'bad'[1]	atamate	ateyamate	'long'	mïnangondï	mïnangondïn
'big'	anïmbam	anïmbuse	'short'	mokas	mokasal
'small'	kote	kosime	'sharp'	kaywï	kaywal
'dry'	kataplam	katapeyal	'dull'	katambus	katambuse
'wet'	nambiwï	nambiwal	'thick'	malmanjï	malmanjïn

The following are examples of such words functioning as attributive adjectives. They immediately follow their respective head nouns and inflect for number (agreeing with the head noun in this regard).

(5.01) namal **anïmbam**

    namal   **anïmbam**
    pig   big
    'big pig'

(5.02) name **anïmbuse**

    name   anïmbuse
    pig.PL   big.PL
    'big pigs'

---

1 There are two common variants of the word 'bad', each with its own plural form. Slight variations in pronunciation for 'good' and 'big' are given in §2.7.

(5.03) kamo **almwan**
 kamo **almwan**
 betel.nut good
 'good betel nut'

(5.04) kame **alwe**
 kame **alwe**
 betel.nut.PL good.PL
 'good betel nuts'

The following examples illustrate predicative uses of adjectives. Here, the property-denoting word comes at the end of the clause. No overt copula is required (nor is one required for predicate nominatives), although it may occur, especially if making a particular TAM distinction is desired (e.g. to signal a past or future state).

(5.05) nja kamo **almwan**
 nja kamo **almwan**
 this betel.nut good
 'This is a good betel nut.'

(5.06) kamo nja **almwan**
 kamo nja **almwan**
 betel.nut this good
 'This betel nut is good.'

5.1.1 Adjectival number morphology

Morphologically, several of the non-plural/plural alternations found among the property-denoting words in Table 5.1 can be placed into one of the noun classes outlined in §3.1–10. For example, a number of plural forms end in *-al*, such as *mokas / mokas-al* 'short' (cf. §3.1). A final *ï* in the non-plural form may be 'lost' in the plural, as in *nambiw-ï / nambiw-al* 'wet' or *kayw-ï / kayw-al* 'sharp' (as is also seen with nouns such *yuw-ï / yuw-al* 'crocodile' §3.1). There may also be traces of the singular suffix *-m*, as in *monga-m / monga-al* 'young' (as found in nouns like *pala-m / pala-al* 'shield', §3.10). There may be some additional irregularity, however, as seen in *kata-pl-am / kata-pe-al* 'dry'. The forms *kat-ïl / kat-iy-al* 'old' show some irregularity as well. The common nominal plural ending *-e* (cf. §3.3) is found (without any additional segments) in just one non-plural/plural pair: *katambus / katambus-e* 'dull'. Two adjectives ('thick' and 'long') have plural endings in -*n*, not found in any nouns (although the suffix found in the plural form *anungw-an* 'mother [PL]' is similar, §3.6). The remaining adjectival forms, which are rather more irregular, are presented in Table 5.2, which includes possible morpheme boundaries.

Table 5.2. Irregular adjectives.

Gloss	Non-plural	Plural
'good'	al-mwan	al-we
'bad'	at-al	at-e-al
'bad'	at-amate	at-e-amate
'big'	anïmb-am	anïmb-use
'small'	ko-te	ko-sime

The adjective 'bad' has two possible non-plural forms, each with its own associated plural form. Each plural form seems to be created (from its respective non-plural equivalent) through a suffix *-e*, which is a very common means of forming plurals in Pondi (§3.3). Strangely, however, both plural forms seem to have morphemes *following* this plural suffix—morphemes (or, at least, forms) that are also present in the equivalent non-plural forms: [al] and [amate]. Their function and etymology are obscure. The alternative analysis—that the roots are *atal* and *atamate*, respectively, and that *e* is an infix in each instance—is equally anomalous, as there are no other known examples of infixation in the language.

5.1.2 The derivational suffix -*wï* '-like'

There is a derivational suffix *-wï* '-like', that can derive adjective-like words. Some examples are presented in Table 5.3.

Table 5.3. The derivational suffix -*wï* '-like'.

Nominal	Gloss	Etymology
nambiwï	'wet'	< nambi 'water'
apungwï	'hot'	< apïn 'fire' (with some irregular sound changes)
kamalïwï	'intelligent'	< kamal 'head' (with an epenthetic [ï] to break up the CC cluster)
mïnangewï	'green'	< mïnange 'taro'[2]
mïndawï	'new'	?

---

[2] The taro plant has green leaves, which in local cuisine are used to make a vibrantly green soup.

Nominal	Gloss	Etymology
kaywï	'sharp'	?
mïndïlwï	'dirty'	?
mïnïlwï	'old (thing)'	?
kïpwï	'mound'	< kïp 'nose'
momiwï	'rice'	< mom-i 'fruit, seed [PL]' (a relatively recent coinage)

Although the first eight words in Table 5.3 denote properties, words like 'mound' and 'rice' are more like prototypical (concrete) nouns.

5.2 Pronouns

Pondi pronouns indicate person, number, and grammatical relation. They do not indicate gender or levels of respect or formality, nor do they make distinctions between inclusivity and exclusivity in the first person non-singular forms.

5.2.1 Personal pronouns

There are three person distinctions among personal pronouns: first, second, and third person. Pondi also makes three number distinctions in its pronominal forms: singular, dual, and plural. While the 3DU form *min* may, perhaps, be traced to a proto-Ulmapo pronominal form (it is in fact identical to the equivalent Ulwa form), the dual forms in Pondi, which I do not believe to be commonly used, are more transparently derived (within Pondi) from other forms. The three-way number distinction among Pondi pronouns is different from the distinction found among common nouns, which exhibit a binary contrast between 'one or two' and 'three or more'. For pronouns, a singular form is used to refer to exactly one referent, whereas the dual form refers to exactly two referents, and the plural form refers to three or more referents.

Pronouns also exhibit a two-way contrast (not found elsewhere in Pondi's grammar) based on grammatical relations—namely, between subjects and non-subjects. For convenience, these non-subject forms may be called 'object pronouns', but it should be kept in mind that they are used to encode not only direct objects, but also objects of postpositions and obliques. The two paradigms (of subject pronouns and non-subject pronouns) are mostly identical. The only differences are found in the 2SG, 3SG, and 3PL forms (I did not manage to elicit sentences with 1DU or 2DU non-subject pronouns, so I cannot be certain of their forms). Whereas the subject pronouns tend to be free forms, the non-subject pronouns cliticise to the following word (or morpheme, in the case of obliques).

Table 5.4 provides the paradigms for subject and non-subject pronouns. The non-subject forms that differ from their equivalent subject forms are given in bold font.

Table 5.4. Personal pronouns.

	Subject pronouns			Non-subject ('object') pronouns		
	singular	dual	plural	singular	dual	plural
1st	nyï	any ~ anin	an	nyï	any ? ~ anin ?	an
2nd	o	wany ~ wanin	wan	**u** ~ [wu]	**wany ? ~ wanin ?**	wan
3rd	mï	min	ndïn	**ma**	min	**ndï**

5.2.2 Reflexive/reciprocal pronouns

There are three reflexive/reciprocal forms (no morphological distinction is made between the categories reflexive ['-self', '-selves'] and reciprocal ['each other', 'one another']). The forms index number (but not person): singular,[3] dual, or plural. Table 5.5 presents the reflexive/reciprocal pronouns.

Table 5.5. Reflexive/reciprocal pronouns.

Number	Pronoun	Gloss
singular	am	'myself, yourself, himself, herself, itself'
dual	ambin	'ourselves [DU], yourselves [DU], themselves [DU], each other'
plural	ambal ~ ambla	'ourselves [PL], yourselves [PL], themselves [PL], one another'

---

3   Of course, the singular form can only have reflexive meaning, not reciprocal.

5.2.3 Possessive pronouns

Possessive pronouns (pronominal determiners) are derived from the set of object pronominal forms plus either the form *-njin* 'thing [NPL]' (which can occur following bare NPs as well) or the formative *is* (likely derived, via metathesis, from the word *se* 'thing [PL]'). The forms with *-njin* are used to refer to a non-plural referent possessum, whereas the forms with *-is* are used to refer to a plural referent possessum. The order of possessive elements in Pondi is always possessor-plus-possessum.

Although the form *-njin* is transparently related to the word *njin* 'thing', I nevertheless analyse the possessive forms as being fully lexicalised as single elements, especially since they exhibit (synchronically non-existent) phonological changes—namely the strengthening of **i* to *i* in the 1SG and 3PL forms (the quasi-degemination of /nnj/ to [nj], as seen in the dual forms, however, is a regular phonological process in the synchronic grammar, §2.5.8).

The forms with *-is* are used to indicate the possession of three or more of an entity. They, too, are formed from the set of object (as opposed to subject) pronominal forms. Like *njin* 'POSS.NPL', the free form *is* 'POSS.PL' may also follow a full NP. In the 2SG form, we see the change of **u-i* to *wu*.

Although possessive pronouns (like personal pronouns) exhibit a three-way number contrast in terms of how they encode the possessor, they exhibit a two-way number contrast in terms of how they encode the possessum. This is the same plural-vs-non-plural contrast that is found among Pondi nouns (Chapter 3).

Table 5.6 provides the paradigm for the possessive pronouns that are used when the possessum is non-plural.

Table 5.6. Possessive pronouns for non-plural possessum.

	Singular	Dual	Plural
1st person	nyinjin 'my'	aninjin 'our [DU]'	anjin 'our [PL]'
2nd person	unjin 'your [SG]'	waninjin 'your [DU]'	wanjin 'your [PL]'
3rd person	manjin 'his/her/its'	minjin 'their [DU]'	ndinjin 'their [PL]'

Table 5.7 provides the paradigm for the possessive pronouns that are used when the possessum is plural.

Table 5.7. Possessive pronouns for plural possessum.

	Singular	**Dual**	**Plural**
1st person	nyis 'my'	aninis 'our [DU]'	anis 'our [PL]'
2nd person	wus 'your [SG]'	waninis 'your [DU]'	wanis 'your [PL]'
3rd person	mays 'his/her/its'	minis 'their [DU]'	ndis 'their [PL]'

There are, additionally, possessive reflexive pronouns in the language: these indicate an anaphoric relationship between the possessum and an antecedent possessor. They may be translated as 'X's own'. I know of only two forms: *ambinjin* 'his/her/its own' (when the possessum is non-plural) and *amblays* 'their own' (when the possessum is plural). I do not know what forms would be used when there is a non-plural possessor but a plural possessum, nor when there is a plural possessor but a non-plural possessum. The following sentences exemplify the use of these possessive reflexive pronouns. The differing translations given in (5.08) show how these forms may have either reflexive or reciprocal meaning.

(5.07) mï ipï **ambinjin** ingip asiyapï

mï	ipï	**ambin-njin**	ingip	asi-apï
3SG.SUBJ	hand	NPL.REFL-POSS.NPL	sternum	hit-PFV

'He$_i$ hit his$_{i/*j}$ chest.'
'He hit his own chest.'

(5.08) min ipï **ambinjin** ingip asiyapï

min	ipï	**ambin-njin**	ingip	asi-apï
3DU	hand	NPL.REFL-POSS.NPL	sternum	hit-PFV

'They hit their own (respective) chests.'
'They hit each other's chests.'

(5.09) **amblays** kulawi mokaw un

ambla-is	kulawi	mokaw	un
PL.REFL-POSS.PL	boy.PL	little	put

'Carry your (own) children!'

5.2.4 Intensive pronouns

In addition to subject and object pronouns, reflexive/reciprocal pronouns, and possessive pronouns, there is a set of intensive pronominal forms. They are derived from the set of object pronouns plus the formative *-am* '-self'. They are used to stress the fact the referent(s) alone is/are the focus of attention. (In Tok Pisin, their equivalents would be, e.g. in the 1SG: *mi wanpela* 'I alone', *mi tasol* 'only I', or *mi yet* 'I myself'.) Table 5.8 presents the paradigm of intensive pronouns. The only phonological changes to be noted are the elision of *ï* in the 1SG and 3PL forms and the fortition of *u* to *w* (preceding *a*) in the 2SG form.

Table 5.8. Intensive pronouns.

	Singular	**Dual**	**Plural**
1st person	nyam 'me myself'	aninam 'us [DU] ourselves'	anam 'us [PL] ourselves'
2nd person	wam 'you yourself'	waninam 'you [DU] yourselves'	wanam 'you [PL] yourselves'
3rd person	mam 'him himself, her herself, it itself'	minam 'them [DU] themselves'	ndam 'them [PL] themselves'

The following sentences illustrate the use of intensive pronouns in Pondi.

(5.10) nyï **mam** ale

    nyï   **mam**   ala-ï
    1SG   3SG.INT   see-IPFV
    'I saw him himself.'

(5.11) mï **nyam** ale

    mï   **nyam**   ala-ï
    3SG.SUBJ   1SG.INT   see-IPFV
    'He saw me myself.'

I only have evidence of these forms occurring as non-subject pronouns. There are, however, three intensive words that may immediately follow a pronoun (or common or proper noun) to serve the same purpose of drawing emphasis to the referent, only used rather when the referent is the grammatical subject. These non-pronominal intensive words are presented in Table 5.9.

Table 5.9. Intensive words.

Number	Pronoun	Gloss
singular	amam	'myself, yourself, himself, herself, itself'
dual	amimin	'ourselves [DU], yourselves [DU], themselves [DU]'
plural	awla	'ourselves [PL], yourselves [PL], themselves [PL]'

The following sentences illustrate the use of these intensive words. In each instance, they emphasise the immediately preceding pronoun.

(5.12) nyï **amam** namal asiyï
  nyï **amam** namal asi-ï
  1SG INT.SG pig hit-IPFV
  'I myself killed the pig!'

(5.13) John **amam** kisïm malï
  John **amam** kisïm mal-ï
  [name] INT.SG jungle go-IPFV
  'John himself went to the jungle.'

(5.14) anin **amimin** kusam amï
  anin **amimin** kusam am-ï
  1DU INT.DU yam eat-IPFV
  'We (two) alone eat yams.'

(5.15) ndïn **awla** malï
  ndïn **awla** mal-ï
  3PL.SUBJ INT.PL go-IPFV
  'They alone went.'

5.2.5 Indefinite/interrogative pronouns

The indefinite/interrogative pronoun that is used to refer to people is *kïman* 'someone, who?', which has the possessive interrogative form *kïmanjin* 'someone's, whose?'. For inanimate referents, there are the interrogative forms *awnjin* 'what? [NPL]' and *awse* 'what? [PL]', which are transparently derived from the question formative *aw-* (§5.7) plus either the non-plural form (*njin*) or the plural form (*se*) of the word 'thing'. They are used only for asking questions. Their indefinite equivalent 'something' is expressed by the word *njin* / *se* 'thing, something' alone.

The quantifier *kwan* 'a(n), some, (an)other' (clearly related to the numeral *kwandap* 'one') can also be used in making less definite reference to a person or entity, to express the concept of 'other', or to create correlative constructions of the form 'the one ... the other', as seen in (5.16). Whereas in the first clause the word *kwan* serves as a determiner (in the NP 'one woman'), in the second it serves a pronominal function ('the other').

(5.16) angwaliyï **kwan** kisïm malï **kwan** ngol pï
　　　 angwaliyï **kwan** kisïm mal-ï **kwan** ngol p-ï
　　　 woman　 INDF　 jungle　 go-IPFV　 INDF　 village　 be-IPFV
　　　 'One woman went to the jungle; the other is in the village.'

As a pronoun (as opposed to determiner, as in the first usage in 5.16), the indefinite form *kwan* can mean 'someone', as in (5.17).

(5.17) meyanga **kwan** kisïm malï
　　　 meyanga **kwan** kisïm mal-ï
　　　 yesterday　 INDF　 jungle　 go-IPFV
　　　 'Someone went to the jungle yesterday.'

5.3 Determiners

In this section I discuss various words in Pondi that in some way indicate the definiteness or specificity of a referent, provide information that situates it in space (relative to some deictic centre), or identify its function (i.e. as subject or non-subject) within a clause. These include deictic demonstratives as well as subject and non-subject (or 'object') markers, all of which index the number of referents.

5.3.1 Deictic demonstratives

Deictic demonstratives in Pondi can be either proximal or distal, and either non-plural or plural, thus forming a matrix of four forms, as given in Table 5.10.

Table 5.10. Deictic demonstratives.

	Non-plural	**Plural**
Proximal	nja 'this'	sa 'these'
Distal	anda 'that'	ala 'those'

These forms, when present, are always the final elements in their respective NPs—that is, they follow the head nouns, to which they point. They do not co-occur with subject markers or object markers (§5.3.2). Their use may be seen in the following sentences.

(5.18) lïl **nja** ambo pal
      lïl   **nja**   ambo   pal
      river   this   NEG   far
      'This river is not far.'

(5.19) nyï kusaw **sa** amnda
      nyï   kusaw   **sa**   am-nda
      1SG   yam.PL   these   eat-IRR
      'I'll eat these yams.'

(5.20) nyï kusam **anda** amnda
      nyï   kusam   **anda**   am-nda
      1SG   yam.PL   that   eat-IRR
      'I'll eat those yams.'

These same deictic determiners may also function as demonstrative pronouns, used in place of NPs, as seen in the following examples.

(5.21) **nja** alïmbam **anda** kote
      nja   alïmbam   **anda**   kote
      this   big   that   small
      'This (one) is big; that (one) is small.'

(5.22) mï ke amngapï **anda** ple yapï
      mï   ke   am-ngapï   **anda**   ple   ya-apï
      3SG.SUBJ sago   eat-PFV   that   speech   talk-PFV
      'He ate and that one (i.e. another person) talked.' (literally 'ate sago')

(5.23) o **alays** se nda ola
      o   **ala**-is   se   n-nda   ola
      2SG.SUBJ those-POSS.PL   thing.PL   take-IRR   don't
      'Don't take other people's things!' (literally 'those [one]'s things')

To my knowledge, there are no dual forms for these deictic demonstratives (cf. pronouns, §5.2.1), nor is there a medial deictic (i.e. to refer to referents that are neither 'near' nor 'far'). Here, 'proximal' should be taken to mean 'near the speaker' and 'distal' should be taken to mean 'not near the speaker' (i.e. there is an ego-centric deictic system). Especially when used as determiners (as opposed to as pronouns), these forms are very commonly reduced to [njï] 'this', [sï] 'these', [andï] 'that', and [alï] 'those'.

Other deictic markers that are derived from these forms include *njakï* 'here, hither' and *andakï* 'there, thither', both transparently containing the postpositional (formative) element *kï* 'at, in, on' (§5.4).

5.3.2 Subject markers and object markers

Pondi also has sets of subject markers and object markers (or, more properly, 'non-subject markers'). These are determiners that follow their respective head nouns, indexing the number of referents. They are identical to the respective sets of subject pronouns and non-subject pronouns. Indeed, they may be thought of simply as third person pronominal forms—in a sense resumptive pronouns, although they occur within the same syntactic phrase as their antecedent head nouns. Subject markers and object markers are never used with pronouns, and thus they are not used for first person or second person referents. Even with third-person referents they do not ever seem to be obligatory. They are perhaps not even that common with subject NPs, although they do seem fairly regular with non-subject NPs. The choice of inclusion or exclusion may reflect alternations in definiteness or specificity, but I do not have enough data to make any strong claims. One function of these markers in the related language Ulwa is to indicate the number of referents in the third person (since Ulwa makes no number distinctions in its nominal forms), but—since Pondi *does* mark nouns for number, these markers would not need to bear this functional load entirely on their own (although they do make a more precise numerical distinction than the one found in nouns, in that they mark 'singular' vs 'dual' vs 'plural', as opposed to 'non-plural' vs 'plural'). Their use can be seen scattered throughout examples in this grammar—for subject markers see examples (4.24, 5.97, 6.22, 6.32, 7.03, inter alia) and for object markers see examples (4.04, 4.13, 5.34, 5.36, 5.39, 5.51, 5.74, 5.99, 6.06, 6.08, 6.54, 7.07, 7.16, 7.17, inter alia).

5.3.3 Quantifiers

We may also discuss here the class of quantifiers, words that provide information concerning the number or amount of a referent, without assigning an exact numerical value (numerals, which do assign exact numerical values, are discussed in §5.9). Table 5.11 presents a list of quantifiers in Pondi.

Table 5.11. Quantifiers.

Quantifier	Gloss
mokan	'all, every, everyone, everything'
yamïn	'all (of), whole'
kïmal	'some'
andeyal	'many, much'

Like other determiners, quantifiers follow their head nouns. The universal quantifier *mokan* 'all' refers to countable entities, as in (5.24). Note that when this quantifier is used in an NP headed by a noun, the noun itself is *not* marked as plural, the quantifier presumably fulfilling the responsibility of indicating number entirely on its own.

(5.24) njimoka **mokan** kayïtï
      njimoka   **mokan**   kayït-ï
      tree   all   fall-IPFV
      'All the trees fell down.'

The form *mokan* 'all' can also function as an indefinite pronoun, referring to 'everyone' or 'everything', as seen in (5.25).

(5.25) **mokan** ngol pï
      mokan   ngol   p-ï
      all   village   be-IPFV
      'Everyone is in the village.'

For non-countable nouns, the quantifier *yamïn* 'all (of), whole' is used. This, too, follows the noun (as in 5.26), and may actually be better considered an adjective.

(5.26) nambi **yamïn**
      nambi   **yamïn**
      water   all
      'all the water'

The quantifier *kïmal* 'some' is illustrated in (5.27). Unlike *mokan* 'all', it follows plural noun forms.

(5.27) kinyal **kïmal** nambi ndïn malï
      kinyal   **kïmal**   nambi   ndï=n   mal-ï
      coconut.PL   some   water   3PL.OBJ=OBL   go-IPFV
      'Some coconuts are floating on the rivers.'

It, too, may function pronominally, as shown in (5.28).

(5.28) **kïmal** kapï nja pï
      kïmal   kapï   nja   p-ï
      some   house   this   be-IPFV
      'Some (people) are in this house.'

The word *andeyal* means both 'many' and 'much'—that is, there is no distinction made between countable and non-countable referents. Generally, the sense of abundance is expressed simply by means of the plural (i.e. 'three or more') form of a noun without any additional modification (5.29). When, however, the word *andeyal* 'many, much' follows the noun, the noun appears in the non-plural form, as shown in (5.30–31).

(5.29) yame kayïtï
      yame   kayït-ï
      tree.PL   fall-IPFV
      '(Many) trees fell down.'

(5.30) njimoka **andeyal** kayïtï
      njimoka   **andeyal**   kayït-ï
      tree   many   fall-IPFV
      'Many trees fell down.'

(5.31) nambi **andeyal**
      nambi   **andeyal**
      water   many
      'much water'

5.4 Postpositions

The only adpositions found in Pondi are postpositions (that is, there are no prepositions—in keeping with the typological expectations of OV languages). Postpositions function to designate relationships between NPs. Most of these seem to be spatial relationships, but other types—such as temporal or benefactive—are possible as well. Table 5.12 contains the postpositions in Pondi of which I am aware.

Table 5.12. Postpositions.

Postposition	Gloss	Notes
kï	'at, in, on'	–
un(kï)	'in, within, inside'	–
at(kï)	'atop, above'	–
imbam(kï)	'under, below'	plural: *iwal*
kos	'near'	< *kwas* 'breast'; cf. English 'abreast'
pal	'far (from?)'	–
mundat	'behind'	–
i	'in front of, before'	spatial
o	'after'	temporal
un	'with'	comitative
ol	'from (a place)'	ablative
to	'from (a person)'	also 'of' (with 'afraid')
lak	'for the sake of, on account of'	< Tok Pisin *laik* 'want [to]'

The form *kï* 'at, in, on' may function on its own as a postposition; it seems also to be an optional element for at least three spatial postpositions: *un(kï)* 'in, within, inside', *at(kï)* 'atop, above', and *imbam(kï)* 'under, below'. This suggests that forms such as *un*, *at*, and *imbam* are (or at least were) nominal elements in nature (i.e. 'interior', 'top', and 'bottom', respectively). In particular, the form *imbam* 'under, below', although functioning as a postposition, seems also to serve (or derive from) a nominal function—namely referring to the area beneath a house.[4] This word has a plural form when referring to the areas beneath multiple houses (*iwal* as opposed to *imbam*). The other two postpositions in

---

4   Pondi houses are built on stilts to prevent them from flooding during the rainy season. The area under the house may be used for storage or as a shaded place to sit.

5. OTHER WORD CLASSES

question—*un* 'in, within, inside' and *at* 'atop, above'—also likely derive from nouns, although they seem to have lost any number distinctions (if ever these were present). The word *kos* 'near' (likely derived from the noun *kwas* 'breast', which is often pronounced [kos]) can be used as a postposition; I do not know whether the word *pal* 'far (from?)' can be used as a postposition (it can serve as a predicate complement). Also, I do not know whether there is a postposition with the temporal sense 'before' (there is, however, the temporal postposition *o* 'after'). The postposition *lak* 'for the sake of, on account of' derives from Tok Pisin *laik* 'want (to)'.

The following sentences exemplify the use of postpositions in Pondi. Object markers, when present, cliticise to the following postposition.

(5.32) taïï kisïm **kï** namal asiyï
        taïï   kisïm   **kï**   namal   asi-ï
        papa   jungle   at   pig   hit-IPFV
        'Papa killed a pig in the jungle.'

(5.33) nyï pisimli **kï** kota ale
        nyï   pisimli   **kï**   kota   ala-ï
        1SG   path   at   poor.thing see-IPFV
        'I saw the poor thing on the path.'

(5.34) yakus mandïn **mawn** pï
        yakus   mandïn   ma=**un**   p-ï
        machete   string.bag 3SG.OBJ=in be-IPFV
        'The machete is inside the string bag.'

(5.35) mï kapï **unkï** ple yapï
        mï   kapï   **un-kï**   ple   ya-apï
        3SG.SUBJ house   in-at   speech   talk-PFV
        'He talked inside the house.'

(5.36) yakus minjamï **mat** pï
        yakus   minjamï   ma=**at**   p-ï
        machete   palm.sp   3SG.OBJ=atop be-IPFV
        'The machete is on the floor.' (literally on a palm sp. that is used to make flooring)

(5.37) sewawi yame **ndatkï** alawe
sewawi yame ndï=at-kï alawa-ï
bird.PL tree.PL 3PL.OBJ=atop-at flock-IPFV
'The birds are flying above the trees.'

(5.38) meyo kapï **maymbam** pï
meyo kapï ma=imbam p-ï
dog.PL house 3SG.OBJ=under be-IPFV
'The dogs are under the house.'

(5.39) meyo kapal **ndiwal** pï
meyo kapal ndï=iwal p-ï
dog.PL house.PL 3PL.OBJ=under.PL be-IPFV
'The dogs are under the houses.'

(5.40) meyanga ndindi njimoka **imbamkï** walwal numle
meyanga ndindi njimoka imbam-kï walwal numla-ï
yesterday dog tree under-at lung throw-IPFV
'Yesterday a dog was panting under the tree.'

(5.41) an nambikal **kos** sangowapï
an nambikal kos sango-apï
1PL riverbank near walk-PFV
'We walked near the riverbank.'

(5.42) komblal njimoka **mundat** pï
komblal njimoka mundat p-ï
child.PL tree behind be-IPFV
'The children are behind the tree.'

(5.43) komblal njimoka **may** pï
komblal njimoka ma=i p-ï
child.PL tree 3SG.OBJ=before be-IPFV
'The children are in front of the tree.'

(5.44) Peter **ano** kisïm malï
Peter an=o kisïm mal-ï
[name] 1PL=after jungle go-IPFV
'Peter went to the jungle after us.'

(5.45) nyï **mawn** ke amï
   nyï   ma=**un**   ke   am-ï
   1SG   3SG.OBJ=with   sago   eat-IPFV
   'I'm eating sago with him.'

(5.46) an ngol **ol** lala wï
   an   ngol   **ol**   la-la   w-ï
   1PL   village   from   put-IRR   want-IPFV
   'We want to leave the village.'

(5.47) Peter **uto** yakus liyï
   Peter   u=**to**   yakus   li-ï
   [name]   2SG.OBJ=from   machete   take-IPFV
   'Peter took the machete from you.'

(5.48) nyï **wanïto** kinyï yawle nda
   nyï   wan=**to**   kinyï   yawle   n-nda
   1SG   2PL=from   coconut   three   take-IRR
   'I'll take three coconuts from you.'

(5.49) nyï namal **lak** kisïm yapï
   nyï   namal   **lak**   kisïm   i-apï
   1SG   pig   for   jungle   come-PFV
   'I went to the jungle on account of a pig.' (i.e. in order to hunt a pig)

Some constructions in Pondi designate spatial relationships without the use of any postpositions. For example, the verb *p-* 'be (at)' (§4.11) can signal the location of a subject (with or without the use of an object marker), as seen in (5.50–51).

(5.50) nyinjin nïmotï Wewak **pï**
   nyi-njin   nïmotï   Wewak   **p-ï**
   1SG-POSS.NPL   friend   [place]   be-IPFV
   'My friend is in Wewak.'

(5.51) tatï ambo kapï **mapï**
   tatï   ambo   kapï   **ma=p-ï**
   papa   NEG   house   3SG.OBJ=be-IPFV
   'Papa isn't (at) home/in the house.'

Similarly, motion verbs (as in §4.12) typically encode goal or destination arguments simply as direct objects, without any sort of postposition (i.e. without any word like 'to') as seen in (5.52).

(5.52) ndïn meyamba kisïm **yapï**
 ndïn meyamba kisïm **i**-apï
 3PL.SUBJ yesterday jungle come-PFV
 'They went to the jungle yesterday.'

Some temporal relationships (especially between physical entities and times of day) can also be expressed without any postpositions, but rather with temporal adverbs, as seen, for example, in (5.52) as well as in (5.53).

(5.53) **kalambo** nyinjin kulam mï kawapï
 kalambo nyi-njin kulam mï kaw-apï
 night 1SG-POSS.NPL boy 3SG.SUBJ sleep-PFV
 'My son slept at night/last night.'

5.5 Adverbs

Adverbs in Pondi can be defined by their unique ability to precede subjects. Adverbs are never required by the argument structure of a verb and may thus always be considered additional information. Although they may serve a number of different functions, they generally provide additional information on the manner in which an action occurs or else they situate an event in time or space.

The allowed pre-subject position of adverbs makes them unique even among the set of obliques, since other such forms (i.e. negators, interrogatives, postpositional phrases, or oblique-marked NPs, §7.3) can never precede the subject. That said, the canonical placement of adverbs is following subjects and preceding objects (that is, in the position held by other obliques, i.e. SXOV). Adverbs bear little structural similarity either to verbs or to nouns (or other nominals): they do not take TAM suffixes or verbal prefixes; nor do they inflect for number or take the oblique-marking enclitic. We may divide adverbs into several subsets, including temporal adverbs, locative adverbs, and other adverbs.

5.5.1 Temporal adverbs

The set of temporal adverbs in Pondi form something of a natural set in that they alone seem more inclined to occur before—rather than after—the subject (although both positions are permitted). They include the forms found in Table 5.13.

Table 5.13. Temporal adverbs.

Adverb	Gloss	Etymology
kïpakï	'earlier, before(hand)'	< kïp 'nose' + a (?) + kï 'at, in, on'
asuwatakï	'later, after(wards)'	< asuwat- 'turn' + a (?) + kï 'at, in, on'
kunas	'later, after(wards)'	< kunï 'buttocks' + as 'tail'
kanam	'now, today'	–
meyamba ~ meyanga	'yesterday'	–
kïmbïlo	'tomorrow'	–

The following sentences exemplify the use of temporal adverbs in Pondi.

(5.54) **kïpakï** kimbe andeyal nambi sangoyï
    kïpakï   kimbe   andeyal   nambi   sango-ï
    earlier   fish   many   water   walk-IPFV
    'Before, many fish used to swim in the river.'

(5.55) John **kïpakï** kisïm yapï
    John   **kïpakï**   kisïm   i-apï
    [name]   earlier   jungle   come-PFV
    'John went to the jungle earlier.'

(5.56) **asuwatakï** nambi ila
    asuwatakï   nambi   i-la
    later   water   come-IRR
    'The water will come later.' (i.e. the river will be higher in the coming wet season)

(5.57) nyï **asuwatakï** nambi pula
    nyï   **asuwatakï**   nambi   pu-la
    1SG   later   water   bathe-IRR
    'I'll bathe later.'

(5.58) **kunas** nyinjin kulam kawla
  kunas nyi-njin kulam kaw-la
  later   1SG-POSS.NPL boy   sleep-IRR
  'My boy will sleep later.'

(5.59) **kanam** anale kisïm malï
  kanam anale kisïm mal-ï
  now   woman.PL jungle go-IPFV
  'The women are going to the jungle now.'

(5.60) ndïn **kanam** se
  ndïn   **kanam** sa-ï
  3PL.SUBJ now   cry-IPFV
  'They are crying now.'

(5.61) **kanam** mï alïmbam
  kanam mï   alïmbam
  now   3SG.SUBJ big
  'He is big now.'

(5.62) **kanam** nyï tatï anin kapï awsapï
  kanam nyï tatï anin kapï a-us-apï
  now   1SG papa 1DU house PRF-build-PFV
  'Papa and I built a house today.'

(5.63) **meyamba** an njimokase ndoliyï
  meyamba an njimokase ndï=oli-ï
  yesterday 1PL stick.PL   3PL.OBJ=cut-IPFV
  'We were chopping wood yesterday.'

(5.64) nyï **meyamba** wanamale
  nyï **meyamba** wanam=ala-ï
  1SG yesterday   2PL.INT=see-IPFV
  'I saw you yourselves yesterday.'

(5.65) **meyanga** anale ambo kusaw ndamngapï
  meyanga anale   ambo kusaw ndï=am-ngapï
  yesterday woman.PL NEG yam.PL 3PL.OBJ=eat-PFV
  'The women did not eat yams yesterday.'

(5.66) **kïmbïlo** nyï kisïm mïla
    kïmbïlo nyï kisïm mal-la
    tomorrow 1SG jungle go-IRR
    'I'll go to the jungle tomorrow.'

(5.67) **kïmbïlo** kin lapïla
    kïmbïlo kin lap-la
    tomorrow rain fall-IRR
    'It will rain tomorrow.'

(5.68) kulawi **kïmbïlo** nungul at sila
    kulawi **kïmbïlo** nungul at si-la
    boy.PL tomorrow grass atop sit-IRR
    'Tomorrow the children will sit on the grass.'

5.5.2 Locative adverbs

I know of the following two locative adverbs in Pondi (Table 5.14), both of which are derived from deictic words.

Table 5.14. Locative adverbs.

Adverb	Gloss	Etymology
njakï	'here, hither'	< *nja* 'this' + *kï* 'at, in, on'
andakï	'there, thither'	< *anda* 'that' + *kï* 'at, in, on'

The following sentences exemplify the use of these locative adverbs.

(5.69) an **njakï** ke
    an **njakï** ke
    1PL here sago
    'We have sago here.'

(5.70) njinulam nja **njakï** alasïla
    njinulam nja **njakï** alas-la
    bird this here fly-IRR
    'This bird will fly here.' (i.e. hither)

(5.71) njinulam **andakï** alatï
    njinulam **andakï** alas-ï
    bird there fly-IPFV
    'A bird is flying there.' (i.e. thither)

(5.72) namuse **andakï** ambo mïnapï

      namuse   **andakï**   ambo   mïna-apï
      meat   there   NEG   cook-PFV

      'The meat there has not cooked.'

5.5.3 Other adverbs

Next we may consider adverbs that contain neither temporal nor spatial information. These adverbs tend to modify sentences by providing additional information on the way in which an event occurs or a state exists. Table 5.15 presents some of the other adverbs that are found in Pondi.

Table 5.15. Other adverbs.

Adverb	Gloss	Adverb	Gloss
apït	'really'	mbïn	'also'
akï	'very'	pisa	'again'
mbole	'maybe'	tïti	'often, always, regularly'

Generally, these remaining adverbs can be viewed as modifying a verbal element, although *akï* 'very' seems to apply only to adjectives (i.e. to strengthen a quality being ascribed to a referent). Although *pisa* 'again' and *tïti* 'often, always, regularly' both, in some sense, encode temporal information, they do not behave like the temporal adverbs listed in Table 5.13: they never occur before the subject. The following sentences exemplify the use of these adverbs.

(5.73) nyinjin kamal **apït** lisingala

      nyi-njin   kamal   **apït**   lisinga-la
      1SG-POSS.NPL   head   really   swell-IRR

      'My head will really swell.' (i.e. will swell greatly)

(5.74) anungwan **apït** kulawi ndonanyï

      anungwan   **apït**   kulawi   ndï=onan-yï
      mother.PL   really   boy.PL   3PL.OBJ=call-IPFV

      'The mothers were really calling the children.' (i.e. shouting loudly to them)

(5.75) njimoka nja kataplam **akï**

      njimoka   nja   kataplam   **akï**
      stick   this   dry   very

      'This stick is very dry.'

(5.76) nyinjin mandïn kokomï **akï**
nyi-njin   mandïn   kokomï   **akï**
1SG-POSS.NPL   string.bag   heavy   very
'My string bag is very heavy.'

(5.77) kïmbïlo ndindi kwandap **mbïn** kisïm mïla
kïmbïlo   ndindi   kwandap   **mbïn**   kisïm   mal-la
tomorrow   dog   one   also   jungle   go-IRR
'One dog will also go to the jungle tomorrow.'

(5.78) kanam **mbïn** minjame kapï pï
kanam   **mbïn**   minjame   kapï   p-ï
now   also   banana.PL   house   be-IPFV
'Today there are also bananas at home.'

(5.79) kïmbïlo an **pisa** ambalandinda
kïmbïlo   an   **pisa**   ambal=andi-nda
tomorrow   1PL   again   PL.REFL=see-IRR
'We'll see one another again tomorrow.'

(5.80) ndïn **pisa** ambangïn sinangapï
ndïn   **pisa**   ambangïn   sinanga-apï
3PL.SUBJ   again   ground   stand-PFV
'They stood on the ground again.'

(5.81) nyï **tïti** ke amï
nyï   **tïti**   ke   am-ï
1SG   often   sago   eat-IPFV
'I eat sago every day.'

(5.82) nyï ambo **tïti** katal le
nyï   ambo   **tïti**   katal   la-ï
1SG   NEG   often   laughter   put-IPFV
'I don't laugh often.'

5.6 Negators

Negators are words that are used to express negative polarity. Although they might not constitute a unified word class, the following three words (Table 5.16) are presented here for the benefit of crosslinguistic comparison.

Table 5.16. Negators.

Negator	Function	Gloss
ambo	negative marker	'no, not' ('NEG')
ola	prohibitive auxiliary verb	'don't!' ('PROH')
mwa	negative response word	'no, nothing'

The negative marker *ambo* 'no, not' is used in declarative and interrogative sentences to signal negative polarity in the clause in which it is found—that is, the negator has scope over the whole clause. Its canonical position is following the subject and preceding the predicate (OV)—that is, S-NEG-O-V. Negation is discussed more fully in §8.4.

Negative imperatives (i.e. prohibitions) are formed not with an imperative verb form, but rather with an irrealis verb form followed by the prohibitive auxiliary verb *ola* 'don't!' (§6.2.1). Prohibitions are discussed further in the section on commands and requests (§8.3).

The interjection *mwa* 'no, nothing' is used to contradict a proposition or answer negatively to a polar ('yes/no') question (questions are discussed in §8.2).

5.7 Interrogative words

The class of interrogative words, which are used in *wh-* (i.e. content) questions, consists of the following (Table 5.17).

Table 5.17. Interrogative words.

Interrogative	Gloss	Etymology
aw	'Q' 'how?'	[question formative]
awnjin	'what? [NPL]'	< *aw* + *njin* 'thing [NPL]'
awse	'what? [PL]'	< *aw* + *se* 'thing [PL]'
awalake	'when?'	< *aw* + *ale* 'day' + *ki* 'on' ?
awate	'why?'	< *aw* + *at* 'cause' ?

Interrogative	Gloss	Etymology
am	'where?'	< *aw* + *m* '?' ?
kïman	'who?'	= 'someone', < *kïmal* 'some' ?
kïmanjin	'whose?'	< *kïman* 'who?' + *njin* 'thing [NPL]'

As is readily apparent from this list, these question words are almost all formed from an interrogative formative *aw-* (akin to *wh-* in English). Alone, this form may mean 'how?'. There are two words for 'what?', depending on the number of the referent being inquired about: the non-plural form is *aw* + *njin* ('thing [NPL]'), whereas the plural form is *aw* + *se* ('thing [PL]'), literally something like 'what thing?' and 'what things?', respectively. The word for 'when?' (*awalake*) seems to derive from *aw-* 'Q' + *ale* 'sun [= day]' + *kï* 'at, in, on' (literally 'on what day?'). The word for 'why?' (*awate*) may derive from *aw-* 'Q' + *at* 'top' (literally 'what top?'). If this is indeed so, then there seems to be a spatial metaphor at play here ('top' > 'cause, reason')—one which is the opposite of that found in English or Tok Pisin (cf. English *ground* or Tok Pisin *as* 'bottom' > 'cause, reason'). The word for 'where?' (*am*) also likely contains (or contained) the question formative *aw-*, but the **w* appears to have been lost before *-m* (whose origin is also obscure to me). Finally, the interrogative words used to inquire of people (*kïman* 'who?' and *kïmanjin* 'whose?') are the only ones that are clearly unconnected to the formative *aw-*. These forms can function as indefinite pronouns in non-interrogative contexts (i.e. 'someone' and 'someone's', respectively). The possessive form *kïmanjin* 'whose?' is clearly derived from *kïman* 'who?' + *njin* 'thing [NPL]' (this latter form is used in deriving all possessive pronouns, §5.2.3). The form *kïman* 'who?' itself appears to be related to *kïmal* 'some', and may indeed be a non-plural form of this word.

Questions are covered in greater detail in §8.2.

5.8 Conjunctions

Pondi conjunctions are presented in Table 5.18.

Table 5.18. Conjunctions.

Conjunction	Function	Gloss
akat	coordination	'and'
o	disjunction	'or' (< Tok Pisin)
mbatï	adversative/consequential	'but, so'

Pondi contains at least one native conjunction, the coordinating conjunction *akat* 'and'. This word does not seem ever to connect clauses (§8.1.1). It can, however, coordinate two phrases, such as NPs. When it does so, it functions as a postpositive element (following the second coordinated NP), as in the following examples.

(5.83) ndindi nyï John **akat** njin
   ndindi nyï John **akat** njin
   dog   1SG [name] and   POSS.NPL
   'John's and my dog'

(5.84) tatï namal yuwï **akat** asiyï
   tatï namal yuwï   **akat** asi-ï
   papa pig   crocodile and   hit-IPFV
   'Papa killed a pig and a crocodile.'

In many ways, the conjunction *akat* 'and' seems to behave rather like a postposition (in which case, we may choose to translate it instead as 'along with' or 'in addition to', yielding alternative translations like 'Papa killed a pig along with a crocodile' for 5.84). The one clue, however, that this word is indeed a conjunction comes from sentences like (5.85), in which it joins two objects and the verb receives the dual object marker proclitic. This example is additionally quite interesting, since it shows the object marker behaving very much as an argument-indexing element.

(5.85) John ipï kamal **akat** mintïtuwapï
   John ipï   kamal **akat** min=tïtuwa-apï
   [name] hand head   and   3DU=scratch-PFV
   'John scratched his arm and his head.'

Disjunctive coordination (whether at the phrase level or at clause level) can be accomplished with the Tok Pisin loan word *o* 'or' as in (5.86).

(5.86) nyï mïla **o** nyï mapïla
   nyï mal-la **o** nyï ma=p-la
   1SG go-IRR or 1SG 3SG.OBJ=be-IRR
   '(Either) I'll go or I'll stay.' (literally 'I'll be at it', with 'it' referring to the village)

Adversative coordination is not well understood, but it may be possible at the clause level with the word *mbatï* 'but'. Although this word closely resembles English *but*, this may just be a coincidence (traditional Tok Pisin uses the word *tasol* 'but' for this adversative meaning). It seems possible for this same word to function as a consequential coordinator (i.e. 'so'). It may be related to the verb *mbat-* 'work, do' (indeed it is the same as the imperfective form of this verb), although I do not believe it to be functioning as an auxiliary or light verb. Elsewhere in the language, auxiliary verbs may only follow irrealis verb forms (whereas *mbatï* can follow verbs marked for any TAM distinction); also, prosodically, *mbatï* does not seem to be part of the preceding verb phrase (or even clause), but rather seems to belong to the following clause. The sentences in (5.87) and (5.88) illustrate its use in joining two clauses. In the first example (5.87) it has an adversative sense, whereas in the second example (5.88) it has a consequential sense.

(5.87) meyamba nyï kisïm yapï **mbatï** nyï ambo namal asiyï
   meyamba nyï kisïm i-apï **mbatï** nyï ambo namal asi-ï
   yesterday 1SG jungle come-PFV but 1SG NEG pig hit-IPFV
   'Yesterday I went to the jungle, but I did not kill a pig.'

(5.88) meyamba mun mayapï **mbata** mï ke amngapï
   meyamba mun ma=i-apï **mbata** mï ke am-ngapï
   yesterday hunger 3SG.OBJ=hit?-PFV so 3SG.SUBJ sago eat-PFV
   'Yesterday he was hungry, so he ate sago.'

The combination of clauses—whether through parataxis or (morphological) subordination is covered more fully in §8.1.

5.9 Numerals

Pondi has a set of cardinal numbers that are used both in counting and to quantify noun phrases, assigning a numerical value to the referent. The number system in Pondi is quinary (base-five), at least for numerals below 25: there are distinct words for the numbers one through four, none of which is derived from another number word. That said, although not derived from other number words, per se, the words for numbers one through four may not all be morphologically simple. The number *kwandap* 'one' appears to derive from the determiner *kwan* 'a(n), some, (an)other', perhaps an elaboration of an earlier Pondi form **kwa(n)* 'one' (cf. Ulwa *kwa* 'one' and Ambakich *koŋ* 'one'). The element **ndap*, oddly enough, appears to be cognate with Ambakich *dop* 'hand'.[5]

---

5 I say 'oddly', because words for 'hand' in each language are used to indicate the number five (of the form 'hand one').

The word for 'two' has two forms, *inin* and *in*, seemingly used in complete free variation. The form *in* may be a simple haplology of *inin*, or, alternatively, the form *inin* may be an iconic reduplication of *in*. If the latter is so, then this may either have occurred in the proto-language or have developed independently in several languages, perhaps through calquing (cf. Ulwa *nini* 'two').

The word for 'three' is *yawle*, which is cognate with the Mwakai word for 'three' (*yora* in the Mongol dialect and *yawor* in the Kaimbal dialect).

The word for 'four' is *nanïnge*, which is clearly cognate with the word for 'four' in the Maruat-Dimiri-Yaul dialect of Ulwa, which is *nanange* (it is *watangïnila* in the Manu dialect of Ulwa).

The word for 'five' is, quite transparently *ipï* 'hand' plus *kwandap* 'one' (i.e. 'one hand'), a clear indication of the hand-counting system that underlies the quinary numerical system. The numbers greater than five are formed through periphrasis. For example, 'six' is *ipï kwandap kwandap ma=at p-ï* 'hand one one 3SG.OBJ=atop be-IPFV' (i.e. 'one hand, one is atop it'). The number 'ten' is expressed as *ipï inin* 'hand two' (i.e. 'two hands'). And so on. Using this system, one can count to twenty-four. Table 5.19 presents the Pondi cardinal numerals from one to twenty-four.

Table 5.19. Pondi numerals up to twenty-four.

	Gloss	**Pondi numeral**
1	'one'	kwandap
2	'two'	inin ~ in
3	'three'	yawle
4	'four'	nanïnge
5	'five'	ipï kwandap
6	'six'	ipï kwandap kwandap mat pï
7	'seven'	ipï kwandap inin mat pï
8	'eight'	ipï kwandap yawle mat pï
9	'nine'	ipï kwandap nanïnge mat pï
10	'ten'	ipï inin
11	'eleven'	ipï in kwandap mat pï
12	'twelve'	ipï in inin mat pï
13	'thirteen'	ipï in yawle mat pï
14	'fourteen'	ipï in nanïnge mat pï
15	'fifteen'	ipï yawle

5. OTHER WORD CLASSES

	Gloss	Pondi numeral
16	'sixteen'	ipï yawle kwandap mat pï
17	'seventeen'	ipï yawle inin mat pï
18	'eighteen'	ipï yawle yawle mat pï
19	'nineteen'	ipï yawle nanïnge mat pï
20	'twenty'	ipï nanïnge
21	'twenty-one'	ipï nanïnge kwandap mat pï
22	'twenty-two'	ipï nanïnge inin mat pï
23	'twenty-three'	ipï nanïnge yawle mat pï
24	'twenty-four'	ipï nanïnge nanïnge mat pï
25	'twenty-five'	?

For higher numbers (which are used almost exclusively for referring to money), Pondi speakers can refer to multiples of ten by using the form *yalïme*, which may derive from *yalïm* 'ironwood tree'.[6] Table 5.20 presents the higher numerals (multiples of ten) in Pondi.

Table 5.20. Pondi higher numerals.

	Gloss	Pondi numeral
30	'thirty'	yalïme yawle
40	'forty'	yalïme nanïnge
50	'fifty'	yalïme ipï kwandap
60	'sixty'	yalïme ipï kwandap kwandap mat pï
70	'seventy'	yalïme ipï kwandap inin mat pï
80	'eighty'	yalïme ipï kwandap yawle mat pï
90	'ninety'	yalïme ipï kwandap nanïnge mat pï
100	'one hundred'	yalïme ipï in

Numerals follow head nouns but precede determiners (such as subject markers or object markers), when these are present. Thus, they function rather like adjectives, modifying nouns.

The following sentences illustrate the use of the numeral *kwandap* 'one' (5.90) and of the related indefinite marker, *kwan* 'a(n)' (5.89).

---

6   The non-plural/plural alternation for 'ironwood tree' is *yal-(ï)m* / *yal-o* (§3.10). Perhaps the form *yalïm* has been reanalysed here as a nominal root, to which the plural suffix *-e* has been added. The relationship between 'ten' and 'ironwood tree' may reflect a traditional system of counting larger numbers that made use of parts of these trees to represent numerals (cf. Ulwa *nali* 'ten', a word which also refers to the spines of sago fronds, which were traditionally used to mark units of ten when counting larger sums).

(5.89) nyï pisa namal **kwan** wanda

nyï	pisa	namal	**kwan**	u=an-nda
1SG	again	pig	INDF	2SG.OBJ=give-IRR

'I'll give you another pig.' (literally 'I'll give you a pig again.')

(5.90) namal **kwandap** kapï imbam pï

namal	**kwandap**	kapï	imbam	p-ï
pig	one	house	under	be-IPFV

'One pig is under the house.'

It is perhaps most common, however, to leave non-plural indefinite referents unmodified by either the indefinite marker or the number 'one', as in the following (5.91).

(5.91) namal nyinjin kusam amngapï

namal	nyi-njin	kusam	am-ngapï
pig	1SG-POSS.NPL	yam	eat-PFV

'A pig ate my yam.'

Instead of the numeral *inin ~ in* 'two', it is possible to use the subject/object marker *min* '3DU'. The two forms do not ever co-occur. When the referent is dual in number (as when it is singular in number), the noun is always marked as 'non-plural' (§6.1.1). The following sentences all include dual referents, marked as such either with the numeral *inin ~ in* 'two' (5.92, 5.94) or with the subject/object marker *min* '3DU' (5.93, 5.95).

(5.92) alkï **inin**

alkï	**inin**
person	two

'two people'

(5.93) alkï **min**

alkï	**min**
person	3DU

'the (two) people'

(5.94) komblam minjamo **inin** amngapï

komblam	minjamo	**inin**	am-ngapï
child	banana	two	eat-PFV

'The child ate two bananas.'

(5.95) komblam minjamo **minamngapï**
　　　 komblam　　minjamo　　**min**=am-ngapï
　　　 child　　　 banana　　　3DU=eat-PFV
　　　 'The child ate the (two) bananas.'

Only with numbers three or greater is it possible for a (plural) determiner (subject marker or object marker) to follow the numeral. Example (5.97) contains the plural subject marker *ndïn*, whereas example (5.96) lacks it.

(5.96) meyo **yawle** kusam amngapï
　　　 meyo　　　**yawle**　　kusam　　am-ngapï
　　　 dog.PL　　 three　　　 yam　　　eat-PFV
　　　 'Three dogs ate the yam.'

(5.97) meyo **yawle ndïn** kusam amngapï
　　　 meyo　　　**yawle**　　**ndïn**　　 kusam　　am-ngapï
　　　 dog.PL　　 three　　　 3PL.SUBJ　　yam　　　eat-PFV
　　　 'Three dogs ate a yam.'

It seems to be optional (when a numeral three or greater occurs in the NP) to mark the noun itself as plural. In the following sentences, the referents—whether subject (5.98) or object (5.99)—are marked as non-plural despite being modified by the numeral *yawle* 'three' (or, perhaps better put, they maintain their base forms, unmarked for number).

(5.98) njimoka **yawle** kayïtï
　　　 njimoka　　**yawle**　　kayït-ï
　　　 tree　　　　three　　　 fall-IPFV
　　　 'Three trees fell down.'

(5.99) nyï nambikul **yawle** ndapapï
　　　 nyï　　　nambikul　　**yawle**　　ndï=ap-apï
　　　 1SG　　 hole　　　　 three　　　 3PL.OBJ=dig-PFV
　　　 'I dug three holes.'

6
PHRASE-LEVEL SYNTAX

This chapter focuses on syntax at the level of the phrase, a set of one or more words functioning together as a syntactic unit (a unit which is taken to be the constituent of a clause, Chapter 7). Although phrases often consist of just a single word, the following sections focus on multi-word phrases, explaining how multiple words interact with one another within a single phrase. I begin with a discussion of noun phrases (§6.1) and verb phrases (§6.2), and then briefly discuss adpositional phrases (§6.3).

6.1 Noun phrases

A noun phrase (NP) consists minimally of a noun (common or proper) or a pronoun (personal or demonstrative). A phrase that has a noun (as opposed to a pronoun) as its head may also contain a determiner (subject marker, object marker, or demonstrative determiner, §5.3), which always comes last in the NP. An NP headed by a pronoun does not permit subject markers or object markers. Adjectives, if present, follow the head and precede determiners. Numerals, like nominal modifiers, follow the head noun and precede determiners such as subject markers or object markers. The only element in an NP that precedes the noun is the possessive pronoun, which indicates the possessor of the referent of the head noun (although it may be preferable to analyse this possessor as a separate NP within which the following NP is embedded). Thus, the canonical order of elements in a Pondi NP is as presented in (6.01).

(6.01) The Pondi NP
[possessor][noun][adjective][numeral][determiner]

NPs may function as subjects (whether the sole argument of an intransitive clause or the more agentive argument of a transitive clause). They may also serve as direct objects of transitive clauses, and as the objects of postpositions. When serving functions other than subject, direct object, or object of a postposition, NPs may (depending on their structure) be marked with the oblique-marking enclitic =*n* (§7.3).

In the following sections I discuss nominal number (§6.1.1) and possession (§6.1.2).

6.1.1 Nominal number

As mentioned in Chapter 3, the number distinction found among Pondi nominals is two-way—between 'one or two' (or 'non-plural') and 'more than two' (or 'plural'). This distinction differs from number distinctions found elsewhere in the grammar, indeed elsewhere within NPs, as determiners exhibit a three-way number distinction—'one' (i.e. singular) vs 'two' (i.e. dual) vs 'more than two' (i.e. plural). When there is an overt indication of nominal number greater than two (i.e. the presence of the quantifier *andeyal* 'many' or a numeral such as *naninge* 'four' following the noun), it is not necessary for the noun to be marked as 'plural' (§5.9). Thus, the contrast found among nouns may be considered one of 'unmarked with respect to number' vs 'marked as referring to more than two referents'.

The different number marking schemes for nouns and determiners can interact within a single NP. Basically, there need not be agreement between the two: the presence or absence of, say, a subject marker, has no effect on the marking of the head noun of the determiner's NP. Thus, the presence of, say, the 3SG.SUBJ marker *mï* indicates that a 'non-plural'-marked (or 'unmarked') noun refers to exactly one referent (6.02); the presence of the 3DU subject marker *min*, on the other hand, indicates that the 'non-plural'-marked noun refers to exactly two referents (6.03); when the 3PL.SUBJ marker *ndïn* is used, however, then there is 'agreement' within the NP, since the noun will also be marked as 'plural' (6.04).

(6.02) kulam mï
     kulam   mï
     boy   3SG.SUBJ
     'the boy'

(6.03) kulam min
      kulam   min
      boy   3DU
      'the (two) boys'

(6.04) kulawi ndïn
      kulawi   ndïn
      boy.PL   3PL.SUBJ
      'the (more than two) boys'

The 'unmarked' nature of the 'non-plural' noun form is illustrated by phrases such as the following (6.05), in which the presence of the numeral *yawle* 'three' obviates the need to mark the noun as plural.

(6.05) kulam yawle ndïn
      kulam   yawle   ndïn
      boy   three   3PLSUBJ
      'the three boys'

The same interaction of number categories can be seen in object NPs, even as the object-marker determiner cliticises to the verb. In (6.06), the object ('pig') is marked as non-plural (to refer to a dual referent), while the object marker is *min*= '3DU', referring to the same dual referent. Example (6.07) is ungrammatical, because the object ('pig') is marked as plural despite referring to a dual referent. In (6.08), the object ('pig') is marked as plural (to refer to a referent of three or more) and the object marker is *ndïn*= '3PL.SUBJ', referring to the same plural referent. Example (6.09), on the other hand, is ungrammatical, because the non-plural form *namal* 'pig' is used despite referring to a referent of three or more (as indicated by the 3PL.OBJ marker *ndi*).

(6.06) tatï alel **namal minasiyï**
      tatï   alel   **namal**   **min**=asi-ï
      papa   spear   pig   3DU=hit-IPFV
      'Papa killed two pigs with a spear.'

(6.07) *tatï alel **name minasiyï**
      tatï   alel   ***name**   **min**=asi-ï
      papa   spear   *pig.PL   3DU=hit-IPFV
      *'Papa killed two pigs with a spear.'

(6.08) tatï alel **name ndasiyï**
      tatï   alel   **name**   **ndï**=asi-ï
      papa   spear   pig.PL   3PL.OBJ=hit-IPFV
      'Papa killed (more than two) pigs with a spear.'

(6.09) *tatï alel **namal ndasiyï**
      tatï   alel   ***namal**   **ndï**=asi-ï
      papa   spear   pig   3PL.OBJ=hit-IPFV
      *'Papa killed (more than two) pigs with a spear.'

6.1.2 Possession

To indicate possession, the possessor immediately precedes the possessum. When the possessor constitutes a single possessive pronoun (e.g. *ninjin* 'my' or *ndinjin* 'their'), we may wish, simply, to treat this element as a determiner (or 'possessive pronoun', §5.2.3). If it is indeed a determiner, then it is the only dependent element in an NP permitted to precede the head noun. When the possessor is expressed not by a pronoun, but rather by a full NP (whether a common noun or a proper noun), then the possessor NP is marked by the free element *njin* 'POSS.NPL' or *is* 'POSS.PL' (the number distinction reflects the number of referents encoded in the possessum NP, not in the possessor NP). The following examples illustrate the use of the free possessive marker *njin* 'POSS.NPL' with a common noun (6.10) and a proper noun (6.11).

(6.10) tatï **njin** kapï
      tatï   **njin**   kapï
      papa   POSS.NPL house
      'papa's house'

(6.11) David **njin** kapï
      David   **njin**   kapï
      [name] POSS.NPL house
      'David's house'

There is no verb in Pondi like the English verb 'have' to indicate possession or ownership. Rather, to express that someone 'has' something, a possessive NP is used, as in the following examples (note that this predicative structure does not differ in any way from the one used for attributive possessive constructions, as in 6.10 and 6.11).

(6.12) tatï **is** kame
      tatï   **is**   kame
      papa   POSS.PL   betel.nut.PL
      'Papa has betel nuts.' (literally 'papa's betel nuts')

(6.13) **mays** imunjï andeyal
      ma-is   imunjï   andeyal
      3SG-POSS.PL   betel.pepper   many
      'It has many betel peppers.' (literally 'its many betel peppers'; 'it' refers here to a string bag)

6.2 Verb phrases

A verb phrase (VP) consists minimally of a verb (which itself contains a stem plus maximally one prefix and maximally one suffix). The verb is always the final element in the VP. If the verb is transitive (and contains an overt object), then the VP contains within it an NP (the direct object of the verb). This NP may be marked with (or indexed by) an object marker, which cliticises to the verb. I do not know whether it is better to analyse these object markers as argument-indexing prefixes (and thus belonging syntactically to the verb) or as belonging syntactically to the object NP—but in either case, they are constituents of VPs. Postpositional phrases (PPs) may also be considered constituents of VPs. When present, they always occur before the verb (and before the direct object, if the verb is transitive). If an auxiliary verb is present, it always immediately follows the main verb. Thus, the canonical order of elements in a Pondi VP is as presented in (6.14).

(6.14) The Pondi VP
      [PP][NP][main verb][auxiliary verb]

In the following sections I discuss auxiliary verbs (§6.2.1), compound verbs (§6.2.2), and equational constructions (§6.2.3).

6.2.1 Auxiliary verbs

There is a small, closed set of auxiliary verbs in Pondi. These are the only words permitted to follow finite verb forms within a given clause. The immediately preceding main verb is always inflected for irrealis mood. The auxiliary verb is thus always the absolute last element in any clause where it is found. At least one auxiliary verb (*w-* 'want, will') is capable of inflecting for (two) TAM distinctions. I have identified the following auxiliary verbs in Pondi (Table 6.1).

Table 6.1. Auxiliary verbs.

Verb	Function	Gloss
w- (wapï, wï)	volitive/conative	'want, will, try' ('VOL')
te	immediate future	'be about to' ('FUT')
ola	prohibitive	'don't!' ('PROH')

Of these, only *w-* 'want, will, try' inflects for TAM—either perfective *wapï* or imperfective *wï* (the latter, due to rounding caused by the preceding labial-velar glide, may be rendered [wo]; I have no evidence of an irrealis form of this auxiliary verb). I take as the basic meaning of *w-* the expression of want, desire, or attempt. Although volition can be encoded by an irrealis verb alone, it can also be encoded by a combination of an irrealis verb with the auxiliary verb *w-*, as in the following examples.

(6.15) meyamba nyï kisïm mïla **wapï**
       meyamba   nyï   kisïm   mal-la   **w-apï**
       yesterday 1SG   jungle   go-IRR   want-PFV
       'I wanted to go the jungle yesterday.'

(6.16) nyï meyamba kapï usïla **wapï** nyï ambo mosapï
       nyï meyamba kapï us-la   **w-apï**   nyï ambo ma=us-apï
       1SG yesterday house build-IRR want-PFV 1SG NEG 3SG.OBJ=build-IRR
       'Yesterday I wanted to build the house, [but] I didn't build it.'

(6.17) Peter anto minjamo nda **wï**
       Peter   an=to   minjamo   n-nda   **w-ï**
       [name]   1PL=from   banana   take-IRR   want-IPFV
       'Peter wants to take a banana from us.'

(6.18) John kapï usïla **wï**
       John   kapï   us-la   **wï**
       [name]   house   build-IRR want-IPFV
       'John wants to build a house.'

Although we could posit an irrealis form */wla/ ([wïla]), it seems that no such form is used; rather, simply an irrealis verb form (without any auxiliary verb) is used to express such notions as 'would want' or 'will desire'.

This same verb is used to encode conative modality—that is, attempts (usually failed)—and may, as such, be translated as 'try', as in the following examples.

(6.19) kanam an kapï usïla **wï**
      kanam   an   kapï   us-la   **w-ï**
      now   1PL   house   build-IRR   want-IPFV
      'Now we are trying to build a house.'

(6.20) tatï alel ningasila **wapï**
      tatï   alel   ningasi-la   **w-apï**
      papa   spear   throw-IRR   want-PFV
      'Papa tried to throw the spear.'

(6.21) meyamba nyï namal asinda **wapï** mwa
      meyamba   nyï   namal   asi-nda   **w-apï**   mwa
      yesterday   1SG   pig   hit-IRR   want-PFV   nothing
      'Yesterday I tried to kill a pig, but I was unsuccessful.'

This final example (6.21) illustrates the frustrative use of *mwa* 'no, nothing', whereby the single word is used to encode the entire clausal meaning of 'but this was to no avail' or 'but this did not work'. (The Tok Pisin word *nogat* 'no' may be used in a similar way.)

The volitional notion of *w-* 'want' seems to have been extended to encode futurity (which, also, can be encoded simply with a single irrealis-marked verb). This may be the result of a well-attested grammaticalisation process (cf. English *will* 'want' > 'future marker'). Alternatively, it may be the result of calquing from Tok Pisin (which has experienced this very grammaticalisation process, such that the verb *laik* 'want' has come to be used also as a future marker). Examples of this immediate future usage of *w-* 'want' include the following.

(6.22) katïl mï kïlïya **wï**
      katïl   mï   kïlï-ya   **w-ï**
      old.man   3SG.SUBJ   die-IRR   want-IPFV
      'The old man is about to die.'

(6.23) kinyï kït oliya **wï**
      kinyï   kït   oli-ya   **w-ï**
      coconut   bottom   cut-IRR   want-IPFV
      'The coconut is about to fall down.' (literally 'cut bottom')

(6.24) popo nja mïnala **wï**
    popo   nja   mïna-la   **w-ï**
    papaya   this   rot-IRR   want-IPFV
    'This papaya is about to rot.' (*popo* < Tok Pisin)

Another function of the auxiliary verb *w-* 'want' is to encode progressive (imperfective) aspect. Although there exists in Pondi an imperfective suffix *-ï* to achieve this same purpose, there are a number of verbs that do not make any morphological distinction between perfective and imperfective aspect. Thus, the addition of the verb *w-* 'want' may help clarify that a progressive or continuous event is being described, as in the following examples.

(6.25) mï sinangala **wï**
    mï   sinanga-la   **w-ï**
    3SG.SUBJ   stand-IRR   want-IPFV
    'He is (in the process of) standing up.'

(6.26) ndïn nïm asïliya **wï**
    ndïn   nïm   asïli-ya   **w-ï**
    3PL.SUBJ   canoe   push-IRR   want-IPFV
    'They are (in the process of) pushing the canoe.'

(6.27) kanam iye kinyï kulam anda **wï**
    kanam   iye   kinyï   kulam   an-nda   **w-ï**
    now   girl   coconut   boy   give-IRR   want-IPFV
    'The girl is now (in the process of) giving the coconut to the boy.'

It may be pointed out here, that—as an alternative to using the auxiliary verb *w-* 'want'—wishes and desires can be expressed with an irrealis verb form alone (§4.4), as in the following examples.

(6.28) nyï ke **amnda**
    nyï   ke   am-**nda**
    1SG   sago   eat-IRR
    'I want to eat.' (literally 'eat sago')

(6.29) kïman nyun **ila**
    kïman   nyï=un   i-**la**
    who   1SG=with   come-IRR
    'Who wants to come with me?'

Unlike the auxiliary verb *w-*, the auxiliary verb *te* 'be about to' does not seem to inflect for any TAM distinctions. Although it is likely cognate with the Ulwa speculative suffix *-t* (which encodes epistemic possibility in that language), it seems rather in Pondi to encode immediate futurity, as in the following examples.

(6.30) ndindi nja wamnda **te**
    ndindi   nja   u=am-nda   **te**
    dog   this   2SG.OBJ=eat-IRR be.about.to
    'This dog is about to bite you!'

(6.31) nyï sila **te**
    nyï   si-la   **te**
    1SG   sit-IRR   be.about.to
    'I'm about to sit down.'

(6.32) kapatupa ndïn alasïla **te**
    kapatupa   ndïn   alas-la   **te**
    hawk   3PL.SUBJ fly-IRR   be.about.to
    'The hawks are about to fly.'

Although this verb generally encodes 'immediate' future time, it may also be used to refer to future time more broadly—or, at least, it is capable of referring to events of the following day, as in example (6.33).

(6.33) tatï kïmbïlo kisïm mïla **te**
    tatï   kïmbïlo   kisïm   mal-la   **te**
    papa   tomorrow jungle   go-IRR   be.about.to
    'Papa will go to the jungle tomorrow.' (perhaps with the sense 'Papa is ready to go to the jungle tomorrow.')

Also, the immediate future auxiliary verb *te* 'be about to' can be used in exhortations (cf. §8.3), as in the following example.

(6.34) an mïla **te**
    an   mal-la   **te**
    1PL   go-IRR   be.about.to
    'Let's go (now)!'

The last auxiliary verb to be considered, *ola* 'don't!', is used in negative commands (i.e. prohibitions). It, too, must follow irrealis-marked verbs, as seen in the following examples.

(6.35) o nyinjin minjamo amnda **ola**
     o   nyi-njin   minjamo   am-nda   ola
     2SG.SUBJ   1SG-POSS.NPL banana   at-IRR   don't
     'Don't eat my banana!'

(6.36) mïla **ola**
     mal-la   **ola**
     go-IRR   don't
     'Don't go!'

The form *ola* 'don't!' is homophonous with the base form (and imperative) of the verb *ola-* 'perceive, hear'. Indeed, it is most likely a grammaticalisation of this verb. Several languages of the region seem to have derived prohibitive markers from verbs of perception or cognition, for example Ulwa *wana-* 'feel' and *wana* 'PROH', and Ambakich *kanak-* 'hear' and *anak* 'PROH'. We can imagine the grammaticalisation process underlying this: at some point there must have been a biclausal construction, the first clause containing an irrealis-marked verb indicating the (hoped) counterfactual event to be prohibited, and the second clause containing an imperative form of a verb of perception (and, by extension, reasoning). Thus, sentences like the one seen in example (6.35) could have originated from biclausal sentences of the form 'before you eat my banana, think!' or 'lest you eat my banana, hark!'. In Ulwa, the grammaticalisation process has gone one step further: the prohibitive marker *wana* has moved from the clause-final verbal position to the canonical negator position (following the subject and preceding the object). More examples of prohibitive constructions are provided in §8.3.

There is no evidence of multiple auxiliary verbs co-occurring in the same VP.

6.2.2 Compound verbs

Compared to some Papuan languages, Pondi does not make frequent use of serial verb constructions (SVCs)—especially not if we take a stricter definition of SVCs that demands that the multiple verbs in a given clause all match in terms of TAM marking. There are, however, a number of compound verb constructions, in which a nominal element is used idiomatically to give a particular meaning to the verb.

In such constructions, a non-referential nominal expression (sometimes referred to as an 'adjunct nominal', Foley 1986:117–128) combines with a verb of rather general meaning to make the meaning of the verb more specific. For example, the verb *ola-* 'perceive' can combine with a number of nouns to refer to different types of sensory perception, such as 'smell', 'taste', or 'feel' (unmodified, the verb *ola-* often has the basic meaning 'hear'). Thus, there are compounds like those in (6.37).

(6.37) nambisola-   'smell' (literally 'odour-perceive')
        imbïnola-   'feel, taste' (literally 'feeling/flavour-perceive')

The following examples illustrate how these compound verbs function in sentences. If an object-marker proclitic is present, it immediately precedes the nominal element (6.40).

(6.38) meyanga nyï ke alwe **nambisole**
       meyanga   nyï   ke   alwe   **nambis-ola-ï**
       yesterday   1SG   sago   good.PL   odour-perceive-IPFV
       'Yesterday I smelled some good food.'

(6.39) nyï ipï **imbïnole**
       nyï   ipï   **imbïn-ola-ï**
       1SG   arm   feeling-perceive-IPFV
       'I'm feeling (my) arm.'

(6.40) meyanga nyï ke ateyamate **ndimbïnole**
       meyanga   nyï   ke   ateyamate   ndï=**imbïn-ola-ï**
       yesterday   1SG   sago   bad.PL   3PL.OBJ=feeling-perceive-IPFV
       'Yesterday I tasted some bad food.'

Another verb commonly used in forming compounds is *numla-* 'throw'. In (6.41), this verb is functioning without any adjunct nominal.

(6.41) alkï alel **ndïnumle**
       alkï   alel   ndï=**numla-ï**
       person   spear   3PL.OBJ=throw-IPFV
       'The person is throwing spears.'

It is possible, however, for this verb stem to combine with various nouns to create a variety of meanings, such as seen in the following compound constructions (6.42).

(6.42) suwate numla-   'spit' (literally 'saliva-throw')
       walwal numla-   'breathe, blow' (literally 'lung-throw')
       pis numla-   'dance' (literally 'leg-throw')

These forms can be seen in the following sentences.

(6.43) kulam **suwate numle**
       kulam   **suwate**   **numla**-ï
       boy   saliva   throw-IPFV
       'The boy spits.'

(6.44) katïl **walwal numle**
       katïl   **walwal**   **numla**-ï
       old.man   lung   throw-IPFV
       'The old man was breathing.'

(6.45) kïmbïlo angwalise **pis numlala**
       kïmbïlo   angwalise   **pis**   **numla**-la
       tomorrow   woman.PL   leg   throw-IRR
       'The women will dance tomorrow.'

In fact, this putative verb stem, *numla-* 'throw', may itself contain an adjunct nominal, in this case *num* '(a) throw', combining with the generic verb *la-* 'put'. Examples of compound verbs formed with *la-* 'put', include the following.

(6.46) kulal la-   'vomit' (literally 'vomitus-put')
       katal la-   'laugh' (literally 'laughter-put')
       kis la-   'mash' (this one is uncertain, since the element *kis*
                    is otherwise unknown)

One particularly interesting compound construction involves the (otherwise unknown) element *pu-* 'bathe'. Although glossed alone as 'bathe', it always occurs with *nambi* 'water'. Simply juxtaposed, the adjunct and verb stem have an intransitive (or reflexive) sense ('bathe [oneself]'), as in (6.47).

(6.47) meyamba kulam **nambi pwapï**
       meyamba   kulam   **nambi**   **pu**-apï
       yesterday boy   water   bathe-PFV
       'The boy bathed (himself) yesterday.'

When employed for encoding a transitive meaning, however, the verb behaves rather more like verbs of 'putting' in Pondi, which take a goal argument as (obligatory) direct object argument and a theme argument as (optional) oblique. The following sentence (6.48) illustrates this use for *pu-* 'bathe'.

(6.48) tatï komblam man **nambi mapwapï**
      tatï   komblam   ma=n   **nambi**   ma=**pu**-apï
      papa   child   3SG.OBJ=OBL   water   3SG.OBJ=bathe-PFV
      'Papa bathed the child.' (perhaps literally 'Papa put the child in water.')

If in fact the verb *pu-* has the meaning 'put' (along with the typical Pondi argument structure associated with verbs of such meaning), then the intransitive sentence (6.48) would literally mean something like 'the boy put (himself) in water yesterday', with the (reflexive) theme argument being simply implied.

6.2.3 Equational constructions

Pondi has no discrete copular verb. Equative sentences (i.e. sentences containing a predicate complement) are formed without any overt verb. That is, the subject (always first in the clause) may be juxtaposed with whatever is predicated of it (always last in the clause). In each of the following equative sentences (6.49–50), the two NPs have the same referent. Two NPs are simply juxtaposed; there is no indication of tense, aspect, or mood (aside from any lexical clues provided in the form of, say, adverbs). The second NP is taken to be the complement.

(6.49) John mï **nïman**
      John   mï   **nïman**
      [name]   3SG.SUBJ man
      'John is a man.'

(6.50) mï **ambo angwaliyï**
      mï   ambo   angwaliyï
      3SG.SUBJ NEG   woman
      'He is not a woman.'

The predicates in such equational constructions can be adjectives, as in examples (6.51) and (6.52).

(6.51) njimoka nja **kataplam**
 njimoka   nja   **kataplam**
 tree   this   dry
 'This tree is dry.'

(6.52) meyamba kusam **almwan**
 meyamba   kusam   **almwan**
 yesterday   yam   good
 'The yam was tasty yesterday.'

6.3 Adpositional phrases

The only adpositional phrases in Pondi are postpositional phrases (PP)—that is, the adposition always immediately follows its object. A PP consists of an NP and a postposition. The NP may consist entirely of a pronoun, in which case the pronoun is of the non-subject variety (if, say, it is a personal pronoun, §5.2.1) and it cliticises to the postposition. When the object is a full NP, it may but need not end with an object marker; when it does, this object marker cliticises to the following postposition.

The following sentences provide examples of a postposition with just a pronoun (6.53), a postposition with a full NP and an object marker (6.54), and a postposition with a full NP but no object marker (6.55).

(6.53) nyï ambo **un** mïla
 nyï   ambo   **u-un**   mal-la
 1SG   NEG   2SG.OBJ=with   go-IRR
 'I won't go with you.'

(6.54) John **alkï ndun** malï
 John   **alkï**   **ndï=un**   mal-ï
 [name] person   3PL.OBJ=with   go-IPFV
 'John is going with the people.'

(6.55) nyï ambinjin **tatï un** name lak sangoyï
 nyï   ambi-njin   **tatï**   **un**   name   lak   sango-ï
 1SG   NPL.REFL-POSS.NPL   papa   with   pig.PL for   walk-IPFV
 'I used to go hunting for pig with my papa.' (literally 'I used to walk with my papa for the sake of pigs.')

This last example (6.55) additionally illustrates how two PPs can function within the same clause: here, we see the comitative postposition *un* 'with', indicating the person with whom the subject acted, as well as the purpose postposition *lak* 'for the sake of', indicating the reason for the action.

It is also possible for two postpositions to combine within a single PP. In all instances, the second postposition is the rather generic word *kï* 'at, in, on', which can follow certain other postpositions, such as *imbam* 'under, below', *at* 'atop, above', or *un* 'in, within, inside' (§5.4). This may reflect the fact that these postpositions have derived from nouns (e.g. in forms such as *at-kï*, the initial *at*—originally 'top'—would have been the object of the postposition *kï* 'at, in, on' (i.e. 'at the top [of]'). Indeed, the form *imbam* 'under, below' seems to retain its nominal nature in exhibiting an alternation between non-plural and plural forms (§5.4). In the synchronic grammar, however, forms like *at* 'atop, above' and *un* 'in, within, inside' may be used as postpositions on their own. The following sentences illustrate how, for example, *at* 'atop, above' can function alone as the head of a PP (6.56); that it is not itself a noun is indicated by the fact that the object marker cliticises to it and not to the following verb (6.57) (i.e. it is not part of compound noun meaning 'the top of the house').

(6.56) kolwal **kapï at** pï
      kolwal   **kapï**   **at**   p-ï
      rat.sp   house   atop   be-IPFV
      'The rat is on the house.'

(6.57) kolwal **kapï mat** pï
      kolwal   **kapï**   **ma=at**   p-ï
      rat.sp   house   3SG.OBJ=atop   be-IPFV
      'The rat is on the house.'

Alternatively, a postposition like *at* 'atop, above' can be part of a larger PP headed by *kï* 'at, in, on', as in (6.58) and (6.59).

(6.58) nyï **mel atkï** sïsuki akalala
      nyï   **mel**   **at-kï**   sïsuki   akala-la
      1SG   palm.sp   atop-at   rubbish   wipe-IRR
      'I will clean up the rubbish on the floor.'

(6.59) sewawi **njimoka matkï** alawe
      sewawi   **njimoka**   **ma=at-kï**   alawa-ï
      bird.PL   tree   3SG.OBJ=atop-at flock-IPFV
      'The birds are flying above the tree.'[1]

Finally, sentence (6.60) illustrates how *kï* 'at, in, on' can function alone—without a word like *at* 'atop, above'—as the head of a PP.

(6.60) kanam ndïn **kapï kï** ke amï
      kanam   ndïn   **kapï**   **kï**   ke   am-ï
      now   3PL.SUBJ house   at   sago   eat-IPFV
      'Now they are eating at home.' (literally 'eating sago')

---

1   The verb glossed here (and in the similar sentence in example 5.37) as 'flock' may actually be indicative of a very limited system of verbal number in Pondi. That is, Pondi distinguishes between *alas-* 'fly [NPL]' and *alawa-* 'fly [PL]'. The exact semantic distinction between the two is unclear—the difference could lie simply in the number of participants, but could, alternatively, depend on whether the event itself is plural, in other words, distributive or iterative (in which case 'flock' is not a great translation, although it still captures something of the plurality of the verb). Pondi's sister language Mwakai has the forms *wura-* 'fly [SG]' and *wurura-* 'fly [PL]'. Indeed, verbal number seems to be a common, though lexically very restricted, feature of Keram languages: Ambakich has *klip-* 'fall [SG]' vs *kanop-* 'fall [PL]'; and Ulwa has *ni-* 'die [SG]' vs *nipunpu-* 'die [PL]'. In all of these pairs, there is a distinct phonological similarity, but no clear derivational process (although some—and especially the Mwakai forms—seem to involve reduplication). With so few attested instances of verbal number in Keram languages, it is difficult to say whether verbal number involves derivation or is merely a lexical distinction (as in *fly* and *flock* in English).

7
CLAUSE-LEVEL SYNTAX

This chapter provides an overview of the syntax of Pondi at the level of the clause. A clause is taken to be a set of elements consisting (minimally) of a verb phrase and a subject (whether overtly expressed or not). Specifically, in this chapter, I discuss basic constituent order (§7.1), core argument alignment (§7.2), obliques (§7.3), ditransitive alignment (§7.4), and monoclausal sentences (§7.5).

7.1 Basic constituent order

The minimally required constituents of an intransitive clause are taken to be a subject (S) and a verb (V). A transitive clause consists, minimally, of these two elements as well as an object (O). Stated in terms defined less by grammatical relations, an intransitive clause consists of a single argument (S) and a verb (V), whereas a transitive clause consists of a more agent-like argument (A), a more patient-like argument (P), and a verb (V). Pondi exhibits the following—fairly rigid—ordering of constituents.

(7.01) Pondi basic constituent order
Intransitive clauses: SV
Transitive clauses: SOV (APV)

In the following examples of intransitive clauses, the verb is in **bold** and the subject is <u>underlined</u>.

(7.02) <u>kulam</u> **sapï**
kulam   sa-apï
boy   cry-PFV
'The boy cried.'

(7.03) <u>katïl mï</u> **kïlïya**
      <u>katïl</u>   mï   **kïlï-ya**
      old.man   3SG.SUBJ   die-IRR
      'The old man will die.'

(7.04) <u>mï</u> **kusanyï**
      <u>mï</u>   **kusan-yï**
      3SG.SUBJ   cough-IPFV
      'He is coughing.'

In the following examples of transitive clauses, the verb is in **bold**, the subject (or more agentive participant) is <u>underlined</u>, and the object (or more patientive participant) is in *italics*.

(7.05) <u>alkï</u> *ndindi* **asiyï**
      <u>alkï</u>   *ndindi*   **asi-ï**
      person   dog   hit-IPFV
      'The person hit the dog.'

(7.06) <u>nanï</u> *njimoka* **tuklupï**
      <u>nanï</u>   *njimoka*   **tukul-apï**
      mama   stick   break-PFV
      'Mama broke a stick.'

(7.07) <u>anale</u> *minjame* ***nd*amnda**
      <u>anale</u>   *minjame*   *ndi*=**am-nda**
      woman.PL banana.PL 3PL.OBJ=eat-IRR
      'The women will eat bananas.'

(7.08) <u>o</u> ***ny*ale**
      <u>o</u>   *nyï*=**ala-ï**
      2SG.SUBJ   1SG=see-IPFV
      'You see me.'

The fact that the object marker *nd(i)* in (7.07) and the object pronoun *ny(i)* in (7.08) are not only emboldened but also italicised in their respective first lines reflects the fact that these forms—although syntactically part of (or entirely constituting) the object NP—are phonologically part of the verb.

7.2 Core argument alignment

The heuristic categories S, A, and O, which are commonly used to determine and compare alignment systems, are taken to be: 1) the single argument of an intransitive clause (S), 2) the more agent-like argument of a transitive clause (A), and 3) the more patient-like argument of a transitive clause (O) (also identified as P in the literature). In Pondi, the S and A arguments pattern alike syntactically, morphologically, and phonologically (thus instantiating a subject relation, §7.1). Pondi may thus be considered to exhibit nominative-accusative alignment.

S and A occur in the same position in the clause (namely, clause-initially), whereas O occurs after S and before the verb. Pondi nouns do not exhibit core argument case morphology. There are, however, two (somewhat distinct) paradigms for personal pronouns (§5.2.1), as well as for certain determiners (§5.3.2). One paradigm is used for subject arguments and for nothing else—that is, this paradigm applies to S and A arguments, but not to O arguments. The other paradigm is used for all non-subject roles (including O arguments). Often, for convenience, I refer to these forms as 'object' forms, although they apply to more than just object arguments—in addition to being used for direct objects of verbs and objects of postpositions, this paradigm is used for oblique NPs (indicated by the oblique-marker enclitic =*n*, §7.3). The two paradigms—subject and object—are highly syncretic, but there are three phonological differences: 2SG.SUBJ *o* vs 2SG.OBJ *u*, 3SG.SUBJ *mï* vs 3SG.OBJ *ma*, and 3PL.SUBJ *ndïn* vs 3PL.OBJ *ndï* (§5.2.1, §5.3.2).

There is no evidence of morphological or syntactic ergativity in the language, nor is there any indication of split-intransitivity or related alignment types (i.e. there is no active–stative/semantic/fluid alignment). The following examples illustrate the contrast in pronominal marking between a more agentive argument (or subject) and the more patientive argument (or object) of a transitive clause. When functioning as a subject, the 2SG form is *o* (7.09). When functioning as an object, the 2SG form is *u* (7.10). (The 1SG form does not vary based on its grammatical relation.)

(7.09) **o** nyasiyapï

o   nyï=asi-apï
2SG.SUBJ   1SG=hit-PFV
'You hit me.'

(7.10) nyï **wasiyapï**
    nyï   **u**=asi-apï
    1SG   2SG.OBJ=hit-PFV
    'I hit you.'

Example (7.11) shows the 3SG forms for the more agentive argument of the transitive clause (*mï*) as well as for the more patientive argument of the transitive clause (*ma*). The single argument of an intransitive clause always resembles the more agentive argument of a transitive clause, regardless of whether the argument is more active (unergative, unaffected, etc., 7.12) or more stative (unaccusative, affected, etc., 7.13).

(7.11) **mï** namal **masiyapï**
    mï   namal   **ma**=asi-apï
    3SG.SUBJ   pig   3SG.OBJ=hit-PFV
    'He hit the pig.'

(7.12) **mï** mbatapï
    mï   mbat-apï
    3SG.SUBJ   work-PFV
    'He worked.'

(7.13) **mï** kusanyï
    mï   kusan-yï
    3SG.SUBJ   cough-IPFV
    'He is coughing.'

Thus, all types of S arguments pattern more closely with A arguments than with O arguments (it is not the case that some Ss are more similar to As, whereas other Ss are more similar to Os depending on semantic or other criteria). Thus, S arguments are alike both syntactically and morphologically, irrespective of whether they are more agentive (unergative) or more patientive (unaccusative).

7.3 Obliques

Core arguments may be defined as the set of all subjects and (direct) objects. Subjects always precede objects, and objects always precede verbs. All other arguments in a clause (that is, noun phrases that are neither subjects nor objects, and all other phrases, such as adverbial phrases) may be referred to as obliques. In Pondi, the canonical position for all obliques is preceding the (direct) object. Generally, obliques immediately precede the object, although some (most notably temporal adverbs, §5.5.1) may precede the subject, thereby coming first in the clause.

There is an enclitic morpheme =*n* 'OBL' that affixes to pronouns and determiners in oblique NPs—that is, to any NP that is neither a subject (or subject complement) nor an object. Although postpositional phrases may be considered obliques, the object of the postposition (at least for these purposes) is considered an object and not an oblique. Only determiners and pronouns may function as hosts for =*n* 'OBL'. This means that oblique full NPs often do not exhibit this clitic—only personal pronouns, deictic demonstratives, and full NPs that end with determiners, such as 'object markers' (here, more properly referred to as 'non-subject markers'). That said, there is exactly one example in my corpus of the oblique marker following a full NP without any determiner present (see example 8.81); thus, either it may in fact be possible for the oblique marker to directly follow nouns or this single example is somewhat ungrammatical or otherwise not fully accounted for.

In the following sentences, oblique NPs (in **bold**) are serving instrumental functions. Only in (7.16) and (7.17) is the enclitic =*n* 'OBL' present, since these NPs contain determiners. In each example, the oblique phrase occurs after the subject and before the object.

(7.14) tatï **yakus** namuse tuklupï
      tatï   **yakus**   namuse   tukul-apï
      papa   machete   meat   cut-PFV
      'Papa cut the meat with a machete.'

(7.15) tatï **kulap** kimbane ndasiyï
      tatï   **kulap**   kimbane   ndï=asi-ï
      papa   fishing.spear fish.PL   3PL.OBJ=hit-IPFV
      'Papa shoots fish with a fishing spear.'

(7.16) tatï **sanglama man** kondiyam oliyï
      tatï   **sanglama**   **ma=n**   kondiyam   oli-ï
      papa   axe   3SG.OBJ=OBL palm.sp   cut-IPFV
      'Papa cuts a palm with an axe.'

(7.17) alkï **sanglamate ndïn** kondiyambune oliyï

alkï	**sanglamate**	**ndï=n**	kondiyambune	oli-ï
person	axe.PL	3PL.OBJ=OBL	palm.sp.PL	cut-IPFV

'People cuts palms with axes.'

Other thematic roles that can be fulfilled by oblique NPs include recipients and beneficiaries. Sentences with recipient NPs are given in §7.4 with the verb *an-* 'give'. Here (7.18) is another example, showing a deictic demonstrative serving as the entire recipient NP. It receives the oblique-marker enclitic.

(7.18) **andan** nyanï

anda=n	nyï=an-ï
that=OBL	1SG=give-IMP

'Give that to me!'

The following (7.19) is an example of a beneficiary NP, also marked with the oblique marker *=n*.

(7.19) kïman **nyïn** nïmbambiyï kanda

kïman	**nyï=n**	nïmbambiyï	ka-nda
who	1SG=OBL	cloth	sew-IRR

'Who can sew the cloth for me?'

In example (7.20), the oblique marker is used to indicate that with which an item is 'full'.

(7.20) manjin mandïn **imunjï man** kusuwate

ma-njin	mandïn	**imunjï**	**ma=n**	kusuwate
3SG-POSS.NPL	string.bag	betel.pepper	3SG.OBJ=OBL	full

'His string bag is full of betel peppers.'

Finally, the argument structure of the verb *mwas-* 'show' admits an oblique NP (§7.4). The precise thematic role fulfilled by this NP depends on one's interpretation, but it could be considered a sort of stimulus or perhaps even an instrument (if we may interpret a sentence such as 'John showed Mary *the ball*' to mean something like 'John furnished Mary['s vision] *with the ball*'). The following is an example of the verb 'show' with a full NP as the instrument/stimulus oblique. Since the NP ends in a determiner (a non-subject marker), it admits the clitic *=n*.

(7.21) **ndindi man** nyïmwas

ndindi	**ma=n**	nyï=mwas
dog	3SG.OBJ=OBL	1SG=show

'Show me the dog!'

Other non-core elements include adverbs and adpositional phrases. These do not receive any oblique marking. Like oblique NPs, these occur before the object and (typically) after the subject (although temporal adverbs often occur before the subject).

7.4 Ditransitive alignment?

Many languages have distinct ways of expressing transfer events—that is, events wherein something is given from one participant to another. In some languages, these constructions make use of ditransitive verbs, which take three arguments: an agent (A), a recipient (R), and a theme (T). Whereas the question of core argument alignment lies in the morphosyntactic patterning of S, A, and O arguments, the main question of ditransitive alignment is whether the O argument of a monotransitive verb patterns more like the R argument or more like the T argument of a ditransitive verb (the O argument is not known ever to pattern more like the A argument).

Pondi, however, does not seem to have any proper ditransitive verbs—that is, there is no verb whose argument structure selects three core arguments. The verb *an-*, which is glossed throughout this grammar as 'give', does not really mean 'give' in the English sense. It is, rather, a monotransitive verb: the subject of this verb encodes the giver/agent and the object encodes the recipient/benefactive (the gift/theme is encoded by an oblique).

The following sentences illustrate the use of the verb *an-* 'give' in Pondi. This irregular verb has a suppletive verb stem (*ala-*), which is used for the imperfective form, *ale* (< /ala-ï/). Furthermore, the verb 'give' is deponent, in that there is no perfective verb form (whether built from the stem *an-* or the stem *ala-*). Rather, the imperfective form *ale* is used to encode perfective aspect as well. In these sentences, it can be seen that the direct object of the verb glossed as 'give' is a recipient argument—whether 'boy' (7.22, 7.23) or 'you' (7.24, 7.25). The direct objects, which—as always—immediately precede the verb, are presented here in **bold**. Note that oblique marking is only overt on NPs that contain pronouns or determiners (§7.3). Thus, in examples (7.22–25), the only morphosyntactic indication of obliqueness (for the recipient argument) is its placement in the sentence (following the subject and preceding the object). In examples (7.26), (7.27), and (7.28), however, which are all imperatives, the recipient arguments are pronouns or determiners and, as such, permit the oblique marker =*n*.

(7.22) meyanga iye kinyï **kulam** ale
       meyanga   iye   kinyï   **kulam**   ala-ï
       yesterday   girl   coconut   boy   give-IPFV
       'Yesterday the girl gave the boy a coconut.'

(7.23) iye kinyal **kulam male**
       iy   kinyal   **kulam**   **ma**=ala-ï
       girl   coconut.PL   boy   3SG.OBJ=give-IPFV
       'The girl gives the boy coconuts.'

(7.24) nyï minjamo **wale**
       nyï   minjamo   **u**=ala-ï
       1SG   banana   2SG.OBJ=give-IPFV
       'I gave you a banana.'

(7.25) nyï minjamo **wanda**
       nyï   minjamo   **u**=an-nda
       1SG   banana   2SG.OBJ=give-IRR
       'I'll give you a banana.'

(7.26) **man** nyanï
       ma=n   nyï=an-ï
       3SG.OBJ=OBL   1SG=give-IMP
       'Give it to me!'

(7.27) **ndïn** nyanï
       ndï=n   nyï=an-ï
       3PL.OBJ=OBL   1SG=give-IMP
       'Give them to me!'

(7.28) **njan** manï
       nja=n   ma=an-ï
       this=OBL   3SG.OBJ=give-IMP
       'Give this to him!'

Like 'giving' events, 'showing' events are also commonly encoded with ditransitive constructions in many languages. In Pondi, the monotransitive verb *mwas-* 'show' is used to encode these events. In such constructions, the agent (the one showing something) is the subject of the clause, the experiencer (the one to whom something is shown) is the object of the verb, and the theme (that which is shown) is expressed in an oblique phrase (indicated by the oblique marker =*n* in NPs with pronouns or determiners). The verb *mwas-* 'show' exhibits phonologically conditioned allomorphy in its stem—namely, s → t / _ ï # (this same change is seen in *alas-* 'fly', which has the imperfective form *alati*). The metathesis in the stem is discussed in §2.6. Like 'give', the verb 'show' is deponent, with the imperfective form serving to encode perfective aspect as well. The following sentences illustrate the use of *mwas-* 'show'; the oblique phrase (in **bold**) always occurs between the subject (shower) and object (experiencer) and—as in (7.33) and (7.34)—is overtly marked as oblique.

(7.29) meyanga nanï **ndindi** tatï momatï
meyanga   nanï   **ndindi**   tatï   ma=mwas-ï
yesterday mama   dog   papa   3SG.OBJ=show-IPFV
'Yesterday mama showed papa the dog.'

(7.30) nanï **kame** kulawi ndïmwatï
nanï   **kame**   kulawi   ndï=mwas-ï
mama   betel.nut.PL   boy.PL   3PL.OBJ=show-IPFV
'Mama shows the boys betel nuts.'

(7.31) nyï **kamo** umwasïla
nyï   **kamo**   u=mwas-la
1SG   betel.nut   2SG.OBJ=show-IRR
'I'll show you a betel nut.'

(7.32) nyï **ambinjin amwï** umwasïla
nyï   **ambin-njin**   **amwï**   u=mwas-la
1SG   NPL.REFL-POSS.NPL   woman   2SG.OBJ=show-IRR
'I'll show you my wife.'

(7.33) nyï **un** ambinjin amwï momasïla
nyï   **u=n**   ambin-njin   amwï   ma=mwas-la
1SG   2SG.OBJ=OBL   NPL.REFL-POSS.NPL   woman   3SG.OBJ=show-IRR
'I'll show you to my wife.'

(7.34) **man** nyïmwas
ma=n   nyï=mwas
3SG.OBJ=OBL   1SG=show
'Show it to me!'

7.5 Monoclausal (or simple) sentences

A simple sentence in Pondi consists (minimally) of one subject and one predicate. The subject may be a pronoun or a full NP, either with or without a determiner (such as a subject marker). The predicate must contain at least one main verb and may contain one auxiliary verb as well. In a transitive clause, there is also an object contained within the verb phrase, and the verb may have an object-marker proclitic preceding it. TAM suffixation appears on the verb (although, in the case of imperative clauses, this marking may be null). There are some compound verbs that consist of nominal adjuncts that associate with verbs. Subjects, too, may consist of multiple elements (typically NPs). Subjects often contain subject markers following the head NP. Other determiners (that is, in addition to subject markers and object markers) are possible as well, whether as part of the subject or as part of the object. In addition to the basic elements of the subject and the verb phrase (including, potentially, an object), the monoclausal sentence may contain obliques. These typically occur between the subject and object, yielding a canonical word order of SXOV.

8

THE SYNTAX OF SENTENCES

The following sections cover a number of syntactic phenomena, most of which deal in some way with multiclausal constructions. I begin by discussing complex sentences in Pondi (§8.1). The remaining sections in this chapter are organised in part by functional concerns. Here I discuss questions (§8.2), commands (§8.3), negation (§8.4), reported speech (§8.5), and conditional sentences (§8.6).

8.1 Complex sentences

Clauses may be combined to form complex (or compound) sentences. The relationship between clauses within a sentence can, generally, be one of coordination or subordination, with the former occurring only rarely in Pondi.

8.1.1 Coordination

Disjunctive coordination of clauses can be accomplished with the conjunction *o* 'or' (borrowed from Tok Pisin), and adversative (or consequential) coordination of clauses can be accomplished with the conjunction *mbati* 'but, so' (§5.8). The conjunction *akat* 'and' is not, however, used to coordinate two dependent clauses. Rather, to accomplish this, parataxis is used, as in the following examples, in which two clauses are juxtaposed without any coordinator or change in verbal morphology.

(8.01) [John namal asiyï] [Peter yuwï asiyï]
[John   namal   asi-ï]   [Peter   yuwï   asi-ï]
[name]   pig   hit-IPFV [name]   crocodile hit-IPFV
'John killed a pig [and] Peter killed a crocodile.'

(8.02) [alkï nïm luwapï] [nyï male]
[alkï   nïm   lu-apï]   [nyï   ma=ala-ï]
person   canoe   carve-IPFV   1SG   3SG.OBJ=see-IPFV
'A person carved a canoe [and] I saw him.'

(8.03) [kanam nyï katïl akï] [nyï ambo name tïlalala]
[kanam   nyï   katïl   akï]   [nyï   ambo   name   tïlala-la]
now   1SG   old   very   1SG   NEG   pig.PL seek-IRR
'Now I'm very old [and] I can't hunt pigs.'

Although Pondi does have an adversative conjunction (*mbatï* 'but'), it is nevertheless common to coordinate an adversative clause to another main clause with simple parataxis as well, as in the following examples.

(8.04) [mï ayapï] [mï pisa ila]
[mï   a-i-apï]   [mï   pisa   i-la]
3SG.SUBJ   PRF-come-PFV   3SG.SUBJ   again   come-IRR
'He's already left, [but] he'll come again.'

(8.05) [nyï kanam mun ambo nye] [nyï asuwatakï kusam amnda]
[nyï kanam mun   ambo nyï=i-ï]   [nyï asuwatakï kusam am-nda]
1SG   now   hunger NEG 1SG=hit?-IPFV 1SG later   yam   eat-IRR
'Now I'm not hungry, [but] later I'll want to eat yams.'

8.1.2 The functional equivalent of relative clauses

I have not found any morphosyntactically defined relative clauses in Pondi. Rather, what may be expressed with a main clause plus relative clause in some languages can be achieved in Pondi with two main clauses, which are simply juxtaposed. The relationship between the two clauses is presumably left for the hearer to deduce, as in the following examples.

(8.06) [nanï apïn njimoka wapï] [mï matuklupï]
[nanï   apïn   njimoka   wa-apï]   [mï   ma=tukul-apï]
mama   fire   tree   burn-PFV   3SG.SUBJ   3SG.OBJ=cut-PFV
'Mama burned the wood that she cut.' (literally 'Mama burned the wood; she [had] cut it.')

(8.07) [nyï namal asiyï] [mï nyinjin kusam amngapï]
[nyï   namal   asi-ï]   [mï   nyi-njin   kusam   am-ngapï]
1SG   pig   hit-IPFV   3SG.SUBJ   1SG-POSS.NPL   yam   eat-PFV
'I killed the pig that ate my yam.' (literally 'I killed the pig; it ate my yam.')

8.1.3 Permissive constructions

Permissive constructions in Pondi are formed in a similar fashion: the first clause contains the verb of 'letting'[1] and has as its subject the person who grants permission and as its object the person being permitted to do something; the subsequent clause has as its subject the person who is permitted to do something and a verb that encodes the action that the person is permitted to perform, as in the following examples.

(8.08) [meyamba nanï kulam mol lapï] [mï kisïm yapï]
[meyamba   nanï   kulam   ma=ol   la-apï]   [mï   kisïm   i-apï]
yesterday   mama   boy   3SG.OBJ=from   put-PFV   3SG.SUBJ   jungle   come-PFV
'Yesterday mama let the boy go to the jungle.' (literally 'Yesterday mama let the boy; he went to the jungle.')

(8.09) [meyamba tatï nyol lapï] [nyï kapï usapï]
[meyamba   tatï   nyï=ol   la-apï]   [nyï   kapï   us-apï]
yesterday   papa   1SG=from   put-PFV   1SG   house   build-PFV
'Yesterday papa let me build a house.' (literally 'Yesterday papa let me; I built a house.')

For permissive constructions in future time, a conditional sentence may be used (§8.6).

I presume that causative constructions work the same way as permissive constructions in Pondi, although I do not have any examples of causative constructions.

---

1 The verbal meaning 'let, allow' is formed by means of the postposition *ol* 'from' and the verb *la-* 'put', literally 'put from', which also provides the verbal meaning 'leave, lose'.

8.1.4 Subordination

It is also possible to combine a main (independent) clause with one or more subordinate[2] (dependent) clauses. Often, there is a temporal relationship between the two clauses—namely, a sequential relationship whereby the event of the second clause follows the event of the first clause. In such sequential clauses in Pondi, the first verb (encoding the first event) receives no TAM marking and is taken to be a nonfinite verb form (or medial verb) (§4.8). If it is a verb whose stem has a sometimes-covert final *-m* (as in *asim-* 'hit, kill'), then this *-m* is here present, as in example (8.10).

(8.10) mï namal **asim** amalï

mï	namal	**asim**	a-mal-ï
3SG.SUBJ	pig	hit	PRF-go-IPFV

'He shot the pig and left.' ('Having shot the pig, he left.')

(8.11) mï kapï **us** amalï

mï	kapï	**us**	a-mal-ï
3SG.SUBJ	house	build	PRF-go-IPFV

'He built the house and left.' ('Having built the house, he left.')

Although these constructions in Pondi in some ways resemble serial verb constructions, they are not best classified as such, since they consist of multiple clauses: each verb heads its own predicate, with its own argument structure, and each predicate can have its own object arguments. The following sentence (8.12) exemplifies how the second verb can have an object (cf. 8.11, in which the first verb has an object).

(8.12) mï **i** kapï usapï

mï	**i**	kapï	us-apï
3SG.SUBJ	come	house	build-PFV

'He came and built the house.' ('Having come, he built the house.')

The medial verbs in these sentences behave in some ways like converbs, and, indeed, it is often difficult to distinguish between the two categories (Haspelmath 1995). Since it does not seem possible to include two

---

[2] I use the term 'subordinate', but it may be the case that these clause types in Pondi are better described as 'cosubordinate' (Foley & Van Valin 1984:241–243): they resemble subordination in that they cannot stand alone and are dependent on a main clause for aspect, mood, and subject reference; they resemble coordination, however, in that they are not embedded within the main clause (or, at least, I have no evidence that they are).

overt subjects in a sentence such as (8.10), a converb-like interpretation (i.e. translated with a participle in English) is often fitting for these constructions.

The presence of TAM marking on both verbs seems to correlate with the presence of two overt subjects, as seen in the contrast in these two sentences, where (8.13) contains a nonfinite medial verb preceding the inflected finite verb and (8.14) contains two inflected finite verbs.

(8.13) mï **i** namal asiyï
 mï i namal asi-ï
 3SG.SUBJ come pig hit-IPFV
 'Having come, he shot the pig.'

(8.14) [mï **amalï**] [mï namal asiyï]
 [mï **a-mal-ï**] [mï namal asi-ï]
 3SG.SUBJ PRF-go-IPFV 3SG.SUBJ pig hit-IPFV
 'He₁ left [and] he₁ shot the pig.'

The first example is thus illustrative of a sort of clause chaining (involving one cosubordinate medial verb), whereas the second example shows two independent clauses joined paratactically (as described in §8.1.1). It should be noted that the phenomenon at hand does not seem to involve switch-reference: the subjects of the two clauses of (8.14) are coreferential. Instead, to indicate two different subject referents (i.e. to say that one person left and a different person shot the pig), one would use a sentence such as (8.15).

(8.15) [mï amalï] [anda namal asiyï]
 [mï a-mal-ï] [anda namal asi-ï]
 3SG.SUBJ PRF-go-IPFV that pig hit-IPFV
 'He₁ left [and] that [one]ⱼ shot the pig.'

8.1.5 Simultaneous action

As mentioned in §4.9, a simultaneous temporal relationship between two clauses can be signalled by the simultaneous suffix *-e*, which affixes to the medial verb stem. The subject of the two clauses may be different, as in the examples given in §4.9. However, the subjects of the two clauses may also be the same, in which case (as opposed to what happens with sequential action, §8.1.4) it is required to repeat the subject, as in example (8.16).

(8.16) [**nyï** kote **mape**] [**nyï** sewawi asiyï]
 [**nyï** kote ma=p-e] [**nyï** sewawi asi-ï]
 1SG small 3SG.OBJ=be-SIM 1SG bird.PL hit-IPFV
 'When I was small, I used to shoot birds.'

Since the medial verb receives no TAM suffix (only the simultaneous suffix -*e*), it can be assumed that it encodes an action in the same time as that encoded by the final verb, whether in past or present time. When, however, the simultaneous events are hypothesised to occur in future time, then the final verb needs to receive the irrealis suffix (§4.4). In such instances the simultaneous suffix is not used, but rather the conditional suffix (§4.10) is employed, as seen in example (8.17).

(8.17) [wan **ise**] [an kisïm masangola]
 [wan i-**se**] [an kisïm ma=sango-la]
 2PL come-COND 1PL jungle 3SG.OBJ=walk-IRR
 'When you come, we'll be walking in the jungle.'

Conditional statements are thus another form of complex sentences in Pondi. They are discussed further in §8.6.

8.1.6 Parataxis

When the speaker wishes to draw neither a conditional nor a temporal (whether simultaneous or sequential) connection between two clauses, then these clauses are simply juxtaposed paratactically. For example, a causal relationship, which may be indicated by the English subordinator *because*, would be left for the speaker to deduce, as in the following examples.

(8.18) [meyamba ndïn ambo kapï usapï] [kin lapapï]
 [meyamba ndïn ambo kapï us-apï] [kin lap-apï]
 yesterday 3PL.SUBJ NEG house build-PFV rain fall-PFV
 'Yesterday they did not build the house; it rained.' (e.g. '*because* it rained')

(8.19) [John Peter asingapï] [mï mokol mays ke liyï]
 [John Peter asi-ngapï] [mï mokol ma=is ke li-ï]
 [name] [name] hit-PFV 3SG.SUBJ stealth 3SG.OBJ=POSS.PL sago take-IPFV
 'John$_i$ hit Peter$_j$; he$_j$ stole his$_i$ food.' (e.g. '*because* he had stolen his food')

To summarise, clauses in Pondi are often compounded paratactically. Coordination can occur without any overt conjunction (although the conjunctions *o* 'or' or *mbati* 'but, so' may optionally be used for disjunctive, adversative, or consequential coordination). Relationships such as causal or concessive relationships require no morphological or syntactic indication. Simultaneous temporal relationships between clauses, however, are indicated by the suffix *-e* on the medial verb; sequential temporal relationships between clauses are indicated by an unsuffixed medial verb; and conditional relationships between clauses are indicated by the medial suffix *-se*.

8.2 Questions

There are two basic types of questions: polar ('yes/no') questions and content ('*wh-*') questions. In polar questions, the truth value of a proposition is queried. These 'yes/no' questions in Pondi are morphosyntactically identical to their declarative counterparts. They differ, however, in that they contain a rising (as opposed to a falling) intonation. The following questions (spoken with different intonation) could function just as well as statements.

(8.20) ndindi kusam amngapï
 ndindi kusam am-ngapï
 dog yam eat-PFV
 'Did the dog eat a yam?' (or, with falling intonation: 'The dog ate a yam.')

(8.21) o kisïm mïla
 o kisïm mal-la
 2SG.SUBJ jungle go-IRR
 'Will you go to the jungle?' (or, with falling intonation: 'You will go to the jungle.')

Negative responses to polar questions may be formed with the word *mwa* 'no, nothing', and may be followed by a full-answer response, as in (8.22).

(8.22) o num olala
 o num ola-la
 2SG.SUBJ garamut hear-IRR
 'Can you hear the *garamut* drum?'
 mwa nyï ambo num olala
 mwa nyï ambo num ola-la
 no 1SG NEG garamut hear-IRR
 'No, I cannot hear the *garamut* drum.'

When the general existence (or immediate presence) of something is being questioned, then the meaning of 'nothing' of this word is apparent; it follows the subject as a predicate complement, as in (8.23).

(8.23) kamo mapï
    kamo   ma=p-ï
    betel.nut 3SG.OBJ=be-IPFV
    'Is there any betel nut?' (literally 'Betel nut is there?')
    kamo **mwa**
    kamo   **mwa**
    betel.nut nothing
    'There is no betel nut.' (literally 'Betel nut [is] nothing.')

Affirmative responses may be formed with an inflected form of the verb *mbat-* 'work, do' (i.e. 'did', 'do/does', or 'will do'), without any expressed subject, as in (8.24).

(8.24) nanï kusam mï lasiyï
    nanï   kusam   mï   l-asi-ï
    mama   yam   3SG.SUBJ DETR-hit-IPFV
    'Has mama boiled yams?' (literally 'hit')
    mbatapï
    mbat-apï
    do-PFV
    'Yes.' (literally 'did'; i.e. 'Yes, mama has boiled yams.')

The other major question type—content questions—do not put forth a proposition whose truth value is queried, but rather request particular information. They do so by making use of so-called *wh*-words. In Pondi, these may better be called *aw*-words, since—with the exception of 'who?' and 'whose?'—they all include a formative element *aw-* (the question word *am* 'where?' seems to have lost the /w/ of this formative, however, §5.7). There is no *wh*-movement in Pondi; all content questions are formed in-situ—that is, with the questioned element occurring in the same place that it would occur in an equivalent declarative sentence. Thus, *awnjin* 'what [NPL]?', *awse* 'what [PL]?', and *kïman* 'who(m)?' all occur in the subject position when the questioned element is the subject of a clause, and they all occur in the object position when the questioned element is an object. Likewise, *kïmanjin* 'whose?' occurs immediately before the possessed NP, just as would any possessive pronoun. The interrogative words *am* 'where?', *awalake* 'when?', *awate* 'why?', and *aw* 'how?', which behave like adverbs, occur in a typical spot for obliques within a clause, namely following the subject and preceding the object.

In each of the following examples, the question word—'who?' (8.25) or 'what?' (8.26)—occurs in the subject position of its clause.

(8.25) **kïman** namal asiyï
    kïman   namal   asi-ï
    who   pig   hit-IPFV
    'Who killed the pig?'

(8.26) **awnjin** kusam amngapï
    aw-njin   kusam   am-ngapï
    Q-thing.NPL   yam   eat-PFV
    'What (animal) ate the yam?'

In each of the following examples, the question word—'whom?' (8.27) or 'what?' (8.28)—occurs in the object position of its clause.

(8.27) alkï **kïman** asiyï
    alkï   **kïman**   asi-ï
    person   who   hit-IPFV
    'Whom did the person kill?'

(8.28) ndindi **awnjin** amngapï
    ndindi   **aw-njin**   am-ngapï
    dog   Q-thing.NPL   eat-PFV
    'What did the dog eat?'

Finally, the following example (8.29) shows a question word ('what?') functioning as a predicate complement.

(8.29) mï **awnjin**
    mï   **aw-njin**
    3SG.SUBJ   Q-thing.NPL
    'What is it?' (literally 'It is what?')

The following sentences illustrate the placement of the other (adverbial) question words—that is, following the subject and preceding the object (if present). The question word *am* 'where?' can inquire into directional location (i.e. 'whither?') (8.30), as well as static location (i.e. 'where?') (8.31); it can also be the object of the postposition *kï* 'at, in, on' (literally 'at where?') (8.32).

(8.30) meyamba o **am** iyapï
   meyamba   o   **am**   i-apï
   yesterday 2SG.SUBJ where   come-PFV
   'Where did you go yesterday?'

(8.31) kulawi **am** pï
   kulawi   **am**   p-ï
   boy.PL   where   be-IPFV
   'Where are the children?'

(8.32) tatï **am kï** kusam amngapï
   tatï   **am**   **kï**   kusam   am-ngapï
   papa   where   at   yam   eat-PFV
   'Where did Papa eat a yam?'

In keeping with the syntactic patterning of temporal adverbs (e.g. *meyamba* 'yesterday', §5.5.1), the question word *awalake* 'when?' can occur either following (8.33) or preceding (8.34) the subject.

(8.33) tatï **awalake** namal asiyï
   tatï   **awalake**   namal   asi-ï
   papa   when   pig   hit-IPFV
   'When did papa kill the pig?'

(8.34) **awalake** tatï kusam amngapï
   awalake   tatï   kusam   am-ngapï
   when   papa   yam   eat-PFV
   'When did Papa eat a yam?'

The adverbial question words *awate* 'why?' (8.35, 8.36) and *aw* 'how?' (8.37) behave in similar fashion.

(8.35) John **awate** Peter asingapï
   John   **awate**   Peter   asi-ngapï
   [name]   why   [name]   hit-PFV
   'Why did John hit Peter?'

(8.36) o **awate** meyamba kisïm yapï
   o   **awate**   meyamba   kisïm   i-apï
   2SG.SUBJ   why   yesterday   jungle   come-PFV
   'Why did you go to the jungle yesterday?'

(8.37) nanï **aw** ke asiyï

    nanï   **aw**   ke   asi-ï

    mama   how   sago   hit-IPFV

    'How is mama cooking the sago?' (literally 'hitting')

Finally, to ask someone's name, one uses the question word *kïman* 'who?' (as opposed to, say, the question word 'what?'). The question word constitutes the predicate complement of the subject NP 'X's name', as seen in (8.38) and (8.39).

(8.38) unjin **ki kïman**

    u-njin   **ki**   **kïman**

    2SG-POSS.NPL   name   who

    'What's your name?' (literally 'Your name [is] who?')

(8.39) manjin **ki kïman**

    ma-njin   **ki**   **kïman**

    3SG-POSS.NPL   name   who

    'What's his name?' (literally 'His name [is] who?')

8.3 Commands and requests

Commands or requests are generally formed by means of an imperative verb form, which is often identical to the bare verb stem (§4.5). Stems with covert final /-m/ retain this segment in the imperative. Verb stems ending in some consonants take a suffix *-ï* 'IMP'. It is not clear whether this is ever obligatory or whether it is merely a means of aiding pronunciation or adding emphasis. It seems to occur invariably with final /l/ and sometimes, but not always, with final /n/ (i.e. it patterns with alveolar sonorants). It is also possible for imperative verb forms to take the perfect prefix *a-* (§4.6), which may add immediacy to the command. Syntactically, commands are formed in the same way as regular declarative sentences, although it is—as in English—common to leave the second person referent implied but not stated. As mentioned in §4.11, the imperative form of the verb *p-* 'be (at)' is irregular: *alap*. In the following pair of imperative sentences, a contrast can be seen (only in the subject pronoun) between singular (8.40) and plural (8.41). Also note that the verb *andi(m)-* 'see' retains its final /-m/.

(8.40) **o** nyandim
    o   nyï=andim
    2SG.SUBJ   1SG=see
    'Look at me!' (addressed to one person)

(8.41) **wan** nyandim
    wan   nyï=andim
    2PL   1SG=see
    'Look at me!' (addressed to multiple people)

The omission of the second person subject pronoun can be seen in examples (8.42) and (8.43), the second of which, (8.43), illustrates the use of the perfect prefix *a-* on the verb.

(8.42) namal nja asim
    namal   nja   asim
    pig   this   hit
    'Hit this pig!'

(8.43) lo **awle**
    lo   **a**-ole
    song   PRF-sing
    'Sing!'

The final -*ï* can be observed in the following examples.

(8.44) kamo kwandap **nyanï**
    kamo   kwandap   nyï=an-**ï**
    betel.nut   one   1SG=give-IMP
    'Give me one betel nut!'

(8.45) wan **amalï**
    wan   a-mal-**ï**
    2PL   PRF-go-IMP
    'Go!' (addressed to multiple people)

In addition to imperative verb forms, it is possible to use irrealis verb forms to express commands or requests. This is unsurprising, since the irrealis mood encodes—among other things—deontic modality (i.e. 'must' or 'should'). Thus, when applied to a second person subject, the irrealis can serve the pragmatic task of issuing a command or request (i.e. 'you must do this' or 'you should do this'). This is seen in the following example.

(8.46)　wan pis **numlala**

　　　wan　　　pis　　　numla-**la**
　　　2PL　　　leg　　　throw-IRR
　　　'Dance!' (addressed to multiple people; literally 'You should/must dance!')

To soften a command (i.e. make a polite request), a conditional verb form (§4.10) may be used instead of an imperative form. This can be viewed as a conventionalised abbreviated sentence—that is, although these pseudo-imperatives are monoclausal constructions, I assume that they derive from full biclausal conditional sentences (§8.6) (e.g. something like 'if you give me one betel nut, I will be grateful' becomes, simply, 'if you give me one betel nut …'). As a conventionalised means of making polite requests, however, these conditional forms are commonly used without expressed second person subjects and also permit the perfect prefix *a-*, as in the first of the following examples.

(8.47)　**ayse**

　　　a-i-**se**
　　　PRF-come-COND
　　　'Please come!'

(8.48)　**nyandimnje**

　　　nyï=andim-**se**
　　　1SG=see-COND
　　　'Please look at me!'

(8.49)　**mamngase**

　　　ma=amnga-**se**
　　　3SG.OBJ=eat-COND
　　　'Please eat it!'

On the presumed reanalysis of the stem *am-* 'eat' to *amnga-*, see §4.10.

Negative commands—that is, prohibitions—are formed with an irrealis main verb plus the auxiliary verb *ola* 'don't!', which is likely, in origin, an imperative form of the verb *ola-* 'perceive' (§6.2.1). As with positive-polarity commands, the second person subject is optional: it occurs in (8.50), but not in (8.51).

(8.50)　o minjamo katmana nja anda **ola**

　　　o　　　minjamo　　katmana　　　nja　　anda　　　　**ola**
　　　2SG.SUBJ　banana　　old.woman　　this　　give-IRR　　don't
　　　'Don't give a banana to this old woman!'

147

(8.51) ke amnda **ola**
    ke   am-nda   **ola**
    sago   eat-IRR   don't
    'Don't eat!' (literally 'eat sago')

Finally, first person imperatives (i.e. exhortations or jussives) are possible as well, although they are not formed with any imperative morphology. Rather, simply, a first person plural pronoun is used with an irrealis verb form (this can be interpreted as a deontic use of the irrealis, i.e. 'we must' or 'we should'), as in the following examples.

(8.52) an ke **amnda**
    an   ke   am-**nda**
    1PL   sago   eat-IRR
    'Let's eat!' (literally 'eat sago')

(8.53) an kisïm **mïla**
    an   kisïm   mal-**la**
    1PL   jungle   go-IRR
    'Let's go to the jungle!'

(8.54) an kapï **mawsïla**
    an   kapï   ma=us-**la**
    1PL   house   3SG.OBJ=build-IRR
    'Let's build a house!'

Negative exhortations are formed in a similar fashion. They are simply negated by the negator *ambo* 'no, not', as in the following examples.

(8.55) an **ambo** ke **amnda**
    an   **ambo**   ke   am-**nda**
    1PL   NEG   sago   eat-IRR
    'Let's not eat!' (literally 'eat sago')

(8.56) an **ambo** kisïm **mïla**
    an   **ambo**   kisïm   mal-**la**
    1PL   NEG   jungle   go-IRR
    'Let's not go to the jungle!'

The immediate future auxiliary verb *te* 'be about to' may be used in exhortations (§6.2.1).

8.4 Negation

Negative declarative sentences in Pondi are formed with the negator word *ambo* 'NEG' ('no, not') (§5.6), which comes (invariably, it seems) immediately after the subject of the clause whose proposition it is negating. That is, in intransitive clauses, it occurs between the subject and the verb; in transitive clauses, it comes between the subject and the object; and in sentences with postnominal obliques (such as adverbs or postpositional phrases), it comes after the subject and before the oblique. Sentences with negative polarity contain propositions concerning events or states that are contrary to perceived reality. Nevertheless, although negated clauses deny the truth of the propositions they contain, these sentences need not be marked morphologically as irrealis. Indeed, negative sentences may reflect the same basic three-way TAM distinction as seen in positive sentences, as illustrated by the following examples: (8.57) has an imperfective-marked verb, (8.58) has a perfective-marked verb, and (8.59) has an irrealis-marked verb.

(8.57) nyï **ambo** kisïm alïmbam sangoyï
 nyï **ambo** kisïm alïmbam sango-ï
 1SG NEG jungle big walk-IPFV
 'I don't walk in the big jungle.'

(8.58) meyamba wan **ambo** njimoka oliyapï
 meyamba wan **ambo** njimoka oli-apï
 yesterday 2PL NEG tree cut-PFV
 'You didn't cut the tree yesterday.'

(8.59) kïmbïlo anale **ambo** minjame ndamnda
 kïmbïlo anale **ambo** minjame ndï=am-nda
 tomorrow woman.PL NEG banana.PL 3PL.OBJ=eat-IRR
 'The women won't eat bananas tomorrow.'

The following sentences illustrate the immediately post-subject placement of *ambo* 'NEG' ('no, not') in sentences with (other) post-subject adverbial or oblique elements, whether a temporal adverb (8.60), a postpositional phrase (8.61), or an oblique NP (8.62).

(8.60) wan **ambo** kïmbïlo njimoka oliya
 wan **ambo** kïmbïlo njimoka oli-ya
 2PL NEG tomorrow tree cut-IRR
 'You won't cut the tree tomorrow.'

(8.61) nyï **ambo** mawn mïla
    nyï   **ambo**   ma=un   mal-la
    1SG   NEG   3SG.OBJ=with   go-IRR
    'I won't go with him.'

(8.62) o **ambo** kamo nyïmwatï
    o   **ambo**   kamo   nyï=mwas-ï
    2SG.SUBJ   NEG   betel.nut   1SG=show-IPFV
    'You haven't shown me the betel nut.'

Constructions that negate predicate nominals work the same way: the negator *ambo* 'NEG' ('no, not') immediately follows the subject, as shown in examples (8.63) and (8.64).

(8.63) unjin nïmotï **ambo** nyinjin nïmotï
    u-njin   nïmotï   **ambo**   nyi-njin   nïmotï
    2SG-POSS.NPL   friend   NEG   1SG-POSS.NPL   friend
    'Your friend is not my friend.'

(8.64) tatï **ambo** kote
    tatï   **ambo**   kote
    papa   NEG   small
    'Papa is not small.'

Negative existential constructions tend not to use *ambo* 'NEG', but rather are formed more idiomatically with the word *mwa* 'no, nothing', stating in effect that the referent in question 'is nothing', as in example (8.65).

(8.65) kanam minjamo **mwa**
    kanam   minjamo   **mwa**
    now   banana   nothing
    'There are no bananas now.' (literally 'Now banana [is] nothing.')

Negative possessive constructions function similarly, as shown in example (8.66).

(8.66) ndïn andakï ke **mwa**
    ndïn   andakï   ke   **mwa**
    3PL.SUBJ   there   sago   nothing
    'Those people there don't have food.' (literally 'Their sago [= food] there [is] nothing.')

Negative commands (i.e. prohibitions)—which use a special auxiliary verb *ola* 'don't!' ('PROH')—and negative exhortations or negative jussives—which are formed with *ambo* 'no, not' ('NEG') and an irrealis verb form—are discussed in §8.3.

8.5 Reported speech

In Pondi, indirect discourse is encoded with multiclausal constructions. The first clause has as its subject the speaker of the reported utterance and a verb of speaking as its verb; the second clause consists of the reinterpreted content of the utterance.

Two important verbs of speaking in Pondi are *ya(w(i))-* 'talk' and *sa- ~ kï-* 'tell'. Both of these verbs are irregular, the first in that there is much variation in the ending on the stem depending on the TAM suffix, and the second in that there is suppletion in the basic stem.[3] The basic paradigms for these verbs are as follows (Table 8.1), with parentheses indicating the verb stem underlying each inflected form.

Table 8.1. Paradigms for verbs of speaking.

Gloss	Verb stems	Imperfective	Perfective	Irrealis
'talk'	ya(w(i))-	yawiyï (yawi-)	yapï (ya-)	yawla (yaw-)
'tell'	sa- ~ kï-	se (sa-)	Ø	kïla (kï-)

The verb *ya(w(i))-* 'talk' can be used in intransitive monoclausal constructions to refer to the act of talking or speaking itself, without any sense of reported speech, as in the following examples.

(8.67) kanam nanï **yawiyï**
kanam   nanï   **yawi**-ï
now   mama   talk-IPFV
'Mama is talking now.'

(8.68) kïmbïlo nyï **yawla**
kïmbïlo   nyï   **yaw**-la
tomorrow   1SG   talk-IRR
'I'll talk tomorrow.'

---

3 Furthermore, as is the case for several other verbs (which may be called deponent), this verb *sa- ~ kï-* 'tell' has no morphologically distinctive perfective form; rather the imperfective form is used to encode perfective aspect as well.

In an alternative construction, this verb takes as an object the noun *ple* 'speech, story, talk'. First, it can be shown how this word can function on its own as a rather normal (although abstract) noun in Pondi, as in these two sentences: in the first (8.69) it functions as part of an object NP; in the second (8.70) it is part of a subject NP.

(8.69) kanam nyï nanï njin **ple** mawle
      kanam   nyï   nanï   njin   **ple**   ma=ola-ï
      now   1SG   mama   POSS.NPL   speech   3SG.OBJ=hear-IPFV
      'Now I'm listening to mama's speech.'

(8.70) wanjin **ple** atamate
      wan-njin   **ple**   atamate
      2PL-POSS.NPL   speech   bad
      'Your speech is bad.' (i.e. 'What you are saying is wrong.')

In (8.71) and (8.72), however, this noun is the object of the verb *ya(w(i))-* 'talk' (literally 'talk speech' or 'talk talk').

(8.71) meyanga John **ple yapï**
      meyanga   John   **ple**   **ya-apï**
      yesterday   John   speech   talk-PFV
      'John talked yesterday.'

(8.72) tatï ke ame **ple yapï**
      tatï   ke   am-e   **ple**   **ya-apï**
      papa   sago   eat-SIM   speech   talk-PFV
      'Papa ate and talked (at the same time).' (literally 'ate sago')

The verb *sa- ~ kï-* 'tell', on the other hand, often functions in transitive constructions. Here, the person being addressed is the object of the verb, as in (8.73).

(8.73) Peter **ukïla**
      Peter   u=**kï**-la
      [name]   2SG.OBJ=tell-IRR
      'Peter will tell you.'

The verb *sa- ~ kï-* 'tell' can occur in multiclausal constructions encoding reported speech, as in the following sentences.

(8.74) [meyanga John **nyïse**] [mï mïla]
　　　 [meyanga　　John　　　nyï=**sa**-ï]　　　[mï　　　mal-la]
　　　 yesterday　　[name]　　1SG=tell-PFV　　3SG.SUBJ　go-IRR
　　　 'Yesterday John told me he would go.' (literally 'Yesterday John told me; he will go.')

(8.75) [nyï **mase**] [nyï mapïla]
　　　 [nyï　　　ma=**sa**-ï]　　　　　　[nyï　　　ma=p-la]
　　　 1SG　　　3SG.OBJ=tell-IPFV　　　1SG　　　3SG.OBJ=be-IRR
　　　 'I told him I would stay.' (literally 'I told him; I will stay.')

(8.76) [Peter **nyïse**] [nanï ke likapï]
　　　 [Peter　　nyï=**sa**-ï]　　　[nanï　　ke　　lik-apï]
　　　 [name]　　1SG=tell-IPFV　　mama　　sago　prepare-PFV
　　　 'Peter told me that Mama prepared sago.' (literally 'Peter told me; mama prepared sago.')

When encoding reported speech without mention of any particular person being addressed, the verb *sa-* ~ *kï-* 'tell' is also used, only without any object. Instead, in the object slot, the form *mbi* occurs. I have only found it here, and do not know its exact meaning or etymology (although it could be related to Ulwa *mbï* 'here'). Perhaps—alternatively—the form *mbisa-* should be simply left unanalysed as a verb meaning 'say'. Such constructions are exemplified in examples (8.77) and (8.78).

(8.77) [Peter **mbise**] [nanï ke likapï]
　　　 [Peter　　　**mbi=sa**-ï]　　　[nanï　　ke　　lik-apï]
　　　 [name]　　　?=tell-IPFV　　　mama　　sago　prepare-PFV
　　　 'Peter said that mama prepared sago.'

(8.78) [Peter **mbise**] [mï minjamo amngapï]
　　　 [Peter　　　**mbi=sa**-ï]　　　[mï　　　　minjamo　am-ngapï]
　　　 [name]　　　?=tell-IPFV　　　3SG.SUBJ　banana　　eat-PFV
　　　 'Peter said that he ate a banana.'

8.6 Conditional sentences

Conditional sentences express hypothetical situations and their presumed results. In Pondi, conditional statements are formed with two clauses, the first (the protasis) expressing the condition, and the second (the apodosis) expressing the consequence. The verb in the protasis contains the conditional suffix *-se* (§4.10), and the verb in the apodosis is marked as irrealis. My data are limited, but it seems that the verb in the protasis (perhaps best thought of as a medial verb), does not inflect in any way for tense, aspect, or mood and that the verb in the apodosis (or the final verb) is always marked as irrealis, again regardless of any TAM distinctions anywhere in the statement: thus there would be no morphosyntactic distinction made among present, past, and future time, nor among implicative, predictive, and counterfactual conditional statements, as illustrated by the following conditional sentences.

(8.79) kin **lapïse** nyï kapï **pïla**
       kin   lap-**se**   nyï   kapï   p-**la**
       rain   fall-COND   1SG   house   be-IRR
       'If it rains, I will stay home.'[4]

(8.80) kin ambo **lapïse** nyï kisïm **mïla**
       kin   ambo   lap-**se**   nyï   kisïm   mal-**la**
       rain   NEG   fall-COND   1SG   jungle   go-IRR
       'If it does not rain, I will go to the jungle.'

(8.81) iye ke ateyamate **amngase** mï kulal n **lala**
       iye   ke   ateyamate   amnga-**se**   mï   kulal   n   la-**la**
       girl   sago   bad.PL   eat-COND   3SG.SUBJ   vomitus   OBL   put-IRR
       'If the girl ate bad food, she will vomit.'[5]

As mentioned in §8.3, conditional verb forms may also be used (in monoclausal constructions) to form polite commands or requests.

---

4   Other possible translations of this sentence include the following: 1) 'If it is raining, I will stay home.'; 2) 'If/when it rains, I stay home.'; 3) 'If it were raining, I would be staying home.'; 4) 'If it had rained, I would have stayed home.'

5   This example is anomalous in that the oblique marker (generally a proclitic =*n*) occurs here without any pronoun or determiner as a host (see §7.3). Note that the verb glossed as 'put'—when it has an explicit object—takes as its object a destination or goal argument, not a theme; theme roles (like 'vomitus' in the present example) are encoded as oblique arguments, so the presence here of *n* is not so strange syntactically, only morphologically, since there is no determiner to host it.

Simultaneous events hypothesised to occur in future time are encoded as conditional statements as well (see example 8.17).

Permissive constructions in future time can also be encoded as conditional statements. In such instances, the verb of 'letting' (§8.1.3) is marked as conditional, and the verb in the following clause is marked as irrealis, as in the following example.

(8.82) kïmbïlo tatï wol **lase** o kapï **usïla**
kïmbïlo tatï u=ol la-**se** o kapï us-**la**
tomorrow papa 2SG.OBJ=from put-COND 2SG.SUBJ house build-IRR
'Tomorrow papa will let you build a house.' (literally 'If tomorrow papa lets you, you will build a house.')

Finally, it may be possible, as an alternative, to express conditional notions as two clauses with irrealis-marked verbs juxtaposed paratactically, as in the following example.

(8.83) o yakus **ningasina**[6] o mol **lala**
o yakus ningasi-**la** o ma=ol la-**la**
2SG.SUBJ machete throw-IRR 2SG.SUBJ 3SG.OBJ=from put-IRR
'If you throw a machete, you will lose it.' (perhaps literally something like 'You might throw a machete; you might lose it.')

I do not know whether such constructions can be used only for implicative conditionals or can be used more widely.

---

6 Here we see an example of the occasional free variation between [l] and [n]; this form is elsewhere pronounced [ningasila].

9
LEXICON

This final chapter provides a basic Pondi word list. First, in §9.1, I provide over 600 Pondi lexical entries, presented alphabetically, each with an English translation. The list includes every Pondi word mentioned elsewhere in this sketch grammar, as well as a number of other words that I have recorded. Then, in §9.2, I provide an English-to-Pondi finder list. Intended to be a quick and simple means of finding words in Pondi, this list does not provide lengthy definitions.

9.1 Pondi-to-English word list

In the following word list, over 600 Pondi words are organised alphabetically, following the conventions of English (and Tok Pisin) alphabetisation. For ease of use, the digraphs <mb>, <nd>, <ng>, <nj>, and <ny> are treated as sequences of two characters each. That is, although each may represent a single phoneme in Pondi, they are alphabetised as if they were each composed of two separate letters. Thus, for example, *ambam* 'arrowhead' comes between *amalo* 'mother' and *amwï* 'woman', even though *ambam* has a different second phoneme (/mb/) from the other two words (/m/). The one exception to this scheme is that word-initial digraphs receive their own letter headings (**mb, nd, ng, nj, ny**). This prevents giving the false impression that, for example, /mb/ is somehow a subset of /m/. The letter <ï> immediately follows <i>.

Pondi verbs are identified with the abbreviation *v.* at the beginning of the English translation. The entry for the Pondi verb takes the form of the verb's stem. If a verb has multiple stems—whether through allomorphy or suppletion—each stem receives its own entry.

The plural forms of nominals (when known) are given in parentheses following the main entry.

When the English gloss is not a translation of the Pondi word but rather a description (i.e. a grammatical gloss), it is set in square brackets (e.g. '[perfect prefix ('PRF')]' is given for the Pondi entry **a-**).

Loan words are flagged as such when known or suspected (with the symbol < indicating the origin language). Where deemed helpful, Tok Pisin definitions are provided for some words (in parentheses following the abbreviation TP) in addition to the English definition.

a

a-	[perfect prefix ('PRF')]	**alas-**	*v.* fly
-a	[irrealis suffix (allomorph of **-la** 'IRR')]	**alasis**	bee
		alat-	*v.* fly (allomorph of **alas-**)
akala-	*v.* wipe, clean	**alaw**	paddle (pl. **alal**)
akat	and (postpositive conjunction)	**alawa-**	*v.* flock, fly
		alawiyï	moon
akï	very	**ale**	sun, day (daytime)
akïkam	ankle (pl. **akïkaw**)	**alel**	spear
akïlamu li-	*v.* hide (intransitive)	**aleyaw**	afternoon
aku-	*v.* scrape (sago palms)	**alï**	bandicoot (pl. **alange**)
al	maggot	**alïmbam**	big, wide (pl. **alïmbuse**) (also **anïmbam**)
al	outside	**alkï**	person
ala	those (demonstrative pronoun)	**almwan**	good (pl. **alwe**) (also **anmwan**)
ala-	*v.* give (suppletive form of **an-**)	**am**	where?
ala-	*v.* see, look (suppletive form of **andim-**)	**am**	myself, yourself, himself, herself, itself (singular reflexive pronoun)
alam	*v.* eat, bite, suck (irregular imperative form of **am-**)	**am-**	*v.* eat, bite, suck
		-am	[intensive pronominal suffix ('INT')]
alap	*v.* be, be at (irregular imperative form of **p-**)	**ama**	mother's brother (maternal uncle) (TP *kandere*)

amalo	mother (pl. **amandïl**)	**amwï**	woman, wife (pl. **amange**)
amam	myself, yourself, himself, herself, itself (singular intensive word)	**an**	we, us (1PL pronoun)
		an-	v. give
		anale	women (plural only)
ambakïse	spider web	**anam**	us [PL] ourselves (1PL intensive pronoun)
ambal	ourselves [PL], yourselves [PL], themselves [PL], one another (plural reflexive/reciprocal pronoun) (also **ambla**)	**anda**	that, that one (demonstrative pronoun)
		andakï	there, thither
		andeyal	many, much
ambalasi-	v. fight (allomorph of **ambalasim-**)	**andi-**	v. see, look (allomorph of **andim-**)
ambalasim-	v. fight	**andim-**	v. see, look
ambam	arrowhead	**angi**	vine sp.
ambangïn	earth, ground, soil	**angunguse**	molar
ambin	ourselves [DU], yourselves [DU], themselves [DU], each other (dual reflexive/reciprocal pronoun)	**angwaliyï**	woman (pl. **angwalise**)
		anin	we two, us two (1DU pronoun)
ambinjin	my own, our [DU] own, your [SG/DU] own, his own, her own, its own, their [DU] own (non-plural reflexive possessive pronoun)	**aninam**	us [DU] ourselves (1DU intensive pronoun)
		aninis	our (1DU possessive pronoun [plural possessum])
ambï	spirit house, men's house (TP *haus tambaran*) (pl. **ambal**)	**aninjin**	our (1DU possessive pronoun [non-plural possessum])
ambla	ourselves [PL], yourselves [PL], themselves [PL], one another (plural reflexive/reciprocal pronoun) (also **ambal**)	**anis**	our (1PL possessive pronoun [plural possessum])
		anïmbam	big, wide (pl. **anïmbuse**) (also **alïmbam**)
amblays	our [PL] own, your [PL] own, their [PL] own (plural reflexive possessive pronoun)	**anjin**	our (1PL possessive pronoun [non-plural possessum])
		anjï	side
ambo	no, not (negative marker, 'NEG')	**anmwan**	good (pl. **alwe**) (also **almwan**)
amimin	ourselves [DU], yourselves [DU], themselves [DU] (dual intensive word)	**anungwï**	mother (pl. **anungwan**)
		any	we two (1DU pronoun)
		ap	mother's sister (maternal aunt)
amnga-	v. eat, bite, suck (reanalysed form of **am-**)	**ap-**	v. dig (a hole)

-apï	[perfective suffix ('PFV')]	**awalake**	when?
apïn	fire	**awase**	day (countable)
apïn am-	v. burn (intransitive)	**awate**	why?
apïn ngane	smoke	**awla**	ourselves [PL], yourselves [PL], themselves [PL] (plural intensive word)
apïn wa-	v. burn (transitive)		
apïnam	sick, ill		
apït	really	**awmbame**	feather (pl. **awmbamate**)
aplate	mushroom	**awmo**	tooth (pl. **awme**)
apmos	heart (pl. **apmosal**)	**awnjin**	what? (non-plural) (pl. **awse**)
apuma	wound, sore		
apumas	bile	**awse**	what? (plural)
apungwï	hot, warm	**ay**	father's sister (paternal aunt)
apusï	sago pith		
as	tail (pl. **asal**)	**ayndana**	dragonfly (pl. **ayndanase**)
asalkotal	wasp sp.		
asangame	pick-axe (for hacking at sago palms)	**e**	
asi-	v. hit, kill, stab, shoot (allomorph of **asim-**)	**e**	blood
		-e	[imperfective suffix (allomorph of **-ï** 'IPFV')]
asim-	v. hit, kill, stab, shoot		
asisuwa-	v. rub	**-e**	[simultaneous suffix 'SIM')]
asïli-	v. push		
asïmbïne	sneeze	**i**	
asïmbïne asi-	v. sneeze	**i**	in front of, before (postposition)
asuwat-	v. turn		
asuwatakï	later, after, afterwards (also **kunas**)	**i-**	v. come
		i-	v. go, flow (suppletive form of **mal-**)
at	top; cause, reason		
at	atop, above (postposition) (also **atkï**)	**i-**	v. hit (?) (used with **mun** 'hunger')
		ilas	sago flour
atal	bad (pl. **ateyal**) (also **atamate**)	**ilongam**	sago sp.
		im-	v. hit (?) (used with **mun** 'hunger')
atamate	bad (pl. **ateyamate**) (also **atal**)		
		imbam	under, below (non-plural) (postposition) (also **imbamkï**)
atïle	amaranth (TP *aupa*)		
atïwï	father (pl. **atïwal**)		
atkï	atop, above (postposition) (also **at**)	**imbamkï**	under, below (postposition) (also **imbam**)
aw	how?		
aw-	[question formative ('Q')]	**imbanje**	liver (pl. **imbanjïl**)

imbïn	feeling, flavour		
imbïnola-	*v.* feel, taste		**ï**
imïngas	betel pepper (TP *daka*) vine (pl. **imïngasal**)	**-ï**	[imperative suffix ('IMP')]
		-ï	[imperfective suffix ('IPFV')]
imundu	grub sp. that lives in trees		
imunjï	betel pepper (TP *daka*)		**k**
in	two (also **inin**)		
ingamo	man (pl. **ingame**)	**ka-**	*v.* sew (allomorph of **kam-**)
ingip	sternum, chest (pl. **ingipi**)		
ingwandambe	man's sister's child (nephew, niece) (reciprocal relation of **ama**)	**kakal**	centipede (pl. **kakalate**)
		kal	traditional mosquito net
		kalam	sky, cloud
inim	vulva (pl. **inimbisi**) (also **inimp**)	**kalambo**	night
		kalami	black
inimp	vulva (pl. **inimbisi**) (also **inim**)	**kalapa-**	*v.* stand, be standing
		kaliye	frog
inin	two (also **in**)	**kalï**	croton shrub; grass skirt (TP *purpur*) (pl. **kalange**)
ipat	back of the hand (pl. **ipasal**)		
ipawn	palm of the hand	**kalpmate**	cold, cool
ipï	arm, hand (pl. **ipal**)	**kalwane**	younger sister
ipï inin	ten	**kalwas**	bone (pl. **kalwasal**)
ipï kwandap	five	**kam-**	*v.* sew
ipï nanïnge	twenty	**kamal**	head (pl. **kamate**)
ipï yawle	fifteen	**kamalïwï**	smart, intelligent
ipïman	grasshopper (pl. **ipïmane**)	**kambale**	coconut shell; dish; skull (pl. **kamblate**)
ipongas	elbow (pl. **ipongasal**)		
-is	[possessive plural suffix ('POSS.PL')]	**kambama**	knee (pl. **kambamase**)
		kamo	betel nut (TP *buai*) (pl. **kame**)
isisal	fingernail		
isï	sago sp.	**kamuliyaka**	millipede (pl. **kamuliyakase**)
isïl	ash, ashes, salt		
iwal	under, below (plural of **imbam**) (postposition)	**kamun**	shoulder (pl. **kamundïl**)
		kanam	now, today
iwalam	garden (pl. **iwalal**)	**kandam**	fig tree (pl. **kandaw**)
iwawe	ti plant (*Cordyline fruticosa*) (TP *tanget*)	**kandam**	venomous green snake sp.
		kandam	sugarcane, sugar (pl. **kandaw**)
iye	girl (pl. **il**)		
		kandul	cress (*Ipomoea aquatica*) (TP *kango*)

kangane	back (of the body); back of a leaf (pl. **kanganase**)	kilal	perspiration, sweat
		kilwata	worm
kapatupa	hawk (TP *tarangau*) (pl. **kapatupal**)	kimbe	fish (pl. **kimbane**)
		kin	small hand drum (TP *kundu*) (pl. **kine**)
kapaw	cassowary casque (horn)		
kapï	house (pl. **kapal**)	kin	rain
kapmonï	spider (pl. **kapmonase**)	kin lap-	*v.* rain
kasake	dream	kinyawal	long, venomous snake sp.
kasane	older sister	kinyï	coconut (pl. **kinyal**)
kasapïn	crab	kis la-	*v.* mash
kasumwï	older brother	kisïm	jungle, woods (pl. **kiso**)
katakïnï	rash, scabies	kï	at, in, on (postposition)
katal	laughter	kï-	*v.* tell (suppletive form of **sa-**)
katal la-	*v.* laugh		
katambule	snail (pl. **katambwase**)	kïkal	ear (pl. **kïke**)
katambus	dull (pl. **katambuse**)	kïkale	white ant, termite; termite nest
kataplam	dry, light (not heavy) (pl. **katapeyal**)		
		kïkïlas	tusk (pl. **kïkïlasal**)
katïl	old (of people), hard (pl. **katiyal**)	kïl	cassowary
		kïlasaw	strap (used around ankles to climb trees)
katïl	old man (pl. **katiyali**)		
katmana	old woman (pl. **katmanase**)	kïlï-	*v.* die
		kïlïmbun	shin
kaw	year	kïmakïn	grub sp. ('sago grub') (pl. **kïmate**)
kaw-	*v.* hoe, break up (ground) (allomorph of **kwa-**)		
		kïmal	some
kaw-	*v.* sleep	kïman	someone; who?
kawal	chicken (pl. **kawate**)	kïmanjin	someone's; whose?
kawal	tree sp. (*Octomeles sumatrana*) (TP *erima*) (pl. **kawate**)	kïmbïlo	tomorrow
		kïmiye	outhouse, toilet
		kïmï	sago pancake (pl. **kïmal**)
kawn	vegetable sp. (*Abelmoschus manihot*) (TP *aibika*) (pl. **kawi**)	kïmïndu	stick used to stir sago (pl. **kïmïndine**)
kayït-	*v.* fall, fall down	kïn	inside, insides
kaywï	sharp (pl. **kaywal**)	kïnambiyï	belly
ke	jellied sago; food	kïp	nose (pl. **kïpi**)
kekal	waist	kïpakï	earlier, before, beforehand
kela	rattan (TP *kanda*); rope	kïpe	breadfruit (pl. **kïpal**)
ki	name	kïpop	upper lip (skin between nose and mouth)

kïpwï	mound (as for planting yams), mountain (pl. **kïpwal**)	kulambïn	flat
		kulap	fishing spear (pl. **kulapisi**)
kïsïl	vine, root	kule	dust, soot
kït	bottom	kule la-	*v.* die (of fire)
kït oli-	*v.* fall down	kulu	lie, untruth (pl. **kulay**)
kïtal	sago sp. (pl. **kïte**)	kulun	wallaby
kïtami	small knife (pl. **kïtamisi**)	kuma	deep (pl. **kumal**)
kïtïmala	blowfly (pl. **kïtïmase**)	kun	fan (pl. **kune**)
kïtupup	wasp sp.	kunas	later, after, afterwards (also **asuwatakï**)
klal	ripe		
klaluwï	white	kunaswï	base (of a shell)
ko	owl	kunawlum	wildfowl (pl. **kunawse**)
koke	clavicle (pl. **kokal**)	kunï	buttocks (pl. **kunal**)
kokomï	heavy (pl. **kokomate**)	kunjangeyat	grave
kokun	snake (pl. **kokune**)	kunu	Tahitian chestnut (*Inocarpus fagifer*) (TP *aila*) (pl. **kunïl**)
kolwal	small rat sp. (pl. **kolwase**)		
kolwane	cockroach (pl. **kolwanase**)		
kolwe	bedbug	kusam	yam (pl. **kusaw**)
kombandïmal	rat sp. that lives near water	kusan	phlegm, cough
		kusan-	*v.* cough
kombïn	wart (pl. **kombïne**)	kusuwate	full
komblam	child, baby (pl. **komblal**)	kut	neck (pl. **kute** or **kutïl**)
kondiyam	palm sp. (TP *buai limbum*) (pl. **kondiyambune**)	kuwï	fish trap (pl. **kuwal**)
		kwa-	*v.* hoe, break up (ground)
kos	near, close	kwame	possum, tree wallaby (one or more species of the *Phalangeridae* family of marsupials) (TP *kapul*)
kosunï	caterpillar (pl. **kosunase**)		
kosuwal	younger brother		
kota	poor thing	kwan	one, someone; a, an; other, another, the other (indefinite pronoun)
kote	small, narrow (pl. **kosime**)		
kotmonde	red	kwandap	one
kukul	semen	kwanjangat	left (not right)
kul	short brown snake sp. (pl. **kuse**)	kwanjïlamba	gecko (pl. **kwanjïlambangane**)
kul	wind, breath	kwanjimo	egg (pl. **kwanjine**)
kulal	thin	kwas	breast (pl. **kwasal**)
kulal	vomitus	kwas nambi	milk
kulal la-	*v.* vomit	kwasal	breast (reanalysed non-plural form of /kwas-al/ 'breasts') (pl. **kwasale**)
kulam	boy, child (pl. **kulawi**)		

kwasï	bow, bow and arrow (pl. **kwasange**)	**m**	
kwasin	leech (pl. **kwasine**)	**ma**	him, her, it (3SG.OBJ pronoun)
l		**makï**	pick-axe handle (pl. **makange**)
l-	[detransitiviser prefix ('DETR')]	**mal**	sago sp. (pl. **malate**)
la-	v. put	**mal-**	v. go, flow
-la	[irrealis suffix ('IRR')]	**malam**	fly, housefly (pl. **malamnje**)
lak	for the sake of, on account of (postposition) (< TP *laik* 'want')	**malam**	scoop (of sago) (pl. **malal**)
		male	fog, dew
		malmanjï	thick (pl. **malmanjïn**)
lak atal p-	v. like	**malo**	waistcloth (possibly < TP *malo* 'grass skirt')
lakal	palm flower (pl. **lake**)		
laluwas	fish sp. (TP *mausgras pis*) (pl. **laluwasal**)	**mam**	him himself, her herself, it itself (3SG intensive pronoun)
lambom	scar		
lap-	v. fall (of rain)	**mamaniny**	correct, right
laplap	right, right-hand	**mambïlanjï**	pan
lawan	flying fox, bat (pl. **lawane**)	**mamngas**	chin (pl. **mamngasal**)
lem	nest	**mandïn**	string bag, net bag (TP *bilum*) (< Kanda *mandim*) (pl. **mandïne**)
li-	v. take, get, catch, hold (suppletive form of **n-**)		
lik-	v. prepare (sago)	**mangal**	thatch (TP *morota*) (pl. **mange**)
lim	palm sp. (TP *limbum*)		
lisinga-	v. swell	**manjin**	his, her, its (3SG possessive pronoun [non-plural possessum])
lïl	river		
lïm	stinger (of an insect) (pl. **lïmïl**)	**mas-**	v. show (allomorph of **mwas-**)
lïsi-	v. pull	**mat-**	v. show (allomorph of **mwas-**)
lo	song		
lo ole-	v. sing	**mays**	his, her, its (3SG possessive pronoun [plural possessum])
lokom	throat (pl. **lokomisi**)		
lonyï	tall ginger (*Etlingera elatior*) (TP *gorgor*)	**mel**	palm sp. (TP *limbum*)
lu-	v. carve, blow (allomorph of **lum-**)	**mete**	guts, intestines
		meyamba	yesterday (also **meyanga**)
lukep	lips	**meyanga**	yesterday (also **meyamba**)
lum-	v. carve, blow	**meyape**	porch, shelf
lunga-	v. ignite, stoke (a fire)	**meyo**	dogs (plural of **ndindi**)

mi	faeces	mokaw	little (also **moko**)
min	belt (pl. **mine**)	moko	little (also **mokaw**)
min	they two, them two (3DU pronoun)	mokol	stealth
		mokol li-	v. steal
minam	them [DU] themselves (3DU intensive pronoun)	moli	armband (pl. **molse**)
		mom	fruit, seed, berry (pl. **momi**)
mingwï	large grub sp. (pl. **mingwal**)	momiwï	rice
minis	their [DU] (3DU possessive pronoun [plural possessum])	momote	grey hair
		momwï	grandmother (< Ap Ma *mom* 'old woman')
minjamï	palm sp. (TP *limbum*)	mon	louse (pl. **mone**)
minjamo	banana (fruit) (pl. **minjame**)	mongam	young (pl. **mongal**)
minjamone	brown frog sp. (pl. **minjamase**)	mukïn	penis
		mukli	vegetable sp. (*Gnetum gnemon*) (TP *tulip*)
minjin	their [DU] (3DU possessive pronoun [non-plural possessum])	mun	hunger; animal (?)
		mundat	behind (postposition)
mï	he, she, it (3SG.SUBJ pronoun)	mundu	cooking tongs (pl. **mundïl**)
mïl-	v. go, flow (allomorph of **mal**)	mwa	nothing, no (negative response word)
mïlïm	tongue (pl. **mïlo**)	mwakï	segment (of sugarcane) (pl. **mwakal**)
mïlïmïnï	mucus		
mïmli	anus (pl. **mïmisi**)	mwalkamïn	stranger
mïmwï	poison, magic	mwas-	v. show
mïna-	v. rot, cook (intransitive)	mwat-	v. show (allomorph of **mwas-**)
mïnam	pandanus (pl. **mïnal**)		
mïnange	taro	mwï	forehead, face; front (pl. **mwal**)
mïnangewï	green		
mïnangondï	long (pl. **mïnangondïn**)	## mb	
mïndami	pus, earwax		
mïndawï	new	mban	basket (pl. **mbane**)
mïndïlwï	dirty	mbat-	v. work, do
mïnïlwï	old (of things)	mbatï	but, so (conjunction)
mïnjamunjï	brain	mbingamï	steps (log with notches cut into it, used to climb into houses) (pl. **mbingamase**)
mo	boil, blister (pl. **mul**)		
mokan	all, every, everyone, everything		
		mbisa-	v. say
mokas	short (pl. **mokasal**)	mbïn	also, too
		mbole	maybe

n

n-	*v.* take, get, catch, hold
=n	[oblique-marking enclitic 'OBL']
namal	pig (pl. **name**)
namban	ghost, spirit (pl. **nambandïl**)
nambi	water
nambi am-	*v.* drink
nambi man mal-	*v.* float
nambi pu-	*v.* bathe
nambi sango-	*v.* swim
nambikal	riverbank
nambikul	hole
nambis	odour
nambisola-	*v.* smell
nambiwï	wet (pl. **nambiwal**)
nambiyï	skin (pl. **nambiyal**)
namïngïlïm	black snake sp. that lives near water
namom	stone axe, stone
namuse	meat, flesh
nanapï	banana leaf (pl. **nanapal**)
nane	thorn
nangal	navel, umbilical cord; strap (of a basket or bag) (pl. **nange**)
nanglange	lightning
nangun	mosquito (pl. **nangune**)
nangungone	Malay apple (*Syzygium malaccense*) (TP *laulau*)
nangwanjï	tadpole
nanï	mama
nanïnge	four
nan-	*v.* wash
nim	canoe (pl. **nimi**) (also **nïm**)
ningasi-	*v.* throw
nï	banana tree (pl. **nal**)
nïm	canoe (pl. **nïmi**) (also **nim**)
nïman	man, husband (pl. **nïmbe**)
nïmbambiyï	cloth (pl. **nïmbambiyal**)
nïmli	creek (pl. **nïmïlse**)
nïmotï	friend (pl. **nïmotandïl**)
num	large slit drum (TP *garamut*) (pl. **numbune**) (also **nump**)
numla-	*v.* throw
nump	large slit drum (TP *garamut*) (pl. **numbune**) (also **num**)
nungakï	banana flower (pl. **nungakal**)
nungul	grass
nungungun	muscle

nd

-nda	[irrealis suffix (allomorph of **-la** 'IRR')]
ndam	them [PL] themselves (3PL intensive pronoun)
ndi-	[allomorph of **ndï** '3PL' in possessive forms]
ndindi	dog (< Kanda *ndanda* 'dog') (pl. **meyo**)
ndinjin	their [PL] (3PL possessive pronoun [non-plural possessum])
ndis	their [PL] (3PL possessive pronoun [plural possessum])
ndï	them (3PL.OBJ pronoun)
ndïn	they [PL] (3PL.SUBJ pronoun)
ndïngïn	hearth (pl. **ndïngïne**)

ng

ngam	ring
-ngapï	[perfective suffix (allomorph of **-apï** 'PFV')]
ngol	village
ngwam	sago sp. (pl. **ngaw**)

nj

nja	this, this one (demonstrative pronoun)
njakï	here, hither
njimoka	stick (pl. **njimokase**); tree (pl. **yame**)
njimoka nambiyï	bark (of a tree)
njin	thing, something (pl. **se**)
-njin	[possessive non-plural suffix ('POSS.NPL')]
njinulam	bird (pl. **sewawi**)

ny

nyam	me myself (1SG intensive pronoun)
nyi-	[allomorph of **nyï** '1SG' in possessive forms]
nyinjin	my (1SG possessive pronoun [non-plural possessum])
nyis	my (1SG possessive pronoun [plural possessum])
nyï	I, me (1SG pronoun)

o

o	or (conjunction) (< TP *o* 'or')
o	after (postposition)
o	you [SG] (2SG.SUBJ pronoun)
ol	from (a place) (postposition)
ola	*v.* don't! (prohibitive auxiliary verb, 'PROH')
ola-	*v.* perceive, hear
oli-	*v.* cut, chop
onan-	*v.* call, summon, shout

p

p-	*v.* be, be at
pa	grandfather
pakïn	bird sp. with a long beak
pakle	turtle (pl. **paklal**)
pal	far
palam	shield (pl. **palal**)
palmo	rib (pl. **palme**)
panjï	piece
papï	leaf; wing (pl. **papal**)
papïmbam	armpit
patale	lime (calcium hydroxide) (TP *kambang*)
pawn	vegetable sp. (a tree of the *Erythrina* genus with edible leaves) (TP *balbal*)
payne	packet (of sago)
pemo	arrow (pl. **peme**)
pi-	*v.* be, be at (allomorph of **p-**)
pis	leg, foot (pl. **pisal**)
pis numla-	*v.* dance
pisa	again
pisaklin	groin
pisamul	upper leg, thigh (pl. **pisamusi**)
pisangamo	toe (pl. **pisangame**)
pisangamo amalo	big toe
pisangane	lower leg (pl. **pisanganate**)
pisapat	top of the foot (pl. **pisapate**)

pisapawn	sole of the foot	**sapalamun**	pick-axe striking end
pisï	ladle	**saw**	bamboo; flute (pl. **sawal**)
pisimli	path, road (pl. **pisimlise**)	**sawklas**	arrow shaft
piyapï	morning	**se**	things (plural of **njin**)
piyaw	red ant	**-se**	[conditional suffix ('COND')]
pïlïk-	v. be afraid, fear		
pïlkan	lizard (pl. **pïlkane**)	**sewawi**	birds (plural of **njinulam**)
pïn	pot (pl. **pïne**)	**si-**	v. sit
pïnaw	urine	**sim**	sago shoot (pl. **simïl**)
pïtï	cane grass (pl. **pïtal**)	**simbanjï**	money
ple	speech, story, talk	**simom**	kidney (pl. **simomnje**)
po	chest	**sinanga-**	v. stand, arise
polas	scab	**sisaw**	yellow snake sp.
popo	papaya (< TP *popo* 'papaya')	**sïlïm**	ladder
		sïpïn	bunch (of bananas) (pl. **sïpïne**)
pul	flatus		
pulï	black ant	**sïsuki**	rubbish, trash
pumbum	crowned pigeon (TP *guria*)	**sumam**	fat, grease (pl. **sumamïnjïl**)
pwas	soft	**suwate**	saliva
		suwate numla-	v. spit

s

sa	these (demonstrative pronoun)		

t

sa-	v. cry, weep	**tatï**	papa
sa-	v. tell	**taw**	fence
sakun	stomach (pl. **sakune**)	**te**	v. be about to (immediate future auxiliary verb, 'FUT')
sakwe	tobacco (areal term)		
sal	mouth (pl. **se**)	**tïlala-**	v. seek, hunt
sambeyo	eel	**tïndïmo**	testicle (pl. **tïndïme**)
sambon	fish sp. (pl. **sambone**)	**tïn-**	v. count
sanï	sago sp.; adze for carving canoes (pl. **sanange**)	**tïti**	often, always, regularly, every day
		tïtuwa-	v. scratch
sangine	trap (for catching land animals) (pl. **sanginase**)	**to**	from (a person) (postposition)'
sanglama	axe, metal axe (areal term) (pl. **sanglamate**)	**tukul-**	v. cut, break
sanglamamun	axe head		
sango-	v. walk		

u

u	fish sp. (TP *bikmaus*)
u	you [SG] (2SG.SUBJ pronoun)
un	in, within, inside (postposition) (also **unkï**)
un	with (postposition)
unjin	your [SG] (2SG possessive pronoun [non-plural possessum])
unkï	in, within, inside (postposition) (also **un**)
un-	*v.* put, carry
us-	*v.* build
usa-	*v.* tie
usi-	*v.* split
ut-	*v.* grind (coconut)

w

w-	*v.* want, will, try (volitive auxiliary verb, 'VOL')
waka-	*v.* lie, lie down
walwal	lung
walwal ningasi-	*v.* breathe, blow (also **walwal numla-**)
walwal numla-	*v.* breathe, blow (also **walwal ningasi-**)
wam	you [SG] yourself (2SG intensive pronoun)
wan	you [PL] (2PL pronoun)
wanam	you [PL] yourselves (2PL intensive pronoun)
wanin	you two (2DU pronoun)
waninam	you [DU] yourselves (2DU intensive pronoun)
waninis	your [DU] (2DU possessive pronoun [plural possessum])
waninjin	your [DU] (2DU possessive pronoun [non-plural possessum])
wanis	your [PL] (2PL possessive pronoun [plural possessum])
wanjin	your [PL] (2PL possessive pronoun [non-plural possessum])
wany	you two (2DU pronoun)
wawl	scale (fish scale); ringworm (tinea) (pl. **wawase**)
-wï	[derivational suffix ('-like')]
wowe	middle
wus	your [SG] (2SG possessive pronoun [plural possessum])

y

-ya	[irrealis suffix (allomorph of **-la** 'IRR')]
ya-	*v.* talk, say
yakamo	finger, claw (pl. **yakame**)
yakamo amalo	thumb
yakun	sago strainer (pl. **yakune**)
yakus	machete, knife (pl. **yakuse**)
yalïm	ironwood tree, hardwood tree (TP *kwila*); post (pl. **yalo**)
yalïme ipï in	one hundred
yalïme ipï kwandap	fifty
yalïme nanïnge	forty
yalïme yawle	thirty
yame	trees (plural of **njimoka**)
yamemon	small bird sp. that sings in the morning
yamïn	all, all of, whole

yan	eye (pl. **yuwal**)	yawpwa	cockatoo (TP *koki*) (pl. **yawpwal**)
yapiyapo	butterfly (pl. **yapiyapose**)	yin	snake sp.
yaw-	v. talk, say (allomorph of **ya-**)	-yï	[imperfective suffix (allomorph of -**ï** ('IPFV')]
yawe	large rat sp.	yul	hair
yawi-	v. talk, say (allomorph of **ya-**)	yumungi	fern sp.
yawkulam	small frog sp. (pl. **yawkuwase**)	yuwali	fishing net (< Kanda *yuwali* 'fishing net') (pl. **yuwalsi**)
yawle	three	yuwï	crocodile (pl. **yuwal**)

9.2 English-to-Pondi finder list

The following is a list of translations from English to Pondi. It is organised alphabetically by the basic English translations for words in the Pondi lexicon. It is intended to be used as a general guide and is by no means exhaustive.

a

a	kwan
above	at, atkï
adze	sanï (pl. **sanange**)
after	o, asuwatakï, kunas
afternoon	aleyaw
afterwards	asuwatakï, kunas
again	pisa
all	yamïn, mokan
also	mbïn
always	tïti
amaranth	atïle
an	kwan
and	akat
animal	mun (?)
ankle	akïkam (pl. **akïkaw**)
another	kwan
ant sp.	kïkale, piyaw, pulï
anus	mïmli (pl. **mïmisi**)
arise v.	sinanga-
arm	ipï (pl. **ipal**)
armband	moli (pl. **molse**)
armpit	papïmbam
arrow	pemo (pl. **peme**)
arrow shaft	sawklas
arrowhead	ambam
ash	isïl
ashes	isïl
at	kï
atop	at, atkï
aunt	ap, ay
aupa	atïle
axe	sanglama (pl. **sanglamate**), namom
axe head	sanglamamun

b

baby	komblam (pl. **komblal**)
back	kangane (pl. **kanganase**)

back of hand	**ipat** (pl. **ipasal**)	black	**kalami**
bad	**atal** (pl. **ateyal**), **atamate** (pl. **ateyamate**)	blister	**mo** (pl. **mul**)
bamboo	**saw** (pl. **sawal**)	blood	**e**
banana	**minjamo** (pl. **minjame**)	blow *v.*	**walwal numla-, walwal ningasi-, lum-, lu-**
banana flower	**nungakï** (pl. **nungakal**)	blowfly	**kïtïmala** (pl. **kïtïmase**)
banana leaf	**nanapï** (pl. **nanapal**)	boil	**mo** (pl. **mul**)
banana tree	**nï** (pl. **nal**)	bone	**kalwas** (pl. **kalwasal**)
bandicoot	**alï** (pl. **alange**)	bottom	**kït**
bark	**njimoka nambiyï**	bow	**kwasï** (pl. **kwasange**)
base	**kunaswï**	boy	**kulam** (pl. **kulawi**)
basket	**mban** (pl. **mbane**)	brain	**mïnjamunjï**
bat	**lawan** (pl. **lawane**)	breadfruit	**kïpe** (pl. **kïpal**)
bathe *v.*	**nambi pu-**	break *v.*	**tukul-**
be *v.*	**p-, pi-, alap**	break up *v.*	**kwa-, kaw-**
be about to *v.*	**te**	breast	**kwas** (pl. **kwasal**), **kwasal** (pl. **kwasale**)
be afraid *v.*	**pïlïk-**		
be at *v.*	**p-, pi-, alap**	breath	**kul**
be standing *v.*	**kalapa-**	breathe *v.*	**walwal numla-, walwal ningasi-**
bedbug	**kolwe**		
bee	**alasis**	brother	**kasumwï, kosuwal**
before	**i, kïpakï**	build *v.*	**us-**
beforehand	**kïpakï**	bunch	**sïpïn** (pl. **sïpïne**)
behind	**mundat**	burn *v.*	**apïn am-, apïn wa-**
belly	**kïnambiyï**	but	**mbatï**
below	**imbam, imbamkï, iwal**	butterfly	**yapiyapo** (pl. **yapiyapose**)
belt	**min** (pl. **mine**)	buttocks	**kunï** (pl. **kunal**)
berry	**mom** (pl. **momi**)		
betel nut	**kamo** (pl. **kame**)		
betel pepper	**imunjï**		
betel pepper vine	**imïngas** (pl. **imïngasal**)		

C

		calcium hydroxide	**patale**
		call *v.*	**onan-**
big	**alïmbam** (pl. **alïmbuse**), **anïmbam** (pl. **anïmbuse**)	cane grass	**pïtï** (pl. **pïtal**)
		canoe	**nim** (pl. **nimi**), **nïm** (pl. **nïmi**)
big toe	**pisangamo amalo**		
bile	**apumas**	carry *v.*	**un-**
bird	**njinulam** (pl. **sewawi**)	carve *v.*	**lu-, lum-**
bird sp.	**pakïn, yamemon**	casque	**kapaw**
bite *v.*	**am-, amnga-, alam**	cassowary	**kïl**

catch *v.*	**n-, li-**
caterpillar	**kosunï** (pl. **kosunase**)
cause	**at**
centipede	**kakal** (pl. **kakalate**)
chest	**po, ingip** (pl. **ingipi**)
chicken	**kawal** (pl. **kawate**)
child	**komblam** (pl. **komblal**), **kulam** (pl. **kulawi**)
chin	**mamngas** (pl. **mamngasal**)
chop *v.*	**oli-**
clavicle	**koke** (pl. **kokal**)
claw	**yakamo** (pl. **yakame**)
clean *v.*	**akala-**
close	**kos**
cloth	**nïmbambiyï** (pl. **nïmbambiyal**)
cloud	**kalam**
cockatoo	**yawpwa** (pl. **yawpwal**)
cockroach	**kolwane** (pl. **kolwanase**)
coconut	**kinyï** (pl. **kinyal**)
coconut shell	**kambale** (pl. **kamblate**)
cold	**kalpmate**
come *v.*	**i-**
cook *v.*	**mïna-**
cool	**kalpmate**
correct	**mamaniny**
cough	**kusan**
cough *v.*	**kusan-**
count *v.*	**tïn-**
crab	**kasapïn**
creek	**nïmli** (pl. **nïmïlse**)
cress	**kandul**
crocodile	**yuwï** (pl. **yuwal**)
croton shrub	**kalï** (pl. **kalange**)
crowned pigeon	**pumbum**
cry *v.*	**sa-**
cut *v.*	**oli-, tukul-**

d

dance *v.*	**pis numla-**
day	**ale, awase**
daytime	**ale**
deep	**kuma** (pl. **kumal**)
dew	**male**
die *v.*	**kïlï-, kule la-**
dig *v.*	**ap-**
dirty	**mïndïlwï**
dish	**kambale** (pl. **kamblate**)
do *v.*	**mbat-**
dog	**ndindi** (pl. **meyo**)
don't *v.*	**ola**
dragonfly	**ayndana** (pl. **ayndanase**)
dream	**kasake**
drink *v.*	**nambi am-**
drum	**kin** (pl. **kine**), **num, nump** (pl. **numbune**)
dry	**kataplam** (pl. **katapeyal**)
dull	**katambus** (pl. **katambuse**)
dust	**kule**

e

each other	**ambin**
ear	**kïkal** (pl. **kïke**)
earlier	**kïpakï**
earth	**ambangïn**
earwax	**mïndami**
eat *v.*	**am-, amnga-, alam**
eel	**sambeyo**
egg	**kwanjimo** (pl. **kwanjine**)
elbow	**ipongas** (pl. **ipongasal**)
every	**mokan**
every day	**tïti**
everyone	**mokan**
everything	**mokan**
eye	**yan** (pl. **yuwal**)

f

face	mwï
faeces	mi
fall v.	kayït-, lap-
fall down v.	kït oli-, kayït-
fan	kun (pl. kune)
far	pal
fat	sumam (pl. sumamïnjïl)
father	atïwï (pl. atïwal)
fear	pïlïk-
feather	awmbame (pl. awmbamate)
feel v.	imbïnola-
feeling	imbïn
fence	taw
fern	yumungi
fifteen	ipï yawle
fifty	yalïme ipï kwandap
fig tree	kandam (pl. kandaw)
fight v.	ambalasi-, ambalasim-
finger	yakamo (pl. yakame)
fingernail	isisal
fire	apïn
fish	kimbe (pl. kimbane)
fish scale	wawl (pl. wawase)
fish sp.	laluwas (pl. laluwasal), sambon (pl. sambone), u
fish trap	kuwï (pl. kuwal)
fishing net	yuwali (pl. yuwalsi)
fishing spear	kulap (pl. kulapisi)
five	ipï kwandap
flat	kulambïn
flatus	pul
flavour	imbïn
flesh	namuse
float v.	nambi man mal-
flock v.	alawa-
flow v.	mal-, mïl-, i-
flower	lakal (pl. lake), nungakï (pl. nungakal)
flute	saw (pl. sawal)
fly	malam
fly v.	alat-, alas-, alawa-
flying fox	lawan (pl. lawane)
fog	male
food	ke
foot	pis (pl. pisal)
for the sake of	lak
forehead	mwï
forty	yalïme nanïnge
four	nanïnge
friend	nïmotï (pl. nïmotandïl)
frog	kaliye
frog sp.	minjamone (pl. minjamase), yawkulam (pl. yawkuwase)
from	ol, to
front	mwï
fruit	mom (pl. momi)
full	kusuwate

g

garamut drum	num, nump (pl. numbune)
garden	iwalam (pl. iwalal)
gecko	kwanjïlamba (pl. kwanjïlambangane)
get v.	n-, li-
ghost	namban (pl. nambandïl)
ginger	lonyï
girl	iye (pl. il)
give v.	an-, ala-
go v.	mal-, mïl-, i-
good	anmwan, almwan (pl. alwe)
grandfather	pa
grandmother	momwï

grass	**nungul, pïtï** (pl. **pïtal**)	his	**mays, manjin**
grass skirt	**kalï** (pl. **kalange**)	his own	**ambinjin**
grasshopper	**ipïman** (pl. **ipïmane**)	hit	**asi-, asim-**
grave	**kunjangeyat**	hither	**njakï**
grease	**sumam** (pl. **sumamïnjïl**)	hoe *v.*	**kwa-, kaw-**
green	**mïnangewï**	hold	**n-, li-**
grey hair	**momote**	hole	**nambikul**
grind *v.*	**ut-**	horn	**kapaw**
groin	**pisaklin**	hot	**apungwï**
ground	**ambangïn**	house	**kapï** (pl. **kapal**)
grub sp.	**imundu, kïmakïn** (pl. **kïmate**), **mingwï** (pl. **mingwal**)	housefly	**malam** (pl. **malamnje**)
		how?	**aw**
		hundred	**yalïme ipï in**
guts	**mete**	hunger	**mun**
		hunt *v.*	**tïlala-**
		husband	**nïman** (pl. **nïmbe**)

h

i

hair	**yul**	I	**nyï**
hand	**ipï** (pl. **ipal**)	ignite *v.*	**lunga-**
hand drum	**kin** (pl. **kine**)	ill	**apïnam**
hard	**katïl** (pl. **katiyal**)	in	**kï, un, unkï**
hardwood tree	**yalïm** (pl. **yalo**)	in front of	**i**
hawk	**kapatupa** (pl. **kapatupal**)	inside	**un, unkï, kïn**
he	**mï**	insides	**kïn**
head	**kamal** (pl. **kamate**)	intelligent	**kamalïwï**
hear *v.*	**ola-**	intestines	**mete**
heart	**apmos** (pl. **apmosal**)	ironwood tree	**yalïm** (pl. **yalo**)
hearth	**ndïngïn** (pl. **ndïngïne**)	it	**mï, ma**
heavy	**kokomï** (pl. **kokomate**)	it itself	**mam**
her	**ma**	its	**mays, manjin**
her(s)	**mays, manjin**	its own	**ambinjin**
her herself	**mam**	itself	**am, amam**
her own	**ambinjin**		
here	**njakï**	## j	
herself	**am, amam**		
hide	**akïlamu li-**	jellied sago	**ke**
him	**ma**	jungle	**kisïm** (pl. **kiso**)
him himself	**mam**		
himself	**am, amam**		

# 9. LEXICON

k

kidney	**simom** (pl. **simomnje**)
kill *v.*	**asi-, asim-**
knee	**kambama** (pl. **kambamase**)
knife	**kïtami** (pl. **kïtamisi**), **yakus** (pl. **yakuse**)
kundu drum	**kin** (pl. **kine**)

l

ladder	**sïlïm**
ladle	**pisï**
later	**asuwatakï, kunas**
laugh *v.*	**katal la-**
laughter	**katal**
leaf	**papï** (pl. **papal**)
leech	**kwasin** (pl. **kwasine**)
left	**kwanjangat**
leg	**pis** (pl. **pisal**)
lie	**kulu** (pl. **kulay**)
lie *v.*	**waka-**
lie down *v.*	**waka-**
light	**kataplam** (pl. **katapeyal**)
lightning	**nanglange**
like *v.*	**lak atal p-**
lime	**patale**
lips	**lukep**
little	**mokaw, moko**
liver	**imbanje** (pl. **imbanjïl**)
lizard	**pïlkan** (pl. **pïlkane**)
long	**mïnangondï** (pl. **mïnangondïn**)
look *v.*	**andim-, andi-, ala-**
louse	**mon** (pl. **mone**)
lower leg	**pisangane** (pl. **pisanganate**)
lung	**walwal**

m

machete	**yakus** (pl. **yakuse**)
maggot	**al**
magic	**mïmwï**
Malay apple	**nangungone**
mama	**nanï**
man	**ingamo** (pl. **ingame**), **nïman** (pl. **nïmbe**)
many	**andeyal**
mash *v.*	**kis la-**
maybe	**mbole**
me	**nyï**
me myself	**nyam**
meat	**namuse**
men's house	**ambï** (pl. **ambal**)
middle	**wowe**
milk	**kwas nambi**
millipede	**kamuliyaka** (pl. **kamuliyakase**)
molar	**angunguse**
money	**simbanjï**
moon	**alawiyï**
morning	**piyapï**
mosquito	**nangun** (pl. **nangune**)
mosquito net	**kal**
mother	**amalo** (pl. **amandïl**), **anungwï** (pl. **anungwan**)
mound	**kïpwï** (pl. **kïpwal**)
mountain	**kïpwï** (pl. **kïpwal**)
mouth	**sal** (pl. **se**)
much	**andeyal**
mucus	**mïlïmïnï**
muscle	**nungungun**
mushroom	**aplate**
my	**nyis, nyinjin**
my own	**ambinjin**
myself	**am, amam**

n

nail	**isisal**
name	**ki**
narrow	**kote** (pl. **kosime**)
navel	**nangal** (pl. **nange**)
near	**kos**
neck	**kut** (pl. **kute** or **kutïl**)
nephew	**ingwandambe**
nest	**lem**
net	**yuwali** (pl. **yuwalsi**)
net bag	**mandïn** (pl. **mandïne**)
new	**mïndawï**
niece	**ingwandambe**
night	**kalambo**
no	**ambo, mwa**
nose	**kïp** (pl. **kïpi**)
not	**ambo**
nothing	**mwa**
now	**kanam**

o

odour	**nambis**
often	**tïti**
old	**katïl** (pl. **katiyal**), **mïnïlwï**
old man	**katïl** (pl. **katiyali**)
old woman	**katmana** (pl. **katmanase**)
on	**kï**
on account of	**lak**
one	**kwandap, kwan**
one another	**ambal, ambla**
one hundred	**yalïme ipï in**
or	**o**
other	**kwan**
our	**aninis, aninjin, anis, anjin**
our own	**ambinjin, amblays**
ourselves	**ambin, ambal, ambla, amimin, awla**
outhouse	**kïmiye**
outside	**al**
owl	**ko**

p

packet	**payne**
paddle	**alaw** (pl. **alal**)
palm of hand	**ipawn**
palm flower	**lakal** (pl. **lake**)
palm sp.	**kondiyam, lim, mel, minjamï**
pan	**mambïlanjï**
pandanus	**mïnam** (pl. **mïnal**)
papa	**tatï**
papaya	**popo**
path	**pisimli** (pl. **pisimlise**)
penis	**mukïn**
perceive	**ola-**
person	**alkï**
perspiration	**kilal**
phlegm	**kusan**
pick-axe	**asangame**
pick-axe handle	**makï** (pl. **makange**)
pick-axe striking end	**sapalamun**
piece	**panjï**
pig	**namal** (pl. **name**)
poison	**mïmwï**
poor thing	**kota**
porch	**meyape**
possum	**kwame**
post	**yalïm** (pl. **yalo**)
pot	**pïn** (pl. **pïne**)
prepare *v.*	**lik-**
pull *v.*	**lïsi-**
pus	**mïndami**
push *v.*	**asïli-**
put *v.*	**la-, un-**

r

rain	kin
rain v.	kin lap-
rash	katakïnï
rat sp.	kolwal (pl. kolwase), kombandïmal, yawe
rattan	kela
really	apït
reason	at
red	kotmonde
regularly	tïti
rib	palmo (pl. palme)
rice	momiwï
right(-hand)	laplap
right (correct)	mamaniny
ring	ngam
ringworm	wawl (pl. wawase)
ripe	klal
river	lïl
riverbank	nambikal
road	pisimli (pl. pisimlise)
root	kïsïl
rope	kela
rot v.	mïna-
rub v.	asisuwa-
rubbish	sïsuki

s

sago flour	ilas
sago pancake	kïmï (pl. kïmal)
sago pith	apusï
sago shoot	sim (pl. simïl)
sago sp.	ilongam, isï, kïtal (pl. kïte), mal (pl. malate), ngwam (pl. ngaw), sanï (pl. sanange)
sago stick	kïmïndu (pl. kïmïndine)
sago strainer	yakun (pl. yakune)
saliva	suwate
salt	isïl
say v.	mbisa-, ya-, yaw-, yawi-
scab	polas
scabies	katakïnï
scale	wawl (pl. wawase)
scar	lambom
scoop	malam (pl. malal)
scrape v.	aku-
scratch v.	tïtuwa-
see v.	andim-, andi-, ala-
seed	mom (pl. momi)
seek v.	tïlala-
segment	mwakï (pl. mwakal)
semen	kukul
sew v.	kam-, ka-
sharp	kaywï (pl. kaywal)
she	mï
shelf	meyape
shell	kambale (pl. kamblate)
shield	palam (pl. palal)
shin	kïlïmbun
shoot v.	asi-, asim-
short	mokas (pl. mokasal)
shoulder	kamun (pl. kamundïl)
shout v.	onan-
show v.	mwas-, mwat-, mas-, mat-
sick	apïnam
side	anjï
sing v.	lo ole-
sister	kalwane, kasane
sit v.	si-
skin	nambiyï (pl. nambiyal)
skirt	kalï (pl. kalange)
skull	kambale (pl. kamblate)
sky	kalam
sleep v.	kaw-

slit drum	num, nump (pl. numbune)	stick	njimoka (pl. njimokase)
small	kote (pl. kosime)	stinger	lïm (pl. lïmïl)
smart	kamalïwï	stoke	lunga-
smell v.	nambisola-	stomach	sakun (pl. sakune)
smoke	apïn ngane	stone	namom
snail	katambule (pl. katambwase)	story	ple
		strainer	yakun (pl. yakune)
snake	kokun (pl. kokune)	stranger	mwalkamïn
snake sp.	kandam, kinyawal, kul, namïngïlïm, sisaw, yin	strap	kïlasaw, nangal (pl. nange)
		string bag	mandïn (pl. mandïne)
sneeze	asïmbïne	suck v.	am-, amnga-, alam
sneeze v.	asïmbïne asi-	sugar	kandam (pl. kandaw)
so	mbatï	sugarcane	kandam (pl. kandaw)
soft	pwas	summon v.	onan-
soil	ambangïn	sun	ale
sole of foot	pisapawn	sweat	kilal
some	kïmal	swell v.	lisinga-
someone	kïman, kwan	swim v.	nambi sango-
someone's	kïmanjin		
something	njin (pl. se)		
song	lo		

t

soot	kule	tadpole	nangwanjï
sore	apuma	Tahitian chestnut	kunu (pl. kunïl)
spear	alel, kulap (pl. kulapisi)	tail	as (pl. asal)
speech	ple	take v.	n-, li-
spider	kapmonï (pl. kapmonase)	talk	ple
spider web	ambakïse	talk v.	ya-, yaw-, yawi-
spirit	namban	tall ginger	lonyï
spirit house	ambï (pl. ambal)	taro	mïnange
spit v.	suwate numla-	taste v.	imbïnola-
split v.	usi-	tell v.	sa-, kï-
stab v.	asi-, asim-	ten	ipï inin
stand v.	sinanga-, kalapa-	termite	kïkale
steal v.	mokol li-	testicle	tïndïmo (pl. tïndïme)
stealth	mokol	that	anda
steps	mbingamï (pl. mbingamase)	thatch	mangal (pl. mange)
sternum	ingip (pl. ingipi)	their	minis, minjin, ndis, ndinjin

9. LEXICON

their own	ambinjin, amblays	trap	kuwï (pl. kuwal), sangine (pl. sanginase)
them	ndï, min	trash	sïsuki
them	minam, ndam	tree	njimoka (pl. yame)
themselves		tree sp.	kawal (pl. kawate)
them two	min	tree wallaby	kwame
themselves	ambin, ambal, ambla, amimin, awla	try *v.*	w-
there	andakï	turn *v.*	asuwat-
these	sa	turtle	pakle (pl. paklal)
they	ndïn, min	tusk	kïkïlas (pl. kïkïlasal)
they two	min	twenty	ipï nanïnge
thick	malmanjï (pl. malmanjïn)	two	in, inin
thigh	pisamul (pl. pisamusi)		
thin	kulal		

U

thing	njin (pl. se)	umbilical cord	nangal (pl. nange)
thirty	yalïme yawle	uncle	ama
this	nja	under	imbam, imbamkï, iwal
thither	andakï	untruth	kulu (pl. kulay)
thorn	nane	upper leg	pisamul (pl. pisamusi)
those	ala	upper lip	kïpop
three	yawle	urine	pïnaw
throat	lokom (pl. lokomisi)	us	an, any, anin
throw *v.*	ningasi-, numla-	us ourselves	aninam, anam
thumb	yakamo amalo	us two	any, anin
ti plant	iwawe		
tie *v.*	usa-		

V

tinea	wawl (pl. wawase)	vegetable sp.	kawn (pl. kawi), mukli, pawn
tobacco	sakwe		
today	kanam	very	akï
toe	pisangamo (pl. pisangame)	village	ngol
		vine	kïsïl
toilet	kïmiye	vine sp.	angi
tomorrow	kïmbïlo	vomit	kulal la-
tongs	mundu (pl. mundïl)	vomitus	kulal
tongue	mïlïm (pl. mïlo)	vulva	inim, inimp (pl. inimbisi)
too	mbïn		
tooth	awmo (pl. awme)		
top	at		
top of foot	pisapat (pl. pisapate)		

W

waist	**kekal**
waistcloth	**malo**
walk	**sango-**
wallaby	**kulun**
want *v.*	**w-**
warm	**apungwï**
wart	**kombïn** (pl. **kombïne**)
wash *v.*	**nan-**
wasp sp.	**asalkotal**, **kïtupup**
water	**nambi**
we	**an**, **any**, **anin**
we two	**any**, **anin**
web	**ambakïse**
weep *v.*	**sa-**
wet	**nambiwï** (pl. **nambiwal**)
what?	**awnjin**, **awse**
when?	**awalake**
where?	**am**
white	**klaluwï**
who?	**kïman**
whole	**yamïn**
whose?	**kïmanjin**
why?	**awate**
wide	**alïmbam** (pl. **alïmbuse**), **anïmbam** (pl. **anïmbuse**)
wife	**amwï** (pl. **amange**)
wildfowl	**kunawlum** (pl. **kunawse**)
will *v.*	**w-**
wind	**kul**
wing	**papï** (pl. **papal**)
wipe *v.*	**akala-**
with	**un**
within	**un**, **unkï**
woman	**amwï** (pl. **amange**), **angwaliyï** (pl. **angwalise**), **anale** (plural only)
woods	**kisïm** (pl. **kiso**)
work *v.*	**mbat-**
worm	**kilwata**
wound	**apuma**

Y

yam	**kusam** (pl. **kusaw**)
year	**kaw**
yesterday	**meyamba**, **meyanga**
you	**o**, **u**, **wan**, **wany**, **wanin**
you two	**wany**, **wanin**
you yourself	**wam**
you yourselves	**wanam**, **waninam**
young	**mongam** (pl. **mongal**)
your	**unjin**, **wus**, **waninjin**, **waninis**, **wanjin**, **wanis**
your own	**ambinjin**, **amblays**
yourself	**am**, **amam**
yourselves	**ambin**, **ambal**, **ambla**, **amimin**, **awla**

SWADESH 100-WORD LIST

The following is a list of 100 basic vocabulary items in Pondi, following Swadesh's (1971:283) list of 100 words. Where I could find no Pondi word for a particular concept, I have provided the closest equivalent (with a gloss to explicate this), and, failing this, a question mark. For nominals, I present the non-plural form (with what I believe to be the root in parentheses following).

1	'I'	nyï
2	'you'	o (2SG.SUBJ), u (2SG.OBJ), wany ~ wanin (2DU), wan (2PL)
3	'we'	an (1PL), any ~ anin (1DU)
4	'this'	nja
5	'that'	anda
6	'who'	kïman
7	'what'	awnjin (NPL), awse (PL)
8	'not'	ambo
9	'all'	mokan
10	'many'	andeyal
11	'one'	kwandap ~ kwan
12	'two'	inin ~ in
13	'big'	alïmbam (alïmb-) ~ anïmbam (anïmb-)
14	'long'	mïnangondï (mïnangondï-)
15	'small'	kote (ko-)
16	'woman'	amwï (am-), angwaliyï (angwali-)
17	'man'	ingamo (ingam-), nïman (nï-)
18	'person'	alkï (alkï-)
19	'fish'	kimbe (kimb-)
20	'bird'	njinulam (NPL), sewawi (PL) (< *sewa-m ?)
21	'dog'	ndindi (NPL), meyo (PL) (< *me-m ?)
22	'louse'	mon (mon-)
23	'tree'	njimoka (NPL), yame (PL) (< *ya-m-o ?)
24	'seed'	mom (mom-) ('fruit, seed')

25	'leaf'	papï (pap-)
26	'root'	kïsïl (kïsïl-) ('vine, root')
27	'bark'	njimoka nambiyï (literally 'tree skin')
28	'skin'	nambiyï (nambi-)
29	'flesh'	namuse (namus-)
30	'blood'	e (e-)
31	'bone'	kalwas (kalwas-)
32	'grease'	sumam (sumam-)
33	'egg'	kwanjimo (kwanji-m-)
34	'horn'	kapaw (kapaw-) ('cassowary casque')
35	'tail'	as (as-) (< *ongas ?)
36	'feather'	awmbame (awmbam-)
37	'hair'	yul (yul-)
38	'head'	kamal (kam-)
39	'ear'	kïkal (kïk-)
40	'eye'	yan (ya-, yu-)
41	'nose'	kïp (kïp-)
42	'mouth'	sal (s-)
43	'tooth'	awmo (aw-m-)
44	'tongue'	mïlïm (mïl-)
45	'claw'	yakamo (yaka-m-) ('finger, claw')
46	'foot'	pis (pis-) ('leg, foot')
47	'knee'	kambama (kambama-)
48	'hand'	ipï (ip-) ('arm, hand')
49	'belly'	kïnambiyï (kïnambi-)
50	'neck'	kut (kut-)
51	'breast'[1]	kwas (kwas-)
52	'heart'	apmos (apmos-)
53	'liver'	imbanje (imbanj-)
54	'drink'	nambi am- (literally 'water-eat')
55	'eat'	am-
56	'bite'	am- ('eat, bite')
57	'see'	andi(m)- ~ ala- (suppletive forms)
58	'hear'	ola-
59	'know'	?
60	'sleep'	kaw-
61	'die'	kïlï-
62	'kill'	asi(m) ('hit, kill')

---

1   Plural ('breasts') in original Swadesh list.

SWADESH 100-WORD LIST

63	'swim'	nambi sango- (literally 'water-walk')
64	'fly'	alas- (allomorph: *alat-*) ~ alawa- (plural form?)
65	'walk'	sango-
66	'come'	i-
67	'lie'	waka-
68	'sit'	si-
69	'stand'	sinanga- ('stand, arise'), kalapa- ('be standing')
70	'give'	an- ~ ala- (suppletive forms)
71	'say'	ya- ~ yaw- ~ yawi- (suppletive forms) ('talk, say')
72	'sun'	ale (ale-)
73	'moon'	alawiyï (alawi-)
74	'star'	?
75	'water'	nambi (nambi-)
76	'rain'	kin (kin-) (also means '*kundu* drum'; metonymic connection?)
77	'stone'	namom (namom-) ('stone axe, stone')
78	'sand'	?
79	'earth'	ambangïn (ambangïn-)
80	'cloud'	kalam (kalam-) ('sky, cloud')
81	'smoke'	apïn ngane (< *apïn* 'fire' + **ngane*, an older word for 'cloud'?)
82	'fire'	apïn (apïn-)
83	'ash'	isïl (isïl-)
84	'burn'	apïn am- (literally 'fire-eat')
85	'path'	pisimli (pisimli-) (< *pis* 'leg, foot' + **m(i)li* 'path')
86	'mountain'	kïpwï ('mound, as for planting yams') (< *kïp* 'nose' + *-wï* '-like')
87	'red'	kotmonde
88	'green'	mïnangewï (< *mïnange* 'taro' + *-wï* '-like')
89	'yellow'	?
90	'white'	klaluwï (< *klal* 'ripe' + *-wï* '-like'?)
91	'black'	kalami (related to *kalam* 'sky, cloud' or *kalambo* 'night'?)
92	'night'	kalambo
93	'hot'	apungwï (apungw-)
94	'cold'	kalpmate (kalpmat-)
95	'full'	kusuwate (kusuwat-)
96	'new'	mïndawï (mïndaw-)
97	'good'	almwan (al-)
98	'round'	?
99	'dry'	kataplam (katapl-, katape-)
100	'name'	ki (ki-)

SWADESH 200-WORD LIST

The following is a list of 200 basic vocabulary items in Pondi, following Swadesh's (1952:456f.) list of 200 words. Where I could find no Pondi word for a particular concept, I have provided the closest equivalent (with a gloss to explicate this), and, failing this, a question mark. For nominals, I present the non-plural form (with what I believe to be the root in parentheses following).

1   'all'   mokan
2   'and'   akat (postpositive)
3   'animal'   ? (*mun ?)
4   'ashes'   isïl (isïl-)
5   'at'   kï (postposition)
6   'back'   kangane (kangan-)
7   'bad'   atal ~ atamate (at-)
8   'bark'   njimoka nambiyï (literally 'tree skin')
9   'because'   (parataxis of two main clauses)
10 'belly'   kïnambiyï (kïnambi-)
11 'berry'   mom (mom-) ('fruit, seed')
12 'big'   alïmbam (alïmb-) ~ anïmbam (anïmb-)
13 'bird'   njinulam (NPL), sewawi (PL) (< *sewa-m ?)
14 'to bite'   am- ('to eat, to bite, to suck')
15 'black'   kalami (related to kalam 'sky, cloud' or kalambo 'night'?)
16 'blood'   e (e-)
17 'to blow'   lu(m)-
18 'bone'   kalwas (kalwas-)
19 'to breathe'   walwal ningasi-, walwal numla- (literally 'to lung-throw')
20 'to burn'   apïn am- (literally 'to fire-eat')
21 'child'   komblam (kombla-)
22 'cloud'   kalam (kalam-) ('sky, cloud')
23 'cold'   kalpmate (kalpmat-)
24 'to come'   i-

25	'to count'	tïn-
26	'to cut'	tukul- ('to cut, to break'), oli- ('to cut, to chop')
27	'day'	ale (ale-) ('sun, day')
28	'to die'	kïlï-
29	'to dig'	ap-
30	'dirty'	mïndïlwï (mïndïlw-)
31	'dog'	ndindi (NPL), meyo (PL) (< *me-m ?)
32	'to drink'	nambi am- (literally 'to water-eat')
33	'dry'	kataplam (katapl-, katape-)
34	'dull'	katambus (katambus-)
35	'dust'	kule (kule-)
36	'ear'	kïkal (kïk-)
37	'earth'	ambangïn (ambangïn-)
38	'to eat'	am- ('to eat, to bite, to suck')
39	'egg'	kwanjimo (kwanji-m-)
40	'eye'	yan (ya-, yu-)
41	'to fall'	kayït-
42	'far'	pal
43	'fat'	sumam (sumam-)
44	'father'	atïwï (atï-)
45	'to fear'	pïlïk- (intransitive; an object of fear can be the object of the postposition *to*)
46	'feather'	awmbame (awmbam-)
47	'few'	?
48	'to fight'	ambalasi(m)- (< *ambal-asi(m)-* 'to hit, to kill, to stab [REFL]')
49	'fire'	apïn (apïn-)
50	'fish'	kimbe (kimb-)
51	'five'	ipï kwandap (literally 'one hand')
52	'to float'	nambi man mal- (literally 'to go with [= by means of] water')
53	'to flow'	mal- ('go')
54	'flower'	lakal (lak-) ('palm flower'), nungakï (nungak-) ('banana flower')
55	'to fly'	alas- (allomorph: *alat-*) ~ alawa- (plural form?)
56	'fog'	male (male-)
57	'foot'	pis (pis-) ('leg, foot')
58	'four'	nanïnge
59	'to freeze'	?
60	'to give'	an- ~ ala- (suppletive forms)
61	'good'	almwan (al-)

SWADESH 200-WORD LIST

62	'grass'	nungul (nungul-)
63	'green'	mïnangewï (< *mïnange* 'taro' + *-wï* '-like')
64	'guts'	mete (mete-)
65	'hair'	yul (yul-)
66	'hand'	ipï (ip-) ('arm, hand')
67	'he'	mï ('he, she, it', 3SG.SUBJ), ma ('him, her, it', 3SG.OBJ)
68	'head'	kamal (kam-)
69	'to hear'	ola-
70	'heart'	apmos (apmos-)
71	'heavy'	kokomï (kokom-)
72	'here'	njakï
73	'to hit'	asi(m)- ('to hit, to kill, to stab')
74	'to hold'	n- ~ li- (suppletive forms) ('to take, to get, to hold')
75	'how?'	aw
76	'to hunt'	tïlala- ('to seek, to hunt')
77	'husband'	nïman (nï-) ('man')
78	'I'	nyï
79	'ice'	?
80	'if'	-se (verbal suffix at end of protasis)
81	'in'	un(kï) (postposition)
82	'to kill'	asi(m)- ('to hit, to kill, to stab')
83	'to know'	?
84	'lake'	?
85	'to laugh'	katal la- (literally 'to laughter-put')
86	'leaf'	papï (pap-) (homophonous with 'wing')
87	'left'	kwanjangat
88	'leg'	pis (pis-) ('leg, foot')
89	'to lie'	waka-
90	'to live'	p- ('to be [at]')
91	'liver'	imbanje (imbanj-)
92	'long'	mïnangondï (mïnangondï-)
93	'louse'	mon (mon-)
94	'man'	ingamo (ingam-), nïman (nï-)
95	'many'	andeyal
96	'meat'	namuse (namus-)
97	'mother'	amalo (ama-), anungwï (anung-)
98	'mountain'	kïpwï ('mound, as for planting yams') (< *kïp* 'nose' + *-wï* '-like')
99	'mouth'	sal (s-)
100	'name'	ki (kɪ-)

101	'narrow'	kote (ko-) ('small')
102	'near'	kos (< *kwas* 'breast', often pronounced [kos], cf. English 'abreast')
103	'neck'	kut (kut-)
104	'new'	mïndawï (mïndaw-)
105	'night'	kalambo
106	'nose'	kïp (kïp-)
107	'not'	ambo
108	'old'	katïl (kati-)
109	'one'	kwandap ~ kwan
110	'other'	kwan
111	'person'	alkï (alkï-)
112	'to play'	?
113	'to pull'	lïsi-
114	'to push'	asïli-
115	'to rain'	kin lap(u)-
116	'red'	kotmonde
117	'right (correct)'	mamaniny
118	'right(-hand)'	laplap
119	'river'	lïl (lïl-)
120	'road'	pisimli (pisimli-) (< *pis* 'leg, foot' + **m(i)li* 'path')
121	'root'	kïsïl (kïsïl-) ('vine, root')
122	'rope'	kela (kela-) ('rattan, rope')
123	'rotten'	mïnapï (perfective form of the verb *mïna-* 'to rot')
124	'to rub'	asisuwa-
125	'salt'	isïl ('ashes, traditional salt made from the ashes of burnt banana leaves')
126	'sand'	?
127	'to say'	ya- ~ yaw- ~ yawi- (suppletive forms) ('talk, say')
128	'to scratch'	tïtuwa-
129	'sea'	?
130	'to see'	andi(m)- ~ ala- (suppletive forms)
131	'seed'	mom (mom-) ('fruit, seed')
132	'to sew'	ka(m)-
133	'sharp'	kaywï (kayw-)
134	'short'	mokas (mokas-)
135	'to sing'	lo ole-
136	'to sit'	si-
137	'skin'	nambiyï (nambi-)
138	'sky'	kalam (kalam-) ('sky, cloud')
139	'to sleep'	kaw-

140	'small'	kote (ko-)
141	'to smell'	nambisola- (literally 'to odour-perceive')
142	'smoke'	apïn ngane (< *apïn* 'fire' + **ngane*, an older word for 'cloud'?)
143	'smooth'	?
144	'snake'	kokun (kokun-)
145	'snow'	?
146	'some'	kïmal
147	'to spit'	suwate numla- (literally 'to saliva-throw')
148	'to split'	usi-
149	'to squeeze'	?
150	'to stab'	asi(m)- ('to hit, to kill, to stab')
151	'to stand'	sinanga- ('to stand, to arise'), kalapa- ('to be standing')
152	'star'	?
153	'stick'	njimoka (njimoka-)
154	'stone'	namom (namom-) ('stone axe, stone')
155	'straight'	?
156	'to suck'	am- ('to eat, to bite, to suck')
157	'sun'	ale (ale-)
158	'to swell'	lisinga-
159	'to swim'	nambi sango- (literally 'to water-walk')
160	'tail'	as (as-) (< **ongas* ?)
161	'that'	anda
162	'there'	andakï
163	'they'	ndïn (3PL.SUBJ), ndï (3PL.OBJ), min (3DU)
164	'thick'	malmanjï (malmanjï-)
165	'thin'	kulal (kul-)
166	'to think'	?
167	'this'	nja
168	'thou'	o (2SG.SUBJ), u (2SG.OBJ)
169	'three'	yawle
170	'to throw'	ningasi-, numla-
171	'to tie'	usa-
172	'tongue'	mïlïm (mïl-)
173	'tooth'	awmo (aw-m-)
174	'tree'	njimoka (NPL), yame (PL) (< **ya-m-o* ?) ('tree, stick')
175	'to turn'	asuwat-
176	'two'	inin ~ in
177	'to vomit'	kulal la- (literally 'to vomitus-put')
178	'to walk'	sango-

179	'warm'	apungwï (apungw-)
180	'to wash'	nan-
181	'water'	nambi (nambi-)
182	'we'	an (1PL), any ~ anin (1DU)
183	'wet'	nambiwï (nambiw-) (< *nambi* 'water' + *-wï* '-like')
184	'what?'	awnjin (NPL), awse (PL)
185	'when?'	awalake
186	'where?'	am
187	'white'	klaluwï (< *klal* 'ripe' + *-wï* '-like'?)
188	'who?'	kïman
189	'wide'	alïmbam (alïmb-) ~ anïmbam (anïmb-) ('big')
190	'wife'	amwï (am-) ('woman')
191	'wind'	kul (kul-)
192	'wing'	papï (pap-) (homophonous with 'leaf')
193	'to wipe'	akala-
194	'with'	un (postposition)
195	'woman'	amwï (am-), angwaliyï (angwali-)
196	'woods'	kisïm (kis-)
197	'worm'	kilwata (kilwat-)
198	'ye'	wan (2PL), wany ~ wanin (2DU)
199	'year'	kaw (kaw-)
200	'yellow'	?

STANDARD SIL–PNG WORD LIST (190 ITEMS)

The following is a list of 190 items (170 words and 20 phrases) in Pondi, based on the standard survey word list used by SIL in Papua New Guinea. The list, developed by Bee and Pence (1962), was revised in 1999 such that the items are grouped according to semantic domains. Where I could find no Pondi word for a particular concept, I have provided the closest equivalent (with a gloss to explicate this), and, failing this, a question mark. For nominals, I present the non-plural form (with what I believe to be the root in parentheses following).

1	'head'	kamal (kam-)
2	'hair'	yul (yul-)
3	'mouth'	sal (s-)
4	'nose'	kïp (kïp-)
5	'eye'	yan (ya-, yu-)
6	'neck'	kut (kut-)
7	'belly'	kïnambiyï (kïnambi-)
8	'skin'	nambiyï (nambi-)
9	'knee'	kambama (kambama-)
10	'ear'	kïkal (kïk-)
11	'tongue'	mïlïm (mïl-)
12	'tooth'	awmo (aw-m-)
13	'breast'	kwas (kwas-)
14	'hand'	ipï (ip-) ('arm, hand')
15	'foot'	pis (pis-) ('leg, foot')
16	'back'	kangane (kangan-)
17	'shoulder'	kamun (kamund-)
18	'forehead'	mwï (mw-) ('forehead, face')
19	'chin'	mamngas (mamngas-) (< *mama 'mouth'? + *ongas, 'tail'?)
20	'elbow'	ipongas (ipongas-) (< *ipï* 'arm, hand' + *ongas 'tail'?)

21	'thumb'	yakamo amalo (literally 'mother finger')
22	'leg'	pis (pis-) ('leg, foot')
23	'heart'	apmos (apmos-)
24	'liver'	imbanje (imbanj-)
25	'bone'	kalwas (kalwas-)
26	'blood'	e (e-)
27	'baby'	komblam (kombla-)
28	'girl'	iye (i-)
29	'boy'	kulam (kula-)
30	'old woman'	katmana (katmana-)
31	'old man'	katïl (kat-)
32	'woman'	amwï (am-), angwaliyï (angwali-)
33	'man'	ingamo (ingam-), nïman (nï-)
34	'father'	atïwï (atï-)
35	'mother'	amalo (ama-), anungwï (anung-)
36	'brother'	kosuwal ('younger brother'), kasumwï ('older brother')
37	'sister'	kalwane ('younger sister'), kasane ('older sister')
38	'name'	ki (ki-)
39	'bird'	njinulam (NPL), sewawi (PL) (< *sewa-m ?)
40	'dog'	ndindi (NPL), meyo (PL) (< *me-m ?)
41	'pig'	namal (nam-)
42	'cassowary'	kïl (kïl-)
43	'wallaby'	kulun (kulun-)
44	'flying fox'	lawan (lawan-)
45	'rat'	kolwal (kolwa-) (smaller sp.), yawe (yawe-) (larger sp.)
46	'frog'	kaliye (kali-)
47	'snake'	kokun (kokun-)
48	'fish'	kimbe (kimb-)
49	'person'	alkï (alkï-)
50	'to sit'	si-
51	'to stand'	sinanga- ('to stand, to arise'), kalapa- ('to be standing')
52	'to lie down'	waka-
53	'to sleep'	kaw-
54	'to walk'	sango-
55	'to bite'	am- ('to eat, to bite')
56	'to eat'	am- ('to eat, to bite')
57	'to give'	an- ~ ala- (suppletive forms)
58	'to see'	andi(m)- ~ ala- (suppletive forms)
59	'to come'	i-
60	'to say'	ya- ~ yaw- ~ yawi- (suppletive forms) ('talk, say')

61	'to hear'	ola-
62	'to know'	?
63	'to drink'	nambi am- (literally 'to water-eat')
64	'to hit'	asi(m)- ('to hit, to kill')
65	'to kill'	asi(m)- ('to hit, to kill')
66	'to die'	kïlï-
67	'to burn'	apïn am- (literally 'to fire-eat')
68	'to fly'	alas- (allomorph: *alat-*) ~ alawa- (plural form?)
69	'to swim'	nambi sango- (literally 'to water-walk')
70	'to run'	?
71	'to fall down'	kayït-
72	'to catch'	n- ~ li- (suppletive forms) ('to take, to get, to catch')
73	'to cough'	kusan-
74	'to laugh'	katal la- (literally 'to laughter-put')
75	'to dance'	pis numla- (literally 'to leg-throw')
76	'big'	alïmbam (alïmb-) ~ anïmbam (anïmb-)
77	'small'	kote (ko-)
78	'good'	almwan (al-)
79	'bad'	atal ~ atamate (at-)
80	'long'	mïnangondï (mïnangondï-)
81	'short'	mokas (mokas-)
82	'heavy'	kokomï (kokom-)
83	'light'	kataplam (katapl-, katape-) ('dry, light')
84	'cold'	kalpmate (kalpmat-)
85	'hot'	apungwï (apungw-)
86	'new'	mïndawï (mïndaw-)
87	'old'	katïl (kati-)
88	'round'	?
89	'wet'	nambiwï (nambiw-) (< *nambi* 'water' + *-wï* '-like')
90	'dry'	kataplam (katapl-, katape-) ('dry, light')
91	'full'	kusuwate (kusuwat-)
92	'road'	pisimli (pisimli-) (< *pis* 'leg, foot' + **m(i)li* 'path')
93	'stone'	namom (namom-) ('stone axe, stone')
94	'earth'	ambangïn (ambangïn-)
95	'sand'	?
96	'mountain'	kïpwï ('mound, as for planting yams') (< *kïp* 'nose' + *-wï* '-like')
97	'fire'	apïn (apïn-)
98	'smoke'	apïn ngane (< *apïn* 'fire' + **ngane*, an older word for 'cloud'?)
99	'ashes'	isïl (isïl-)
100	'sun'	ale (ale-)

101	'moon'	alawiyï (alawi-)
102	'star'	?
103	'cloud'	kalam (kalam-) ('sky, cloud')
104	'rain'	kin (kin-) (also means '*kundu* drum'; metonymic connection?)
105	'wind'	kul (kul-)
106	'water'	nambi (nambi-)
107	'vine'	kïsïl ('vine, root')
108	'tree'	njimoka (NPL), yame (PL) (< *ya-m-o* ?) ('tree, stick')
109	'stick'	njimoka (njimoka-)
110	'bark'	njimoka nambiyï (literally 'tree skin')
111	'seed'	mom (mom-) ('fruit, seed')
112	'root'	kïsïl ('vine, root')
113	'leaf'	papï (pap-) (homophonous with 'wing')
114	'meat'	namuse (namus-)
115	'fat'	sumam (sumam-)
116	'egg'	kwanjimo (kwanji-m-)
117	'louse'	mon (mon-)
118	'feather'	awmbame (awmbam-)
119	'horn'	kapaw (kapaw-) ('cassowary casque')
120	'wing'	papï (pap-) (homophonous with 'leaf')
121	'claw'	yakamo (yaka-m-) ('finger, claw')
122	'tail'	as (as-) (< *ongas* ?)
123	'one'	kwandap ~ kwan
124	'two'	inin ~ in
125	'three'	yawle
126	'four'	nanïnge
127	'five'	ipï kwandap (literally 'one hand')
128	'ten'	ipï inin (literally 'two hands')
129	'taro'	mïnange (mïnange-)
130	'sugarcane'	kandam (kanda-)
131	'yam'	kusam (kusa-)
132	'banana'	nï (n-) ('banana tree'), minjamo (minja-m-) ('banana fruit')
133	'sweet potato'	?
134	'bean'	?
135	'axe'	sanglama (sanglam-) ('metal axe'), namom (namom-) ('stone axe, stone')
136	'knife'	yakus (yakus-) ('machete'), kïtami (kïtam-) ('small knife')
137	'arrow'	pemo (pe-m-)
138	'net bag'	mandïn (mandïn-)
139	'house'	kapï (kap-)

STANDARD SIL–PNG WORD LIST (190 ITEMS)

140	'tobacco'	sakwe (sakwe-)
141	'morning'	piyapï
142	'afternoon'	aleyaw
143	'night'	kalambo
144	'yesterday'	meyamba ~ meyanga
145	'tomorrow'	kïmbïlo
146	'white'	klaluwï (< *klal* 'ripe' + *wï* '-like'?)
147	'black'	kalami (related to *kalam* 'sky, cloud' or *kalambo* 'night'?)
148	'yellow'	?
149	'red'	kotmonde
150	'green'	mïnangewï (< *mïnange* 'taro' + *wï* '-like')
151	'many'	andeyal
152	'all'	mokan
153	'this'	nja
154	'that'	anda
155	'what?'	awnjin (NPL), awse (PL)
156	'who?'	kïman
157	'when?'	awalake
158	'where?'	am
159	'yes'	(inflected form of the verb *mbat-* 'work, do')
160	'no'	mwa
161	'not'	ambo
162	'I'	nyï
163	'you (SG)'	o (2SG.SUBJ), u (2SG.OBJ)
164	'he'	mï ('he, she, it', 3SG.SUBJ), ma ('him, her, it', 3SG.OBJ)
165	'we two'	any ~ anin
166	'you two'	wany ~ wanin
167	'they two'	min
168	'we'	an
169	'you (PL)'	wan
170	'they'	ndïn (3PL.SUBJ), ndï (3PL.OBJ)
171	'He is hungry.'	(mï) mun may ~ (mï) mun me
172	'He eats sugarcane.'	mï kandam nambi amï
173	'He laughs a lot.'[1]	mï tïti katal le
174	'One man[2] stands.'	alkï kwandap kalape
175	'Two men stand.'	alkï inin kalape
176	'Three men stand.'	alkï yawle kalape

---

1   The adverb *tïtï* in the Pondi translation means 'often' or 'always'.
2   Every translation of 'man' or 'men' is given with the Pondi word *alkï* 'person, people', which is the common way of referring to a man (or woman) unless special reference to gender is required.

177	'The man goes.'	alkï[3] malï
178	'The man went yesterday.'	meyamba alkï yapï[4]
179	'The man will go tomorrow.'	kïmbïlo alkï mïla
180	'The man eats the yam.'	alkï kusam mamï
181	'The man ate the yam yesterday.'	meyamba alkï kusam mamngapï
182	'The man will eat the yam tomorrow.'	kïmbïlo alkï kusam mamnda
183	'The man hit the dog.'	alkï ndindi masiyapï
184	'The man didn't hit the dog.'	alkï ambo ndindi masiyapï
185	'The big man hit the little dog.'	alkï alïmbam ndindi kote masiyapï
186	'The man gave the dog to the boy.'	alkï ndindi (man) kulam malï
187	'The man hit the dog and went.'	alkï ndindi asim yapï
188	'The man hit the dog when the boy went.'	kulam male alkï ndini asiyï
189	'The man hit the dog and it went.'	alkï ndindi masiyapï mï yapï
190	'The man shot and ate the pig.'	alkï namal asim mamngapï

---

3   This subject *alkï* 'person'—and all following subjects—can be followed by the subject marker *mï* '3SG.SUBJ'.
4   Here, as in sentences 187 and 189, the verb form *(a)malï* can be used instead of *yapï*.

REFERENCES

Barlow, Russell. 2016. Pondi (aka Langam) language recordings. Pacific and Regional Archive for Digital Sources in Endangered Cultures (PARADISEC). Available online at catalog.paradisec.org.au/collections/RB6.

Barlow, Russell. 2018. *A grammar of Ulwa*. PhD dissertation, University of Hawai'i at Mānoa. Available online at hdl.handle.net/10125/62506.

Barlow, Russell. 2019a. Agent demotion through inverted word order: Syntactic passives in Ulwa. *Studies in Language* 43(4). 1015–1037. doi.org/10.1075/sl.19010.bar.

Barlow, Russell. 2019b. A syntactic motivation for valency reduction: Antipassive constructions in Ulwa. *Oceanic Linguistics* 58(1). 1–30. doi.org/10.1353/ol.2019.0001.

Barlow, Russell. 2020. Notes on Mwakai, East Sepik Province, Papua New Guinea. *Language and Linguistics in Melanesia* 38. 37–99. Available online at langlxmelanesia.com/llm-vol-38-2020.

Bee, Darlene & Alan R. Pence. 1962. Toward standardization of a survey word list for Papua and New Guinea. In James C. Dean (ed.), *Studies in New Guinea linguistics by Members of the Summer Institute of Linguistics (New Guinea Branch)*, 64–75 (Oceania Linguistic Monographs 6). Sydney: University of Sydney.

Brooks, Joseph Daniel. 2016. The few and the plenty: A typologically rare number opposition in Chini. Paper presented at the 8th Austronesian and Papuan Languages and Linguistics conference. SOAS, London, May 14.

Comrie, Bernard, Martin Haspelmath & Balthasar Bickel. 2008. *The Leipzig Glossing Rules: Conventions for interlinear morpheme-by-morpheme glosses*. Revised edn. Leipzig: Department of Linguistics of the Max Planck Institute for Evolutionary Anthropology and Department of Linguistics of the University of Leipzig. Available online at www.eva.mpg.de/lingua/resources/glossing-rules.php.

Corbett, Greville G. 1991. *Gender*. Cambridge: Cambridge University Press. doi.org/10.1017/CBO9781139166119.

Corbett, Greville G. 2000. *Number*. Cambridge: Cambridge University Press. doi.org/10.1017/CBO9781139164344.

Eberhard, David M., Gary F. Simons & Charles D. Fennig. 2020. *Ethnologue: Languages of the world, twenty-third edition*. Dallas: SIL International. Available online at ethnologue.com.

Foley, William A. 1986. *The Papuan languages of New Guinea*. Cambridge: Cambridge University Press.

Foley, William A. 2005. Linguistic prehistory in the Sepik-Ramu Basin. In Andrew Pawley, Robert Attenborough, Jack Golson & Robin Hide (eds), *Papuan pasts: Studies in the cultural, linguistic and biological history of the Papuan-speaking peoples*, 109–144. Canberra: Research School of Pacific and Asian Studies, The Australian National University.

Foley, William A. 2018. The languages of the Sepik-Ramu Basin and environs. In Bill Palmer (ed.), *The languages and linguistics of the New Guinea area: A comprehensive guide*, 197–432. Berlin: De Gruyter Mouton. doi.org/10.1515/9783110295252-003.

Foley, William A. & Robert D. Van Valin, Jr. 1984. *Functional syntax and universal grammar*. Cambridge: Cambridge University Press.

Hammarström, Harald, Robert Forkel, Martin Haspelmath & Sebastian Bank. 2020. *Glottolog 4.2.1*. Jena: Max Planck Institute for the Science of Human History. Available online at glottolog.org.

Haspelmath, Martin. 1995. The converb as a cross-linguistically valid category. In Martin Haspelmath & Ekkehard König (eds), *Converbs in cross-linguistic perspective: Structure and meaning of adverbial verb forms – adverbial participles, gerunds*, 1–55. Berlin: Mouton de Gruyter.

Kulick, Don & Angela Terrill. 2019. *A grammar and dictionary of Tayap: The life and death of a Papuan language* (Pacific Linguistics 661). Berlin: De Gruyter Mouton. doi.org/10.1515/9781501512209.

Laycock, Donald C. 1971. Notebook D25: Selected research papers of Don Laycock on languages in Papua New Guinea: Kis, Langam, Miyak (Kyenele), Pinai. Pacific and Regional Archive for Digital Sources in Endangered Cultures (PARADISEC). Available online at catalog.paradisec.org.au/collections/DL2/items/036.

Laycock, Donald C. 1973. *Sepik languages: Checklist and preliminary classification* (Pacific Linguistics: Series B 25). Canberra: Research School of Pacific and Asian Studies, The Australian National University.

Lee, Nala H. & John R. Van Way. 2016. Assessing levels of endangerment in the Catalogue of Endangered Languages (ELCat) using the Language Endangerment Index (LEI). *Language in Society* 45. 271–292. doi.org/10.1017/S0047404515000962.

Lee, Nala H. & John R. Van Way. 2018. The Language Endangerment Index. In Lyle Campbell & Anna Belew (eds), *Cataloguing the world's endangered languages*, 66–78. London: Routledge. doi.org/10.4324/9781315686028-5.

Lewis, M. Paul & Gary F. Simons. 2010. Assessing endangerment: Expanding Fishman's GIDS. *Revue roumaine de linguistique* 55(2). 103–120.

Maddieson, Ian. 2013a. Consonant inventories. In Matthew S. Dryer & Martin Haspelmath (eds), *The world atlas of language structures online*. Leipzig: Max Planck Institute for Evolutionary Anthropology. Available online at wals.info/chapter/1.

Maddieson, Ian. 2013b. Vowel quality inventories. In Matthew S. Dryer & Martin Haspelmath (eds), *The world atlas of language structures online*. Leipzig: Max Planck Institute for Evolutionary Anthropology. Available online at wals.info/chapter/2.

Maddieson, Ian. 2013c. Consonant-vowel ratio. In Matthew S. Dryer & Martin Haspelmath (eds), *The world atlas of language structures online*. Leipzig: Max Planck Institute for Evolutionary Anthropology. Available online at wals.info/chapter/3.

Nichols, Johanna, David A. Peterson & Jonathan Barnes. 2004. Transitivizing and detransitivizing languages. *Linguistic Typology* 8(2). 149–211. doi.org/10.1515/lity.2004.005.

Swadesh, Morris. 1952. Lexico-statistic dating of prehistoric ethnic contacts: With special reference to North American Indians and Eskimos. *Proceedings of the American Philosophical Society* 96(4). 452–463.

Swadesh, Morris. 1971. *The origin and diversification of language*, ed. by Joel F. Sherzer. Chicago: Aldine-Atherton. doi.org/10.4324/9781315133621.

UNESCO Ad Hoc Expert Group on Endangered Languages. 2003. *Language vitality and endangerment*. Document submitted to the International Expert Meeting on UNESCO Programme Safeguarding of Endangered Languages. Paris, 10–12 March 2003. Available online at ich.unesco.org/doc/src/00120-EN.pdf.

Usher, Timothy. n.d. Keram River. A section of *New Guinea World*. Online manuscript. sites.google.com/site/newguineaworld/families/keram-and-ramu-rivers/keram-river.

Wade, Martha Lynn. 1984. *Some stratificational insights concerning Botin (Kambot), a Papuan language*. MA thesis, University of Texas at Arlington.

Wilkinson, Richard James. 1959. *A Malay-English dictionary: Romanised*. London: Macmillan.

Wonderly, William, Lorna F. Gibson & Paul L. Kirk. 1954. Number in Kiowa: Nouns, demonstratives, and adjectives. *International Journal of American Linguistics* 20. 1–7. doi.org/10.1086/464244.

www.ingramcontent.com/pod-product-compliance
Lightning Source LLC
Chambersburg PA
CBHW041925220426
43670CB00032B/2961